P9-COO-808

Dawn of Desegregation

The Reverend Joseph Armstrong De Laine, circa 1970.
Courtesy of South Caroliniana Library

Dawn of Desegregation

J. A. De Laine and *Briggs v. Elliott*

Ophelia De Laine Gona

The University of South Carolina Press

© 2011 University of South Carolina

Published by the University of South Carolina Press
Columbia, South Carolina 29208

www.sc.edu/uscpress

Manufactured in the United States of America

20 19 18 17 16 15 14 13 12 11   10 9 8 7 6 5 4 3 2 1

Library of Congress Cataloging-in-Publication Data

Gona, Ophelia De Laine.
   Dawn of desegregation : J.A. De Laine and Briggs v. Elliott / Ophelia De Laine Gona.
     p. cm.
   Includes bibliographical references and index.
   ISBN 978-1-57003-980-5 (cloth : alk. paper) 1. Briggs, Harry, d. 1986—Trials,
litigation, etc. 2. Elliott, R. W.—Trials, litigation, etc. 3. DeLaine, Joseph A. (Joseph
Armstrong), 1898–1974. 4. Segregation in education—Law and legislation—South
Carolina—Clarendon County—History—20th century. 5. African Americans—
Civil rights—South Carolina—Clarendon County—History—20th century. 6. Civil
rights movements—South Carolina—Clarendon County—History—20th century.
7. African American clergy—South Carolina—Clarendon County—Biography.
8. African American civil rights workers—South Carolina—Clarendon County—
Biography. I. Title.
   KF228.B75G66 2011
   344.73'07980975781—dc22

                                                                          2010048790

This book was printed on Glatfelter Natures, a recycled paper with 30 percent
postconsumer waste content.

In Memoriam
Joseph Armstrong De Laine
July 2, 1898–August 3, 1974

His was a voice crying in a wilderness,
Questioning an unjust, intolerable system
That cruelly brutalized and dehumanized
The very souls of his people.

Courageously taking a perilous stand,
He put truth in its proper perspective,
Never straddling the fence,
But boldly calling the shots as he saw them.
A respected leader, he challenged the status quo,
But resolutely kept his covenant with God.

Buttressed and undergirded
By unselfish motives, Christian dedication,
And an unassailable moral character,
He forged onward, carrying on when hope was gone
With raw courage and steely fortitude,
Far beyond the call of duty.

With burning zeal and dogged determination,
He used himself as a catalyst and a human sacrifice,
Stimulating and inspiring people,
Setting in motion a powerful correctional force
That came out of Clarendon to revolutionize
Thought and social practice throughout a nation.

Teacher, clergyman, and good shepherd.
A prime mover and a martyr
In the 20th century struggle for justice and equality.
His life was a testament
To an unshakeable belief in his church's motto,
"God, our father; Christ, our redeemer; man our brother."
His memory is a tribute
To honest leadership, tenacious faith, personal sacrifice,
    and abiding love.

                    Ophelia De Laine Gona,
                after an essay by L. Charles Williams

"A few of us were not the type to accept
injustice or unjust methods."
J. A. De Laine

Contents

Illustrations

Preface

A powerful corrective force
came out of Clarendon.
AFTER L. CHARLES WILLIAMS

As the United States of America approached the fiftieth anniversary of the Supreme Court's momentous 1954 *Brown v. Board of Education of Topeka* (*Brown*) decision, my brothers—Joseph A. De Laine, Jr., and Brumit B. De Laine—and I were troubled. We knew that, of the five different legal cases that shaped that historic decision, *Briggs et al. v. Elliott et al.* (*Briggs*) was the seminal one. The first of the *Brown* cases to arrive at the Supreme Court, *Briggs* came out of poor, rural Clarendon County, South Carolina. Even before it was argued in the courts, *Briggs* had already caused a major revolution in South Carolina's education system. As the case that changed the NAACP's approach to fighting segregation, as the case responsible for others being heard at the same time, as one of the *Brown* cases, and as the one that provided the most damning evidence of the ills of segregation, *Briggs* had a key role in ending public school segregation and in laying the groundwork for the civil rights movement of the 1950s and 1960s. Yet, despite the fact that *Briggs* changed the course of human events, its key role in shaping the nation's future had been largely overlooked. My brothers and I were mindful of this because we were aware of the leadership role our father, the late Rev. Joseph Armstrong "J. A." De Laine, had assumed in *Briggs,* the case that signaled the dawn of desegregation.

The twenty *Briggs* plaintiffs did not spontaneously decide to sue for the end of public school segregation. Instead *Briggs* was the outcome of a long, arduous struggle for justice, a crusade fraught with perils and retaliation. Before *Briggs* got to the courts, many people had lost their jobs and their homes, or had their lives threatened. And for more than a decade subsequently, danger and reprisals continually plagued the plaintiffs, their leaders, and their supporters.

On the eve of the anniversary of the *Brown* decision, my brothers and I worried that the names and struggles of the *Briggs* heroes would soon be lost to memory.

We wanted it to be appreciated that legal segregation began its long overdue collapse, not because of a case generally associated with Kansas, but because a few humble, poorly educated people in an out-of-the way South Carolina place dared to take a stand for equality. We felt that everyone should know more of the human price that had been paid to end legal segregation in schools. Additionally we wanted our father's writings and notes regarding the genesis of *Briggs* to be interpreted correctly. We jointly decided that I should research and document the facts. This was something that our father—fervent in his desire to have the complete story of *Briggs* told—had asked me to do forty-five years earlier. I didn't do it then because I didn't know how.

Over the intervening years, others—including my father—did what I did not. They wrote about *Briggs*, not always accurately. Even so, no one adequately explained how and why *Briggs* happened. Now that I am making a serious effort to do what was requested of me, most players in this remarkable drama have gone to their eternal resting places and I have reached my twilight years. My father, Rev. De Laine, has been dead thirty-five years and my mother almost ten. To write this account, I needed more than my own incomplete recollections. I had to seek whatever written sources I could find and to tap the memories of the few participants who still lived. Fortunately, despite the burning of our Summerton home in 1951 and his abrupt departure from South Carolina in 1955, my father left published materials and extensive personal records that included letters, legal documents, and undated news clippings relevant to the *Briggs* case. Because he made carbon copies of practically every document he typed (using only his index fingers) and kept many of them, there were often different versions of the same document.

Using the writings and the files he left, as well as oral histories provided by eyewitnesses to that unique page in history, I was able to identify the major events and circumstances in the heroic saga of *Briggs*. Collating the facts, I wrote—as faithfully as I could—this account of how *Briggs* came into being. Given the passage of time between the events and their documentation, the fallibility of human memory, and the existence of a few conflicting sources, what I have written can only be an approximation of what actually happened. In two or three instances, I had to make judgment calls regarding the truth.

In contemplating the hardships and misery that the petitioners suffered in retaliation for their act, I asked myself over and over, "Why did they do it? What force could have been strong enough to make those twenty plaintiffs, so far removed from the mainstream of American life, risk their lives and livelihoods to challenge the establishment?" Before reaching the end of my first draft, I began to understand how my father's unyielding persistence, fearless leadership, constant encouragement, abiding faith, and personal sacrifices inspired the steadfast courage of others that resulted in two educational revolutions: the regional one in South Carolina and the national one throughout the United States. The plaintiffs and their supporters took their brave stand because my father convinced them it was the right thing to do. The story of *Briggs* is my father's story. Without him and his efforts, *Briggs* would never have been. Without *Briggs*—the lawsuit that came out of Clarendon—American history since 1954 would have been much different. The desegregation movement in America's public schools would have had to wait, to arise at another time under different circumstances. This is the story of the dawn of that movement, the story of J. A. De Laine and the lawsuit called *Briggs*.

A Note on the Writing of this Book

To focus my writing while telling the story of the *Briggs* case, I needed to decide for whom I was writing. That was a challenging task because I want everyone to understand and appreciate how it happened. In the end I decided to write for a certain forty-five-year-old woman who has an inquiring mind and an interest in people's struggles for equality. I am confident that anyone who chooses to read this account will share many of her interests. With her in mind, I have tried to accurately relate the events that played a role in this fascinating, but little heralded, page in history. Believing that the woman for whom I have written will have neither the time nor interest to read original sources, I have not documented most references. I have, however, attempted to include enough information for anyone who wishes to study this topic further.

My father's personal records included letters, published materials, legal documents, and undated news clippings. It was his habit to make carbon copies of practically every document he typed, and he kept many of them, including different drafts of the same document. Along with oral histories, these records were the sources of practically all of my information. Although some documents currently remain in the possession of my brothers and me, many have been donated to the South Caroliniana Library at the University of South Carolina in Columbia. More than 350 of these have been digitized and can be found in the Joseph A. De Laine Papers, University Libraries Digital Collection, University of South Carolina, Columbia, at http://www.sc.edu/library/digital/collections/delaine.html. Documents from the period 1942 through 1956 provided most of the information on the genesis of the *Briggs* lawsuit.

Rev. De Laine's published materials consisted almost exclusively of the more than 150 installments of his account, "Our Part in a Revolution," which were published in the *AME Christian Recorder* (Nashville), 1966–70. Fortunately he kept clippings of many of the published installments, as well as drafts, because they are not readily available through libraries. The most complete set of issues of the *AME Christian Recorder* from that period was found in the United Methodist Archives Center at Drew University in Madison, New Jersey.

For the most part, dialog has been written just as my father wrote it or as I heard it, although occasionally quoted material was edited to make it more intelligible. In some instances, quotations were constructed from narratives. Nonstandard English was used in a few cases to emphasize the ordinariness of the Clarendon heroes. The names used to refer to individuals are the names by which I knew them.

Acknowledgments

Great care has been taken to ensure the highest possible level of accuracy in recounting the events of this fascinating saga, which happened mainly between 1940 and 1955. Reconstruction of the incidents and their chronology relied heavily on details and, many times, words drawn from the papers of the late Rev. Joseph Armstrong "J. A." De Laine, my father. Some of his writings were published from 1968 to 1972 in the *AME Christian Recorder* as a series of installments entitled "Our Part in a Revolution." I am grateful to the editor of that publication for permission to use those sources, and I humbly acknowledge my father as my coauthor.

Over a period of more than ten years, I engaged in a number of lengthy conversations—often scribbling notes—with my mother, Mattie Belton De Laine, and with her brother, David G. Belton, Jr., both of whom are now deceased. They provided valuable insight and background details about the way things once were, and the forces that caused them to be that way. That knowledge helped me elaborate on more static, recorded facts. For both information and clarification, I relied heavily on my brothers, Joseph A. De Laine, Jr., and Brumit B. De Laine. During the 1940s and 1950s, they frequently accompanied our father in his travels and, thus, one or the other of them was an eyewitness to a number of key events. In later years they spent a great deal of time with my father and the people who knew him. They also conducted formal interviews with several *Briggs* plaintiffs and supporters. Both freely contributed time, resources, and knowledge during my research and writing. This account could never have been written without their gracious and ever willing help.

Daisy De Laine Block and Marguirite L. De Laine provided facts about family history and local individuals. Conversations with others who were intimately acquainted with one or more aspects of the *Briggs* case, or who knew my father, yielded particulars and amplification regarding events leading to the lawsuit, my father's personality, and ancillary incidents. These individuals included Roberta Mack Prince, Jessie Pearson, Zolia Johnson, Inez Jones Pearson, Leroy Hooks, Ferdinand Pearson, Albert Fuller, and Reverdy Wells.

Descendants of *Briggs* plaintiffs who graciously supplied information about their parents (whose names are in parentheses) were Denia Stukes Hightower

(Willie "Bo" Stukes), Celestine Parson Lloyd (Bennie Parson), Susan Ann Lawson Johnson (Susan Lawson), Nathaniel Briggs (Harry Briggs), John Wesley Richburg (Rebecca Richburg), Sarah Ellen Ragin Williams (Hazel Ragin), and Daisy Oliver Rivers (Mary Oliver). Descendants of *Briggs* supporters who helped in a similar manner were James Morris Seals (J. W. Seals), Euralia Brown Craig (James Brown), Clara Gipson McKnight (Johnny Gipson), as well as Beatrice Brown Rivers and Geneva Brown Finney (Henry and Theola Brown).

Correspondence with other individuals, namely, John Hurst Adams (son of E. A. Adams), Millicent E. Brown (daughter of J. Arthur "Joe" Brown), Joseph Elliott (grandson of R. W. Elliott), Tom Hanchett, and Miles Richard, also helped in my awareness of certain personalities, events, and historical conditions.

Willard Strong, the publications specialist at Santee Cooper (South Carolina's state-owned electric and water utility), assisted with the Santee Cooper Hydroelectric Project's history. Librarians at the Caroliniana Library, Drew University, Clarendon County Archives, and the National Archives at Atlanta were most gracious and helpful in my searches for additional sources.

My brothers checked several versions of the manuscript for accuracy. Shantha Farris critically read several versions and often served as my "muse," inspiring me to see implications I had overlooked, to add explanations I had omitted, and to write when I wanted to do other things. Nana Jacklin Christmas, Laura Damon, Mary Lou Lustig, Amos G. Gona, and Raj P. Gona read various versions of the manuscript. Their editorial diligence and expertise in finding errors, redundancies, and just plain bad writing, as well as in challenging my insight, were invaluable. The staff of the University of South Carolina Press, especially my acquisitions editor, Alex Moore, and my project editor, Karen Beidel, further nurtured and refined the manuscript with tact and expertise to bring it to a publishable form. The contributions of all of these individuals; the constant support of Amos G. Gona, Shantha Farris, Raj P. Gona, Kira Farris, and Brad Farris; and the encouragement of countless others are gratefully acknowledged.

I

Before

1. *Briars of Discrimination*

Injustice will not forever be borne silently.
W. B. Harvey

In an undated speech, Rev. J. A. De Laine wrote, "A long story is behind the first of the five cases [the *Briggs* case] which caused the courts to reverse 'Separate-But-Equal.' The story takes its beginning in 1946 and continues until the present day. On the banks of the Santee River in South Carolina, where the Santee Hydro-Electric Dam was built, colored children were not transported to and from school like other schoolchildren. Neither did they have comfortable buildings where they could warm their little bodies when they arrived at school. In the Jordan section of Clarendon County, the backed-up waters flooded some of the bridges and thus colored children had to paddle a boat across the water and walk the rest of the way to their inferior school. A minister of the community tried every possible source to have this condition adjusted." Rev. De Laine—the man I usually called Daddy—was that minister.

CLARENDON

In 1946 Clarendon was one of the poorest counties of South Carolina, which in turn was one of the nation's poorest states. Nothing of particular significance had happened in Clarendon County's 607 square miles since 1780 when Gen. Francis Marion (the Swamp Fox of Revolutionary War history) and his brigade ambushed British troops on River Road near the Santee River.

More than two-thirds of Clarendon's approximately 31,500 residents, including our family, were descended from slave women. Mostly poor and uneducated, the majority of these people of color lived in the lower part of the county, many on farms that belonged to descendants of slave owners. Large numbers of the population whose ancestors had been held in involuntary bondage dwelled in unpainted, two- or three-room cabins that sometimes sheltered families of six or more. They tilled the same soil and grew the same crops as their ancestors had done a century earlier. The children helped the adults with farm chores, enabling families to survive from one year to the next. Only in winter, when the ground

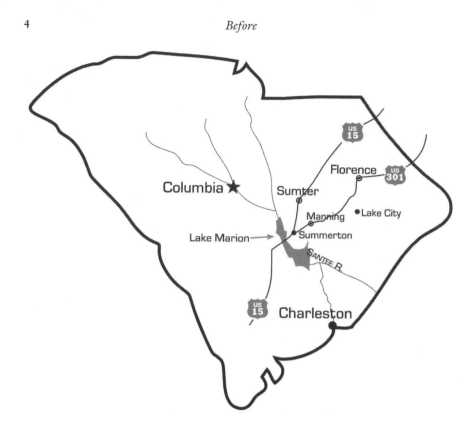

Map of South Carolina. The illustration shows the approximate extent of
Lake Marion, which was dammed in the 1940s. Illustration by the author

lay fallow, were children free to go to school. Even then the farm chores had to
be done before leaving for school, as well as upon returning. Rain or shine, summer or winter, cows had to be milked, hogs fed, and eggs collected.

The primary crop was cotton, with tobacco being a close second. Paid a penny
a pound, expert cotton pickers might top three hundred pounds a day. Most
laborers, however, didn't make it to the two-hundred-pound mark, so they took
home less than two dollars for a day's work. Earlier in the year, a family might
have earned another hundred or so dollars from tying tar-laden tobacco leaves or
doing other equally dirty work.

Life was a little better for the few black people who were landowners. With
a little help, a lot of hard work, and the best possible circumstances, a husband
and wife might harvest six or seven bales of cotton by the end of the season. The
sale of that cotton might gross a little more than two thousand dollars for almost
seven months of backbreaking plowing, seeding, chopping, weeding, and picking. From this money all expenses had to be met and debts paid.

Most black people who didn't labor in the fields did other menial tasks, such
as loading trucks, sawing wood, cooking, cleaning, or caring for children. They

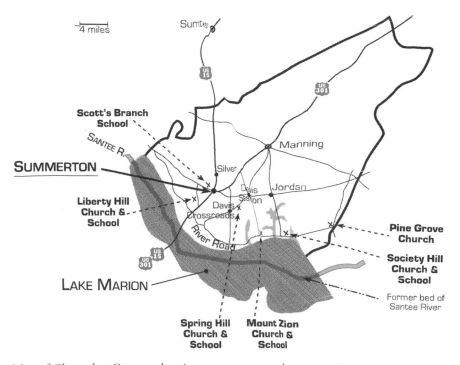

Map of Clarendon County, showing most towns and communities mentioned in the text. The locations of several schools and churches are also shown. The riverbed that formed the county's southern border before the impoundment of Santee River waters in the 1940s is also indicated. Illustration by the author

were not prepared to do any other work because the education of practically all black people ended before seventh grade.

Clarendon's white people owned most of the land and the businesses. They were the money lenders, as well as the collectors. They were the lawmakers, the judges, and the law enforcers. They were also the ones who were permitted to vote in the Democratic Party primary, who were served first in stores, who were allowed to go to toilets at gas stations, and whose children could ride to school on buses. That was the way things had been for generations, and the entire social system—economic, political, educational, and customary—was designed to keep them that way, preserving what some people called the "time-honored southern way of life."

For black people, however, that way of life fostered a festering discontent that was sown by the thorny briars of discrimination, fertilized with the manure of disenfranchisement, and kept warm by the heat of an inner rage generated each time a fully grown man was called "boy." That discontent germinated in fields and forests, at cookstoves and washtubs, on wagons, in rowboats, and beside army jeeps. Nurtured by the anger of war veterans who were denied the democratic rights for which they had fought, cultivated by the frustration of individuals wronged by an unjust legal system, and watered by tears of men and women who didn't know where their ancestors had come from—but who knew without a doubt that their children were destined for a dead-end future—the discontent grew until it ripened into *Briggs et al. v. Elliott et al.,* a school desegregation lawsuit.

A State of Education?

Clarendon's 6,500 black schoolchildren attended about sixty ramshackle one-, two-, three-, or four-room structures and three or four larger ones that were divided among more than thirty independent school districts. Each school district was under the auspices of an officially appointed trustee board, composed of white men who had little interest in the shabby black schools. As in other areas of the South, another set of men—black and self-appointed—actually saw to the welfare of the schools. These volunteer trustees had to beg for every penny of assistance they got from the official trustees. More often than not, their requests for aid to the indigent schools were denied by the officials with declarations such as "I'm real sorry, but y'all's school already got as much as we can spare."

This unidentified, two-room elementary school building, with its small windows and separate classroom doors, was typical of many black schools before 1951. The foundation pillars that supported the structure may have been bricks or logs. Note the absence of a chimney. Courtesy of the De Laine Family Collection

When cold winter air seeped through the cracks between a classroom's floorboards, the classroom teacher or the principal had to see that a fire was lit. If there was no wood for a fire, students were sent to collect and cut firewood. If educational supplies were needed, the instructors had to be resourceful, inventive, and willing to purchase school supplies from their meager monthly salaries.

Two hundred years earlier, in 1740, South Carolina's legislators banned education of black people in an effort to curb the threat of slave rebellions. When the slaves were emancipated more than a century later, practically all of them were unable to read. During the brief period of Reconstruction, many gained a rudimentary education in free public schools. But, too soon, political power shifted to politicians who had no regard for universal education. They drastically reduced all education funding and virtually eliminated centralized control of the state's schools.

In 1895 South Carolina adopted a constitution that made racial segregation mandatory. Around the same time, the United States Supreme Court condoned the practice of segregation with its *Plessy v. Ferguson* decision. Racial separation of public facilities was declared lawful if the facilities were equal. With the practice of "separate but equal" thus given legal status, Jim Crow laws and Black Codes further disenfranchised African Americans in the South. Deprived of practically all rights as United States citizens, black people were denied a voice in their government, relegated to the fringes of society, and essentially stripped of any recourse for justice. Using the crutch of "separate but equal," South Carolina's Act of Separation went a step further and made it a crime for black and white children to attend the same schools.

At the beginning of the twentieth century, practically all South Carolina schools were poorly equipped and in a state of disrepair. White politicians saw little need to educate black children who were destined to become laborers and farmers. So, as the years passed, the racially separate school systems became less and less equal. Practically all support for black education came from private sources: philanthropists, missionaries, fraternal organizations, and churches. Erected on private property, even the school buildings for black children were paid for with money raised largely (sometimes completely) by parents. Some philanthropies, such as the Julius Rosenwald Fund, encouraged both parental and public support by requiring cash contributions from black communities to build schools and agreements from the white-run school boards to operate them. These places for the education of black children came to be considered part of the public school system, despite their having been built on private land with nongovernmental money. Nevertheless the public school boards supported them grudgingly.

Academic performance by the state's children lagged behind that of the rest of the nation, with black children faring far worse than white children. In an effort to improve matters, school attendance was made compulsory in 1921. Of course no attempt was made to enforce the law for black children; they had too few schools and no means of transportation to get to them. Three years later the state's legislature passed the 6-0-1 law, with the hope that education would improve in poor school districts. The state would pay for six months of school if a school district paid for one additional month of instruction. There was no required contribution from the county, as represented by the zero. The 6-0-1 plan also facilitated consolidation of schools and provided assistance to purchase school buses.

As a result of this law, numerous small schools were abandoned and replaced by brick or stone buildings to which rural children were transported by bus. Once there the students enjoyed the luxuries of indoor toilets, drinking fountains, central heating, and yet-to-be-filled libraries. Janitors, paid by public funds, kept the school buildings in good condition, and lunchroom aides served hot lunches. The results were good. Attendance rose, fewer children repeated grades, and not as many students dropped out of school. Only one thing prevented the new system from being ideal.

That one thing? The authorities didn't consolidate, or even improve, the black schools. Although the number of black schools in Clarendon County had increased during the twenty years following the passage of 6-0-1, conditions remained essentially unchanged. Black schools were still dilapidated, small, and poorly lit. White children rode buses to school; black children didn't. White schools had janitors; black schools often didn't even have fuel to make fires.

By 1944 most Clarendon school districts had increased the length of the school year for black children from three to at least six months, with a couple of districts making it as long as seven and a half months. But not one of Clarendon's black schools was open for eight and a half months—as the white schools were. Many rural children didn't begin school until they were nine or ten years old, when they were able to walk several miles along the unpaved roads that, depending on the weather, were either muddy or dusty. Even then they couldn't get to school if the weather was bad or if farmwork had to be done. The spotty attendance resulted in few students being promoted annually and some first-grade students being teenagers.

In their overcrowded classrooms, students often sat squeezed together on long benches behind equally long tables. If many children were in school, they just pushed closer together so everyone could have a seat. On winter days body heat supplemented the warmth from stoves that were stuffed with leaves and twigs collected by male students or filled with wood cut by fathers or maybe even stoked with a little coal bought by teachers. Most schoolbooks, rented from the district, were dog-eared discards from the white schools. If the books were new (which wasn't often), they were stamped "FOR USE IN COLORED SCHOOLS." Apparently those books had information that was forbidden to white children.

South Carolina's segregated facilities for education were far from equal and everyone knew it. For example, practically every penny generated for education in Clarendon County was used for the education of white children. State funds for white teachers' salaries and other educational needs were supplemented by local money. On the other hand, the salaries of Clarendon's black teachers were paid solely by the state. No public money was allocated for supplies in black schools, and black school budgets had to include student fees to pay for essentials such as brooms, coal, and chalk. Many white people didn't think black people deserved equality —either of school facilities or of teacher salaries. A clipping from a June 1943 issue of the *Sumter Daily Item* included the statement "The white taxpayers will, soon or late, conclude that they cannot carry the great burden of sustaining a school system for 814,000 colored people whose relative contribution to the tax fund is small."

Although the economy of Clarendon County depended on the labor of black people and although its black students outnumbered white students by a ratio of three to one, in 1945 the county's white school property was valued at more than four and a half times that of black school property. The previous year the county's black schools received a combined grand total of $19.00 from public funds for "new buildings / building alteration / grounds." Also in that year county spending for fuel, water, light, power, and janitorial supplies at black schools was $300. Averaged out among the 67 black schools, the amount came to a little less than $4.50 per school. County records for the following year, show that $51.00 of the budget for black schools was spent on "wages, operation and repair" of school buses, although the county operated no buses for black children! The sum worked out to less than a penny per student. In contrast an average of $8.99 per child was spent on transportation for white students in the same year.

Another thing that South Carolina's General Assembly did when it passed 6-0-1 in 1924 was to establish a four-tiered salary scale for teachers based on both gender and race. Salaries of white males were at the top; those of black males were less than half those of white females; and black women were at the bottom. In 1940 the average yearly salary for the 2,915 classroom teachers in 1,758 white schools was $1,067. During the same year the average pay for the 5,780 teachers in 2,343 black schools was $535. The situation was similar in other southern states.

When the U.S. Supreme Court ruled favorably on a Virginia salary equalization lawsuit in 1940, South Carolina's legislators publicly announced that no one could force them to equalize black teachers' salaries. To emphasize their stand, they approved salary supplements for white teachers and completely ignored the black educators. Knowing that South Carolina's white people did not take kindly to the idea of equal salaries, the black leaders of the statewide black teachers' organization refused to press for salary equity. State education authorities even sent representatives to the black teachers' meetings to discourage black teachers from suing, and the black association's leader cautioned members, "These white folks aren't going to let you make as much money as they make. You're a fool if you try to get them to do it. All you gonna do is to get fired." Only after electing new leaders was the teachers' association able to engage the NAACP to file a lawsuit for equal salaries.

The South Carolina teachers won two lawsuits with favorable decisions by Judge J. Waties Waring in the federal district court. After his 1945 ruling that tiered salary scales were discriminatory, South Carolina's lawmakers had to find a way to make salaries uniform. Using the premise that white teachers were better trained than black teachers, the decision was made to base state aid for salaries on individual qualifications. Under the new rules, each teacher would be placed in a class (from I to a low of V) determined by education and given a grade (from A to D) according to achievement on the National Teachers Examination. Within that framework their final salaries would be determined according to years of teaching experience. A situation should no longer exist in which elementary school teacher salaries averaged $998 for white males, $856 for white females, $411 for black males, and $372 for black females.

Much discussion preceded adoption of the new certification standards. A March 27, 1946, article in Columbia's *State* (South Carolina's major newspaper), quoted Senator W. B. Harvey of Beaufort as saying, "If we pass this . . . and the Negroes fail to qualify for higher salaries, I warn you, they will claim they were given unequal educational facilities. They will say . . . give us schools equal to yours . . . and they'll say it in court and the courts will sustain them."

The senator also publicly acknowledged, "The real reason for this . . . is to set up, by a legalized method, a standard by which . . . the majority of . . . white teachers can qualify for higher salaries, and the Negroes cannot, thus legalizing a difference in their salaries." Then, accurately foretelling the future, he advised, "Injustice will not forever be borne silently. The day is not far distant, if we don't correct injustices, when the Negro will try to correct them at the ballot box."

It wasn't just the conditions of school buildings and teacher's salaries that kept African Americans in Clarendon and the rest of South Carolina uneducated. Transportation was a major problem. Often the rural students couldn't get to school to take advantage of the meager learning opportunities. Black students who graduated from one of Clarendon's elementary schools could continue their education only by attending a distant high school, one perhaps as much as ten miles away. With no means of transportation, students needed to board in town. Most families couldn't afford that expense. Some young people tried walking to high school, finishing their chores before dawn, then taking the straightest route to the school, cutting across fields along the way. On days when the fields were too muddy, they walked along the road. School buses carrying white children splashed mud on them as they passed. Then, adding insult to injury, the young riders—filled with scorn learned from their parents (and perhaps bored with the monotonous, bumpy rides)—diverted themselves by trying to hit the walking black children with spit or soda-bottle caps while yelling the most degrading epithets they knew. By the time the black students got to school, after as much as an hour and a half of walking, they were late, dirty, tired, and angry. After school they walked home where evening chores awaited. Most young people soon gave up the quest for more education.

State authorities knew their failure to provide black children with school bus transportation was discriminatory. When the topic of school buses was considered in the state senate in 1943, Senator Harvey advised, "Transportation is the one most vulnerable spot we have [regarding] discrimination against Negroes. . . . It takes the same muscular effort for a colored boy to walk three miles to school as a white. . . . We can get around the difference in teacher salaries on the basis of certification of fitness. . . . But on school bus transportation, as an attorney I could not file an answer to a charge of discrimination."

A considerable number of rural black parents worried about school transportation for their children and often talked over the problem with each other. In school the teachers thought about it, although rarely voicing their anguish. On Sundays the preachers—sometimes teachers themselves—generally mentioned the problem only while praying for God to "give us the strength to carry on." There seemed to be no outside solution to the problem so, at several places in the state, groups of parents addressed the problem by pooling resources and providing their own transportation for their children.

THE PRIMARY GATE

The matter of voting rights was as important to black leaders as the condition of the children's education. Like most southern states, South Carolina was overwhelmingly Democratic. As a consequence, the outcome of every general election was predetermined by the outcome of the Democratic Party's primary election. However, black people were not allowed to vote in the party's primary elections and, therefore, had no voice in government. A similar situation existed in other southern states. Lonnie E. Smith, a black man, sued for the right to vote in the Democratic Party's primary elections in Texas. On April 3, 1944, the U.S. Supreme Court ruled that the Texas Democratic Party could not exclude black voters from participating in its primary elections. Because it was governed by a number of state regulations, the party was ruled to be acting as an arm of the state.

South Carolina's white people were angry. They rebelliously declared their Democratic Party had excluded black people from primary elections since the 1890s, and they vowed to never open the elections to them. Immediately after the Texas ruling, the South Carolina governor, Olin D. Johnston, announced, "History has taught us that we must keep our white Democratic primaries pure and unadulterated." In a rallying cry, he declared, "We South Carolinians will use the necessary methods to retain white supremacy in our primaries and to safe-guard the homes and happiness of our people. . . . White supremacy will be maintained."

Hell-bent on keeping the state's black people from having a voice in government, Governor Johnston promptly recommended that South Carolina's laws be made foolproof enough for the Democratic Party to circumvent the Court's ruling. So, eleven days after the Supreme Court's decision, South Carolina's General Assembly met in a special six-day session, and the lawmakers proved their expertise in manipulating the law. In a concentrated and coordinated affirmation of the governor's declaration, more than 140 state laws that regulated either the Democratic Party or its primary elections were repealed. The action allowed the party to operate as a bona fide private club, making it exempt from the Supreme Court's ruling. By the seventh day, the legislators' work was done. Presumably they rested.

SUMMERTON

Before the massive gates of the Santee Dam were closed in 1941 and the rising waters formed the new Lake Marion, one of Clarendon's borders was the Santee River. Ten miles north of the river lay an insignificant little town called Summerton. At the time it didn't even have a traffic light. Appearing as a tiny speck on the South Carolina map, Summerton was about equidistant from Columbia and Charleston, the state's largest cities. Of the three incorporated towns in the county, Summerton was the second largest, with about 1,500 individuals residing inside its official boundaries. The homes of most black "townspeople" were just beyond the town limits. The rest of the area's population lived up to nine miles from town—near hamlets and villages with names like Davis Crossroads, Davis Station, and Silver.

Three black schools fell within Summerton's school district. The buildings were erected in 1935 or later, after parents raised enough money to "qualify" for supplementary public funds. All three schools accommodated the elementary grades, but only the ten-room Scott's Branch School offered high school classes for black students. It was built just outside the town limits after the old four-room school was accidentally destroyed by fire in 1935.

In 1946 Scott's Branch had real desks, not tables like the other two schools. The desks were the old-fashioned kind with a fold-up seat attached to the front of a metal frame and a desktop attached behind. Purchased from the white schools after being discarded, they were covered with ink stains and carved initials. Their joints were so loose that a child using the desk had trouble writing when the child on the attached seat moved. Long boards were suspended between two desks when there weren't enough seats. To serve its six-hundred-plus students, the school had two outhouse toilets, each with four or five seats. The single schoolyard pump, so heavily used that the ground around it was muddy before midmorning, was replaced with outdoor running water taps around 1945.

In the years approaching the middle of the twentieth century, Jim Crow laws, disparities in allocation of funds for education, and lack of school transportation were keeping Clarendon's African Americans uneducated in the same way that levying fines for teaching black people to read had done two hundred years earlier. With no voice in government, the people of Clarendon seemed dammed to an eternal state of poverty and ignorance.

DE LAINE

In 1946 the time was right for a man like Rev. Joseph Armstrong "J. A." De Laine to assume the mantle of civic leadership. An unpretentious man who walked with God and—sometimes—with a pistol by his side, his concern for the unlettered rural people of Clarendon County and their children succeeded in inspiring some of them, igniting their allegiance so much that they dared to do the unthinkable. They undertook a formidable quest to make change happen, to claim their "piece of the pie." Their journey took them from asking for school bus transportation to challenging public school segregation, the legal and widespread practice of "separate but equal" in the nation's education systems.

The earliest known De Laine ancestor is said to have been an African who came to American shores as a free mariner in the late 1700s or early 1800s. Probably jumping ship, he remained in the Charleston area, where a number of free black people lived, until he acquired a white "protector" and moved inland to the future Clarendon County. There, using the name Charles De Laine, he worked in the building trades. He sired a son, also named Charles, who earned his living repairing mills. Since the millwright Charles was a free man who often traveled around the countryside at a time when almost all nonwhites were confined to plantations as slaves, the name De Laine became widely known.

After Emancipation, the De Laines became landowners, tradesmen, and operators of small businesses. One of them—Henry Charles, my paternal grandfather—became a preacher and pastor in the African Methodist Episcopal (AME) Church, a denomination founded by free black people in 1787 because of racial harassment. In the years following Emancipation, AME churches proliferated in South Carolina. My grandfather probably found it easy to accept the church's motto—"God, Our Father; Christ, Our Redeemer; Man, Our Brother"—for the men of his family had never been held in bondage. For my Grandmother Tisbia, who bore my father and twelve other children, the part that said "Man, Our Brother" was only common sense. Both of her parents had been born as slaves, fathered by their mothers' owners.

The eighth child of Grandma Tisbia and Grandpa H. C. was my father. Called JA by family members, he was born on July 2, 1898, near Manning, Clarendon's county seat. In spite of the Jim Crow laws, his parents imbued their children with a sense of self-sufficiency, a belief in the brotherhood of men, and an expectation of justice. Although family members accepted the practice of segregation, they refused to be subservient—or to be summarily deprived of their rights.

When JA was fourteen, he soundly beat a white boy who touched one of his sisters inappropriately. In the South Carolina of 1912, black boys who did such things were subject to punishment. JA was sentenced to a dozen lashes with a cane, administered by his school principal. The other boy would not be punished. Refusing to submit to the unfair discipline, JA left home, hopped on a freight train, and "rode the rails" like a hobo until he reached Atlanta.

There he eked out a precarious living and attended night classes at the "Colored" YMCA. After several years he came home and, working in family enterprises, learned carpentry and business skills. By that time his father had become a presiding elder for the AME Church's Manning District, a group of thirty-some churches whose location coincided almost exactly with Clarendon County's boundaries. Having a religious bent, JA eagerly accompanied his father when he visited the churches, and people throughout the county became acquainted with the personable, outgoing young man.

Around 1917 he went to the state capital, Columbia, to pursue a teacher-training course at Allen University, an AME Church college. For the next fourteen years, he worked as a carpenter, teacher, and entrepreneur—supporting himself, helping relatives, and buying property. Simultaneously he nurtured his spiritual development, becoming licensed to preach by the AME Church in 1923, and receiving his first assignment as a church pastor in 1925.

While at Allen he was exposed to the idea that black churches were duty bound to provide more than spiritual nourishment and was taken under the wing of civic activist E. A. Adams, a minister and faculty member. When he earned his bachelor of arts degree at thirty-three years of age, Rev. De Laine became one of the less than 1 percent of the nation's black people who were college graduates. He was immediately recruited into a special part-time program for agriculture teachers that, when completed, would make him eligible to become principal of a training (vocational high) school for black students.

In 1931, the year he graduated, he married Mattie Belton, a graduate of a teacher-training course. Three years later, while serving as principal of a Baptist-controlled training school, he was asked to change religious denominations and become a Baptist. Never one to alter his allegiance for personal gain, Rev. De Laine refused. The Baptist elders who ran the school did not renew his contract.

Undaunted, he returned to Clarendon County with his wife and his infant son (my older brother, who was named after my father but always called Jay). Many Clarendon people remembered him from his youth, and others were familiar with the name De Laine. He had matured and was more learned, but his convictions were much the same as when he first left home. He believed in respecting everyone, keeping his word, looking others in the eye, and accumulating little or no debt. He felt he had a duty, as a Christian leader, to be involved in the community. And he was convinced that God would guide and protect him, that Jesus Christ would redeem his soul, and that the brotherhood of men was not defined by color.

His bishop assigned him to serve as pastor of the small Spring Hill circuit of two churches. Both churches were located about five miles from Summerton. There was no parsonage. The usual practice in the AME Church was for a pastor to remain at an assignment for eight years. Since he needed a place to live, Rev. De Laine confidently used his own money and carpentry skills to help build a three-bedroom parsonage at Spring Hill.

He was hired as principal and head teacher of the six grade, three-room Bob Johnson Elementary School, near the village of Davis Station. The road to the shack that housed the school passed within a few feet of the homes of the Pearson brothers, Levi and Hammett. During his first year at the school, the new principal hired Mr. Hammett's son, fourteen-year-old Jessie, to fell small trees, cut the wood, and start fires in the school's stoves. Jessie later observed that "a strong friendship developed between Pop, Uncle Levi, and Rev. De Laine. But Rev. De Laine was a real practical man—he hired me because I was responsible and lived nearby, not because Pop was his friend."

By the end of 1939, the family had expanded to include me and my younger brother, Brumit (known as BB). Rev. De Laine had moved on to become principal of the eight grade Liberty Hill School while Mis' De Laine, as Mother was called, continued teaching at the little school in the dilapidated Masonic lodge beside Spring Hill Church. The four-room Liberty Hill school building was new, having replaced the hovel where Rev. De Laine had occasionally taught when he was a student at Allen. The school was close to Liberty Hill AME Church, a stately edifice designed and built by my great uncle Pete when my grandfather was the church's pastor.

Our family was well off by local standards. As Rev. De Laine saw it, however, security was a matter of being free of debt and having an income made possible by property ownership. To that end he had bought a farm near Spring Hill and, with a trustworthy farm manager, started establishing a modern, highly productive farm.

His neat little world was turned topsy-turvy in December 1940 when his pastoral assignment was unexpectedly changed to the Pine Grove / Society Hill circuit. With a combined membership of almost nine hundred, it was the county's third largest AME appointment and appropriate for a man of his education and experience. He should have been delighted, but he wasn't. Located on Santee River Road southeast of Summerton, Society Hill was fourteen miles from our house; Pine Grove was nine miles farther. Both churches were in the remotest

Spring Hill Elementary School continued to be housed on the first floor of this building, the Spring Hill Prince Hall Masons' lodge, until 1950. The lodge stood on the grounds of Spring Hill AME Church. In this photograph, taken circa 1940, teachers Mattie De Laine and Helen Richburg (wife of Rev. E. E. Richburg) are standing with their students. The girl in the front row, middle, is the author as a child. Courtesy of South Caroliniana Library

part of the county; to get to either entailed a long, uncomfortable journey along unpaved back roads. Furthermore neither offered living accommodations. The change undermined Rev. De Laine's financial strategy because his master plan had not included building a family home for two more years.

However, a man like my father is rarely caught completely unprepared. He immediately bought an excellently situated lot in Summerton, less than twenty feet outside the town limits and directly across from Scott's Branch, the "town's" school for black children. Four months later we moved into the house, even before it had inside walls. Some day it was supposed to become my mother's dream house, but for the time being, we had no electricity (it had not yet come to the area), an outside water pump (the water mains didn't come to our side of town), and no telephone (they were still a rarity in Clarendon).

As a conscientious pastor, Rev. De Laine made it a point to visit the members of his church regularly. Roberta Mack was a teenager when he was assigned to Society Hill, her family's church. She described him as a humble man and observed, "Some people act high and mighty when they get a little education or money, but Rev. De Laine wasn't like that. He didn't act like he was better than other people. He went to people's houses no matter what kind of place they lived in. And he'd sit and talk, or help out with the work—whatever the family was doing."

She recalled how the people of Society Hill really liked my father—even though he wasn't the kind of "hollering preacher" they were accustomed to. "He was always showing us how to live our daily lives—teaching when he was preaching, and teaching when he wasn't." People came to him with their troubles, knowing that whatever they told him in private would never be repeated. But some things couldn't remain private. If, for example, an unmarried girl got pregnant, Rev. De Laine counseled her at home and then set a Sunday for the people to welcome her back. Believing that people should get along together, he always taught cooperation. When church members had arguments, he tried to help them resolve the issues, facing problems before they became large.

My father was actively involved in statewide AME Church affairs and the black teachers' professional association. He avidly read the black-owned publications, keeping abreast of social issues. Like other socially concerned ministers, he used black news media as educational resources for parishioners, sometimes reading entire articles to virtually illiterate congregations who had no representation in the mainstream press.

He once read an editorial entitled "Are Teachers Children or Fools?" Thinking the article was full of common sense, he invited the writer to speak to his congregation. After the speech he received a warning that "somebody was going to get a bullet in the belly." Unintimidated, Rev. De Laine claimed, "That was the beginning of my involvement with affairs about Negro Rights. I began to work to raise money to help with the teachers' salary case." In Clarendon County he was the only teacher who openly advocated financing a plaintiff in a salary equalization case. Although he collected a little money at one county teachers' meeting, he said, "We raised more money from others than from teachers." One teacher told the county superintendent of education that Rev. De Laine was trying to stir up a fight between white and colored teachers, and accused him of being a Communist agitator.

Americans dreaded Communism. The establishment often branded the NAACP as a Communist front, and many southerners were convinced that NAACP members were trying to undermine democracy. With NAACP leaders pushing for change, the organization was growing stronger in South Carolina, despite a fear that deterred some people from supporting the organization. To avoid the negativity associated with the NAACP, a less controversial organization called the Negro Citizens' Committee (NCC) was used as a cover.

The president of South Carolina's NCC was E. A. Adams, Rev. De Laine's confidant and former teacher. In 1942 Dr. Adams and the state NCC secretary, James N. Hinton, who was also executive director of the South Carolina Conference of NAACP Branches, dispatched another activist to persuade my father to organize a Clarendon NAACP branch. Rev. De Laine agreed on the need for a county branch, but he had his hands full—pastoring, teaching, and operating a farm with four tenants. Saying, "The job is too big for me to undertake alone," he helped his visitor seek cooperation from the county's other two leading AME pastors.

The three pastors immediately formed a temporary organization, but the two others who were chosen must have been reluctant for my father made no further mention of them. By mid-1943 he had recruited six strong NAACP supporters. They were Hammett and Levi Pearson, James W. "J. W." Seals (another AME pastor), home demonstration agent Sarah Daniels, Professor McFadden, and Mrs. House. According to Rev. De Laine, the small group was effective, "but there was a great price to be paid to get the message to people. Because we had no telephones, contact had to be door to door or on the street on Saturday evenings."

He enthusiastically applied for a NAACP charter although there was a hitch in finding a meeting place. Pastors of Clarendon's larger, centrally located churches were reluctant for the controversial organization to use their premises. Finally permission came from Edward Frazier, pastor of Summerton's small St. Mark AME Church. The first formal meeting of the nascent NAACP branch was held in the modest structure.

Unfortunately Rev. De Laine fell ill a few months later and was hospitalized for an extended period. Dr. Adams came from Columbia to preach for him on Sundays. His farm manager continued overseeing farm operations. Mother took care of the family and her job. But no one had the skills, personality, and inclination to lead the fledgling NAACP branch effectively. It withered and died.

2. *Spokesman for the Disenfranchised*

I wanted a piece of the pie.

JESSE PEARSON

W hen Rev. De Laine was assigned to Society Hill Church in 1940, a major change was in the making for church members. A hydroelectric plant was being built nearby on the Santee River. By the time he arrived, the basin of one of two planned reservoirs had been cleared and its dam built. Work had just begun on the second basin, the one that would become the future Lake Marion. Within a few months the enlargement of World War II hostilities caused the hydroelectric facility to be declared necessary for national defense, and its completion became urgent. The eight-mile-long Santee River dam was hastily finished, and the last of its massive gates closed on November 12, 1941. The water impounded by the world's longest earthen dam began to flood adjacent areas before the basin had been completely cleared.

Each rain pushed the water farther inland and the imprisoned water flooded the Santee's tributaries, inching higher as it lapped at support pillars of rickety wooden bridges. Covered with canebrakes, prickly brambles, and thousands of stumps and dead trees, the basin floor was hidden by the deceptively gentle surface of the new lake. In the five years after the dam's gates closed, the water obliterated the rickety bridge where River Road crossed Church Branch beside Society Hill Church and the adjacent Society Hill School. At first people used the bridge to ford their way across the water. As the water got deeper and the bridge couldn't be seen, they used the bridge railings as markers for the old road. However, when the tops of the railings sank out of view, the people were cut off from the other side altogether, leaving those who lived on the far side of the water as much as five or six miles by road—a half-hour wagon journey—from the church and school. Rowboats were pressed into service to make the trip shorter.

When Roberta Mack was a student at Society Hill School, she walked four miles to school, crossing the Church Branch bridge. After she graduated from eighth grade in 1941, she was hired as the school's first cook. When she got married, she quit the job. By that time the lake was almost filled. The edge of the water was within a thousand feet of Society Hill Church, and she had started paddling a boat across, just as some others did.

Most adults feared the boat trip, remembering the numerous perils that lurked unseen below the water's placid surface. As time passed, their concern about the water subsided. They carried on with their daily lives as always, adjusting their activities to the rhythm of the seasons. In August, when limp brown tassels signaled the ripeness of the corn kernels, the leaves were also ready to be stripped from corn stalks for fodder. It was the time of year when many children from "up north" visited their grandparents and cousins "down on the farm," safe from temptations of the big cities.

One Sunday during the August after Mis' Roberta got married, Viola Johnson's grandson drowned while the Society Hill congregation was in the church. Unnoticed by the grown-ups, the boy and several other children had slipped out and gone to play by the water.

Mis' Roberta recalled, "Mis' Viola's grandson and another boy got in the boat and went out. According to the other boy, they were fooling around, daring each other to jump in the water. The one that drowned was just visiting his grandma for the summer. I believe he thought he could swim over to her house just across the water. He took off his clothes and jumped in." Shuddering, she continued. "That boy never did come up. His body got caught in some of the stuff that was covered by the water."

The tragedy had nothing to do with school. Except for where, when, and how the drowning happened, it might have been dismissed as "just one of those things." However, Rev. De Laine was inside Society Hill Church at the time, and he knew that, by failing to restore a satisfactory travel route, the authorities had left a dangerous condition behind. Always the teacher, he was particularly worried about the children who came to the nearby school. If another bridge wasn't going to be built, he thought that at least a school bus should have been provided. Although he had no official connection with Society Hill School, he felt obliged to do something. It was, he believed, only a matter of time before another accident happened.

The church elders delegated him and two of their group to seek relief for the problem. Rev. De Laine composed a letter to a county official that all three men signed. No satisfactory response came. Determined to have officials fulfill their obligation regarding public safety, he wrote to the local school trustees, then to the county superintendent of schools. All claimed to be powerless to do anything even though the white children of the area rode to school daily on public school buses.

For more than two years, Rev. De Laine worked to gain relief for the children of the Society Hill section, writing to the road supervisor, state officials, and officials at the hydroelectric project. Then he wrote to officials in the federal government, all the way up the hierarchy until he reached U.S. Attorney General Thomas Clark. Mis' Roberta said that whenever he received a reply, "He read the letters in church so we would all know what was going on." There never was any relief, and the children continued to use the boat to get to school.

After the end of the Second World War in 1945, large numbers of veterans returned to their homes. Around the time of the drowning, Summerton's black veterans were trying to take advantage of the GI Bill's educational benefits and to improve their agriculture skills. However, the local education authorities failed to make it possible for them to do so. This angered the young men. As Jessie Pearson—Hammett Pearson's son and one of the veterans—observed, "I had fought for my country, and I wanted a piece of the pie. Not the whole pie. Just my piece. And they didn't want to give it to me!"

The veterans approached Rev. De Laine with their problem. To help them, he wrote a letter to the state superintendent of education that inquired how they could get agriculture classes. The letter was signed by Jessie, his cousin Ferdinand, and several other veterans. A reply from the state office said the local school board was responsible for finding an instructor and making classes available. Despite also receiving a communication to this effect, the local authorities took no action, asserting that no teacher was available. Using advice from my father, the veterans located an eligible teacher and told him how to apply for the job. The ploy was successful. As Ferdinand recalled, "The GI classes started almost a year after I got home. But soon afterwards, seven teachers and about one hundred veterans were involved."

My father was pleased to have helped the veterans. Most likely, none of them had completed ninth grade before enlisting.

In 1943 or 1944, two groups of Clarendon parents (one from the Davis Station area, the other from a few miles farther east in the Jordan section) brought up the subject of transportation for black schoolchildren with their respective local authorities. The authorities denied the requests, saying, "There just isn't enough money."

Recognizing the futility of expecting assistance from public funds, somebody suggested that the parents themselves buy a school bus, as had been done elsewhere. To consider the proposal, seventeen Davis Station area families assembled at New Light Baptist Church. Before the work-worn men and women dispersed, the Houses—Wilbur and James—had come to an agreement with Hammett and Levi Pearson, Preston Lemon, "Sugar" Madison, "Toss" Green, Isaiah De Laine, Heyward Lindsay, and eight other families whose names have been lost to history. They would pool their money and buy a used bus.

Someone said that the old, rusting vehicle the parents bought had been used as a chicken coop and for hay storage. When the bus had been cleaned up, the parents discovered a part was needed before the vehicle could carry the children. With their money low, one of the volunteer trustees asked an official for assistance in repairing the bus.

The request could not have been completely unanticipated. A clipping found in my father's files from the *Sumter Daily Item* (reprinted from the March 13, 1943, edition of the *Charleston News and Courier*) shows that perhaps a year before the Davis Station parents' request, the state senate had discussed the topic of school transportation for black children. In spite of, or perhaps because of, those concerns at the state level, the parents were given a few dollars to buy the necessary bus part. They were also warned that the county had no more money to give them.

Rev. De Laine thought the parents' approach was reasonable. In more than fourteen years as a school principal, he had learned that change doesn't just happen. If black parents wanted something done for their children, they would probably have to do it themselves. Many times he had requested money to buy school essentials only to be told, "Sorry, Preacher, there ain't no more money available for your school this year." Going back to his shabby school, he would use his ingenuity to solve the problem. He often recalled the time when, "I bought window sashes and materials for the school and . . . did the work myself with the children helping during school hours [and] I couldn't even get the officials to pay for the materials." The situation was hard to accept, but as a strong advocate of "taking what you have and making what you want," Rev. De Laine knew that, until the authorities were forced to act equitably and fairly, the solution for the transportation problem was up to the parents.

Too old and too neglected for too many years, the Davis Station bus sometimes started in the morning and sometimes didn't. Sometimes it conked out as it bumped along the rutted route, and sometimes it got almost to the school before it stopped. When it did arrive at its morning stops, children quickly got on, not wanting the engine to die while waiting for them. If it didn't arrive and the sun had climbed too high, the waiting students knew it was time to turn around and go home. Despite the deficiencies of the ancient bus, it was a disappointment when no amount of tinkering could resurrect it and the children again had to walk—sometimes getting rides on passing wagons and pickup trucks.

Having once proven their ability to buy a bus, the parents knew they could do it again. They located a reconditioned school bus that cost $700. Its purchase would be a financial strain for the farmers, the most affluent among them probably having annual gross incomes of around $1,500. They reached out, and other parents joined them. Even my father's farm manager, Johnny Gipson from the Davis Crossroads area, joined the group. The bus would make it possible for his eldest daughter to live at home, six miles from school, instead of with us during her last year of high school.

By the spring of 1946, the students were again riding to school. The bus route started at the House settlement, went about two miles out to Davis Station, made a loop of about six miles, and passed by Triumph Holiness Church. After going back through Davis Station, it went five miles over to Davis Crossroads, three more miles up to U.S. Route 301, and finally ended with the one-and-a-half-mile stretch to Scott's Branch, just beyond the western edge of Summerton. A few children walked more than two miles to get to their bus stop.

More reliable than the first, the new bus still broke down too often. The continual outlay of two dollars a day for the driver's salary—plus gasoline money—was a big drain on the families' meager finances. The parents needed help with operational costs, but no one felt confident enough to approach the officials. However, they all knew my father and were aware of his efforts to establish an NAACP branch, as well as of what he was trying to do at Society Hill. Some even knew how he had helped the veterans. For some he had been the teacher of their children, and for others their pastor. Many remembered him from his youth. All held him in high regard.

Because he was an educated man who would listen to their concerns and who was unafraid of the authorities, Rev. De Laine was asked to become spokesman for the Davis Station parents. Believing that God helps those who try, he willingly accepted the responsibility. With a committee, he went to the county superintendent of schools, L. B. McCord, to ask for assistance in maintaining and operating the parent-owned bus. The superintendent, who was also pastor of the Manning Presbyterian Church, listened. Then he told the committee what the men who held power in the South commonly believed, something to the effect that, "Y'all Nigras don't pay enough taxes for us to give you any more money. It's just not right for y'all to expect us white people to pay even more taxes so you can run a bus for Nigra children." Whatever his actual words were, Mr. McCord's answer translated into an unequivocal "NO."

3. The Challenge

Here am I, send me.
ISAIAH 6:8

During the year Rev. De Laine said the story of *Briggs* began—1946—he turned forty-eight years old. He was the principal of a little elementary school in Silver, three miles north of Summerton, and still the pastor of Pine Grove / Society Hill circuit. He earned his second bachelor's degree, a bachelor of divinity, that year. It was the year of the drowning, the year the veterans got their agriculture classes, and the year the parents recruited him as their spokesman. And it was the year the new certification standards for teachers' salaries went into effect.

Like any sensible man, my father's goals were to provide a decent living for his family and to live to reach a ripe old age. No matter how much the country of his birth deprived him of his constitutional rights, he strove to honor it by being an honest man, a good citizen, and an exemplary Christian leader. A compassionate man, he wanted to improve the lives of those around him. A caring teacher, he helped expand the horizons of children and adults. Believing in justice, he did his bit to enable his people to have a voice in their government, which had been said to be "of the people, by the people, and for the people." Thinking of himself as a shepherd, not a savior, he put his trust in God and sought divine guidance every morning. With a mind thus shaped, he was the right man in the right place, doing the right thing at the right time. Perhaps the farthest thought from his mind as he worked with the parents was to become a savior or a martyr.

Because the new regulations clearly showed how education governed certification and influenced salaries, teachers—including my mother—flocked to colleges, taking both evening and summer courses to improve their credentials. Ever since earning her teaching certificate in 1930, Mother had worked off and on toward a college degree. We children spent most of our summers at her parents' home in Columbia while she attended the combined Benedict College / Allen University Summer School. When she registered for the summer session in June 1947, she had completed three-fourths of the necessary credits.

My father also registered for a course that summer, simply because a course titled Race and Culture was to be taught by someone he greatly admired. However, before the first week was over, the original professor was replaced by George A. Singleton, the Philadelphia-based editor of two AME publications and a man with whom Daddy was already acquainted. Soon a significant amount of discussion in the class was being devoted to the problems of Clarendon's black people.

One Thursday toward the end of June, a general assembly was held on Allen's campus. The speaker was James N. Hinton, executive director of the South Carolina Conference of NAACP Branches. As he addressed the audience, composed mainly of teachers, Mr. Hinton talked about NAACP efforts to end the all-white Democratic primary and about a lawsuit against the University of South Carolina Law School. Then he elaborated on public school education in South Carolina. According to Rev. De Laine's notes, Mr. Hinton took as his text how the white man's heel still pressed the faces of black people into the mud. The fiery orator declared that limitations on education were preventing African Americans from advancing. Withholding education, he proclaimed, was one of the surest methods of keeping a people down.

He said that the white man was afraid of educated black people because, no longer satisfied with menial jobs, they competed for white men's jobs. If that happened, who would work the white man's fields? Who would clean his house or nurse his children? Black people, he asserted, could never break the bonds of servitude until they were educated.

Enumerating the ugly facts, Mr. Hinton swayed his listeners. Conditions in black schools were disgraceful, and the counties gave black schools almost no support. Mr. Hinton undoubtedly asked rhetorical questions, answering them with more questions of the same damning sort. He would have asked his audience, "Why don't white officials do more?" The question would have been followed by another. "With only a few tattered books, no other teaching supplies, and not even fuel for heat, a Negro teacher has almost nothing to work with. Isn't this a way of denying education?"

Mr. Hinton made the teachers think—and become uncomfortable with their thoughts—as he posed questions like, "What about the problem of children getting to the high schools once they graduate from elementary schools? Isn't the failure to provide bus transportation still another way of discouraging children of color from discovering the liberating messages that come with education? Doesn't this lack of opportunity lead to a lack of education that results in keeping Negroes down?"

He reminded his listeners that the NAACP had successfully launched legal action to improve black education in other southern states. Then he got to his point: it was high time for change in South Carolina. Black people *had* to get more than a basic education. Educational opportunities *had* to be equalized. Starting an effort for equalization with bus transportation for high school students, he posited, would be the least inflammatory beginning and—echoing Senator Harvey's 1946 statement—the hardest request for white people to deny. After all, he reminded the audience, every county in the state sent white children to school by bus. What legal rationale could those in power use for not providing the same for black children?

Finally he tossed out a challenge. With words clearly intended to raise the hackles of those who considered themselves leaders, it was a dare to start a battle. In essence he threw down a gauntlet with the bold assertion, "No schoolteacher or preacher in South Carolina has the courage to find a plaintiff who will test the legality of South Carolina's bus-transportation practices."

Although the forum was perfect for focusing attention on the bus situation, the teachers must have thought Mr. Hinton had taken leave of his senses. Every one of them knew that any teacher involved in such a scheme would be fired. There were even places in South Carolina where such an action would be a death sentence.

However, the NAACP man might have planned his words as a prod to a specific person. Almost certainly he knew my father would be in the audience. As Clarendon's contact for the NAACP and state NCC, Rev. De Laine had undoubtedly talked with both Mr. Hinton and his associate, Dr. Adams, about what was happening at Society Hill and Davis Station. Furthermore Dr. Adams and Dr. Singleton, the professor for the Race and Culture course, had a long history of collaboration on socially significant issues. Dr. Singleton had even visited one of my father's churches on River Road. It's possible that Mr. Hinton was invited as a direct outcome of discussions in the Race and Culture class.

In any case my father picked up the gauntlet almost before it fell, a plan already forming in his mind. He knew exactly whom he would ask to become a plaintiff. Three days later, with my brother Jay tagging along, Daddy went to see his friends Hammett and Levi Pearson. Intelligent, but almost illiterate, the men—who worked together as closely as two fingers on one hand—were among the Davis Station parents who bought the school bus. They and their older sons (the two veterans) were landowners and members of the NAACP.

Rev. De Laine explained what he had in mind, saying the plaintiff would need someone to "run for him if he couldn't run," someone to help protect him if there were threats. The brothers needed no coercion; their only concern was financial support. They told my father, "We don't have enough money to run a lawsuit and we can't trust white lawyers to look out for us."

Rev. De Laine replied, "Suppose I get the legal talent, would you take the local abuse?"

Mr. Hammett, the risk taker, quickly accepted. "Yes, I'll do it."

Having given the matter considerable thought, my father replied, "Hammett, you're a little hot headed. Suppose Levi does the suing and you run for him if the goings get too rough?"

Mr. Levi obligingly agreed, "Sure. If you get the money."
That happened on Sunday, June 22, 1947.

A favorable outcome to a legal challenge for school bus transportation seemed promising because the lawsuit would go to the federal district court presided over by J. Waties Waring. During slightly more than five years on the bench, Judge Waring's decisions always supported equal treatment and protection as set forth by the United States Constitution. On one occasion, to the outrage of other white people, he ruled in favor of a black man, finding a white person guilty of violating the Thirteenth Amendment. The use of codes to identify potential jurors by race was forbidden in his court. And, shockingly, Judge Waring had appointed a black man as his court bailiff. His evenhanded application of the law had made him a hero to South Carolina's black people.

With such a rosy outlook, Rev. De Laine took Mr. Levi to see Mr. Hinton and Harold Boulware, the attorney for the state's NAACP Conference of Branches, the very next week. Although recent legal battles had left the NAACP's state coffers almost empty, the men were able to make plans for proceeding because A. J. Butler, executive secretary of the teachers' organization, was also at the meeting. Mr. Levi would sign a petition asking Clarendon County to provide school bus transportation for his children. Mr. Boulware would represent him. My father would act as intermediary. And Mr. Butler would ask the teachers' association for financial assistance. In the meantime Rev. De Laine would finance the effort as necessary, with the understanding he would be reimbursed after the lawsuit was filed.

Mr. Boulware set legal action in motion, using the following supporting facts as supplied by my father:

1. Mr. Levi had three children who attended Scott's Branch School, about eight miles from the Pearson house.
2. Mr. Levi's children had attended Bob Johnson Elementary School, about a quarter mile from their house.
3. Bob Johnson School was in Clarendon School District 26, where there was no high school.
4. Black students from District 26 attended high school at Scott's Branch in Clarendon School District 22.
5. Clarendon County provided no public transportation for black children.
6. White children in the area where Mr. Levi lived were transported to school by buses provided by the county.

Using these facts, a two-page petition—dated July 28, 1947—was drawn up. In it Levi Pearson "prayed that school bus transportation be furnished, maintained, and operated out of public funds in School District Number 26, Clarendon County, South Carolina, for use of the named children." The petition

was submitted to three school authorities—Clarendon School District 26 superintendent Vander Stukes, Clarendon County superintendent of education L. B.
McCord, and the secretary of the South Carolina Board of Education. A hearing
was requested, on behalf of Mr. Levi, within the next three weeks.

Despite several mail reminders, months passed without a reply from any of
the addressees. On October 1, Mr. Boulware wrote to Rev. De Laine that he was
"processing the law . . . to file suit." A letter was enclosed for Mr. Levi to sign.
Two and a half months later, Mr. Levi signed a letter dated December 16, 1947,
and addressed to "Whom It May Concern." It stated, "I have done all of the fol-
lowing-up [with] the trustees and county officers that I am going to do. All further business contact will be referred to Attorney Boulware." In his letter Mr.
Levi reconfirmed his commitment to the endeavor with the statement, "Mr.
Vander Stukes or any other person, assumes too much when they assume that I
am not interested in the Bus Transportation Suit."

News of Mr. Levi's unprecedented action raced around the farms of Davis
Station and Jordan. Black people—at least some of them—were jubilant. Some
others were doomsayers, people whose concept of the future extended no further
than the expected displeasure of their bosses. Still others naively believed that, in
a few short weeks, their children would be riding to school on buses, just like the
white children. Interest in the NAACP escalated, although not to the point that
the organization gained large numbers of members.

The lawsuit was not filed for several months. On February 5, 1948, Rev.
De Laine wrote to Mr. Hinton, warning that the people's interest was growing
cold. He implied that they couldn't afford to lose grassroots support and the
chance to mobilize the people. Furthermore he was continuing to spend money,
expecting the people to raise money to repay him. He said that news of the filing
of the transportation lawsuit would "give great courage to many who are waiting
on leadership."

Mr. Hinton replied that the local school board had finally scheduled the
requested hearing for February 27, 1948. He expressed hope that the appropriate
legal papers would arrive from the NAACP's national office before the hearing.
He also requested that Rev. De Laine say nothing about money "until the case is
actually filed in court. We will then call on people . . . for support." While my
father's financial concerns might have been assuaged, the letter had disturbing
news. Mr. Boulware wanted him to attend the school board hearing.

Showing his involvement by being at the meeting would have severely undermined Rev. De Laine's ability to continue his civic work. He immediately shared
his concern with Mr. Boulware on February 13. A reply came promptly, stating,
"I quite agree that it would not be . . . wise. . . . I should have thought of this
before asking you." Nevertheless he made it clear that Rev. De Laine was a part
of the process, asking him to "personally see to it that Mr. Pearson meets me at
the school. . . . I shall stop at your house on my way back."

At the end of the first week of March, the case still had not been filed. Rev. De Laine regretted that because he believed the bus transportation case was key to increasing support for the NAACP in the county and to encouraging involvement in the voting initiative. Although voting and school bus transportation were both used to keep black people as second-class citizens, Rev. De Laine had not yet begun to appreciate how strongly his leadership in one of those areas was influencing his stature in the other.

2

Quest for Equality
1947–1951

4. *Ups and Downs*

O sometimes the shadows are deep,
and rough seems the path to the goal
"The Rock Is Higher Than I," old gospel song

S outh Carolina's six-day legislative marathon in 1944 had succeeded in craft-
ing a way to deny representation to black people, yet remain within the law.
The Democratic Party had legally become the Democratic Club. To vote in the
Democratic primary, it was necessary to first enroll in the newly formed club,
something that could be done only at white-owned locations. Efforts by NAACP
members to join were repeatedly unsuccessful—until the day George Elmore,
looking as Caucasian as the men handling the registration (thanks to his forefathers), walked into a party office and signed his name. When someone discovered Mr. Elmore had "one drop" of black blood, his name was immediately
purged from the membership rolls.

NAACP lawyers sued, and in July 1947 Judge Waring ruled that the Democrats were unconstitutionally excluding black people. Although it was immediately appealed, the decision was upheld. Ecstatic NAACP members started
educating people how to register and vote. In Clarendon County, Rev. De Laine
was coordinator for the effort. His Clarendon recruitment effort was successful,
and, when the books opened for registration on March 1, 1948, many black citizens went to register. My father wasn't among them. He was ill and had to remain at home.

Despite their good turnout, almost none of the black people succeeded in registering. Rev. De Laine reported "much unfairness on the part of the registration
board," a literacy test being the major stumbling block. Inez Jones Pearson, a
high school graduate, failed the test after being made to read the entire Constitution twice. Sarah Daniels, the college-educated home demonstration agent,
was told she couldn't read well enough. The two black high school principals suffered the same fate.

A few days later my father wrote to Mr. Boulware. Although he asked if there
had been a response to the *Pearson* bus petition, Daddy seemed more concerned
with the voting issue. Based on his new knowledge of tactics used to keep African

Americans from registering, he outlined a plan that would require him to take the literacy test when he went to register. Since he held a Permanent Professional Teacher Certificate and had earned a B on the National Teachers Examination, he reasoned he would be a good person to start a lawsuit "should they be so stupid as to [say] I cannot read well enough."

He also had a backup plan. If the registrars allowed him to pass the test, he would "try to get someone else, if possible, to burst the cap." But, as he explained in a March 6 letter to Mr. Boulware, "We have a great problem in this county; we have no leadership and an abundance of ignorance." Only a small percentage of black people in the county could read well enough to qualify using the literacy test. Furthermore, my father added, "They keep the Negroes out, and register all the whites, even when some whites are not present."

Somehow, even in the face of such blatant bias, he maintained his deep belief in fairness, hoping the local authorities would see the error of their ways and be shamed into changing and doing what was right. His next sentence stated, "I also feel like making a somewhat patriotic speech while we are waiting [to register]." He wanted to "send a petition or resolution to the [election] board, or wherever necessary, asking for a better interpretation of the Constitution and better opportunities to get before the registration committee."

The fact that the county's three leading black educators had been turned down when they tried to register must have made my optimistic father think the teachers could be roused from their apathy. He considered "making a fighting speech in the County Teachers' Meeting" to stir up support for the NAACP and the voting effort, but left that decision up to the lawyer, writing, "I cannot tell what I will do until I have your advice."

The news that a black man was suing for school bus transportation broke in the *State* newspaper in March 1947. The lawsuit, *Levi Pearson v. Clarendon County and School District No. 26,* had finally been filed in the U.S. Eastern District Court of South Carolina. Although news of the lawsuit made white people angry, Mr. Levi became a hero among South Carolina's black residents.

Rev. De Laine wasted no time in taking advantage of his friend's new popularity. He had Mr. Hinton ask Mr. Levi to serve as nominal president of Clarendon's reorganized NAACP branch. Mis' Daniels would serve as vice president. Rev. De Laine, the secretary, and Rev. Seals, the treasurer, would do most of the work. In early April the four officers agreed to pay J. S. "Flutie" Boyd, a retired teacher, to "guide Negro aspirants for registration." My father wrote to him, "We use the name Citizen Committee but it is really the NAACP." He enclosed the draft of a letter he intended to send to the board of registration— after the NAACP approved—to let the registrars know an advocate would accompany any black people who came to register.

During March and early April, Rev. De Laine was busy. In addition to teaching and pastoring, he was engaged in a number of other activities. Besides the voting effort, he had the farm where he had started to shift from growing cotton and tobacco to producing beef. With an investment of more than six thousand dollars, he had acquired breeding cattle and started to clear a grazing range. At Allen University he served on the Board of Control, and he filled the capacity of grand master for his Prince Hall Masons' lodge. The letter-writing campaign on behalf of the Society Hill community continued, and, with the bus case still in the works, he had to support Mr. Levi in every way he could.

That last activity explains why he was in his car at Mr. Levi's house on Friday, April 9. He was coaching his friend for the bus transportation trial. With Mr. Levi at the driver's door, the two men were deep in conversation when another car rolled down the lane, passing the house before stopping. One of the occupants called out. Recognizing the man, Mr. Levi said, "There's Mr. McCord now."

L. B. McCord, county superintendent of education, had come almost ten miles into the country from Manning to see the black farmer. With him were Vander Stukes, superintendent of Clarendon School District 26, and the county auditor. Hoping he would not be recognized, Rev. De Laine slid out of his car and stealthily hurried into the Pearson house. There, sitting beside an open window, he eavesdropped on the conversation.

The three men had brought devastating news. Mr. Levi's taxes for the previous year had been credited to District 5—not to District 26, which he was suing.

When the visitors left, Rev. De Laine, Mr. Levi, and Mr. Hammett tried to make sense of what had happened. How was it possible that Mr. Levi's taxes hadn't been paid to District 26? Although Mr. Levi distinctly remembered paying his taxes to District 26 previously, he couldn't find tax receipts to verify it. Confused, the men looked at Mr. Hammett's receipts—his house was only a few yards from Mr. Levi's and even farther away from the old school. His recent tax receipt was credited to District 26.

The men discussed the situation, considering possible plans of action. Finally my father drove home. The letter he wrote to Mr. Boulware began, "You will be surprised just as we were this morning."

Recapping the afternoon's events, he observed that the officials must have been preparing their bombshell for months. Why else, he opined, would ninth and tenth grades have suddenly been added to the already overcrowded Felton-Rosenwald School at the far end of District 5? The only conceivable reason was so the authorities could claim that high school classes were available in the district where Mr. Levi paid taxes.

"Recently," the last paragraph in his letter stated, "I have gone out so far until I doubt that anything will save me as a teacher next year." Although he would hate to be fired, he said, "I doubt that will stop me. It may cause me to fight harder." Almost as an afterthought, he added, "I was turned down from registration." The amount of his poll tax had not been recorded on the receipt.

Mr. Boulware might have been surprised about Mr. Levi's taxes, but preparations for the *Pearson* case continued. Mr. Hammett's offer to take Mr. Levi's place was not entertained. Nor was anything said about Mr. Levi's offer to start all over with a petition to District 5.

Twenty days after the authorities visited the Pearson farm, Rev. De Laine again wrote to Mr. Boyd regarding the voting thrust. "Mr. Hinton promised to write to the Board about the irregularities and he also promised to write to you. I hope he will not fail to do so." A check for fifteen dollars was enclosed, along with the comment, "Common sense tells me that this is not paying you for the service asked of you." Perhaps it was only a nominal fee set by Mr. Boyd because another sentence stated, "I am very glad you see it in the light of a personal sacrifice." The letter also said, "We have published it in six places that you will be present to assist Negro aspirants for registration."

Rev. De Laine had previously made plans to be out of the state for almost a month on both church and personal business. In anticipation of his absence, he counseled Mr. Boyd to "be cautious, smooth and discreet in your dealings, but firm in your guidance. . . . If we need Lawyer Boulware, we will have him on the first Monday in June." By that time my father planned to be back.

But when he returned, everything had changed.

During the time since Judge Waring ruled that black people must be allowed to register for the Democratic primary, South Carolina's politicians had worked diligently to find ways to circumvent the law. On May 19, 1948, the state Democratic Party/Club changed its membership rules, and the names of all African Americans were removed from its rolls. The new rules said black people could vote as nonmembers—if they took a "segregation" oath. Every prospective voter was required to swear belief in "social, religious, and educational separation of races" and in "the principle of States Rights," as well as opposition to a proposed federal law that prohibited discrimination in federal workplaces.

It was discouraging. But nine days later there was again reason for optimism. On May 28, Mr. Boulware sent a communication, stating that the bus transportation case would be argued on June 9. The lawyers needed Mr. Levi for consultation before the trial, and my father was to transport him to Charleston. It looked as if the tax situation had not affected the case.

The shocker came at the pretrial proceedings, one day before the scheduled trial. Thurgood Marshall, the NAACP's lead lawyer who had come from the national office, requested dismissal of the case. Judge Waring granted the request, and the development made headline news. According to rumor, when the state senator from Clarendon heard the radio announcement, he threw his foot on his desk and laughed, saying, "Old nigger don't even know where he live."

The reason Mr. Boulware and Mr. Marshall allowed the *Pearson* case to continue to pretrial will probably never be known. Could it be they suspected Mr. Levi's property had been gerrymandered, but couldn't prove it? My father claimed his hair turned white that day. He had spent almost a year building the *Pearson* case up in the minds of people who looked to him for leadership. He had held meetings and made promises. In his excitement he had even told people that the law was clear and the county would have to provide transportation for all children.

Sincerely believing everything he told the people, he had not hesitated to spend his own money to bring the case to court, anticipating repayment when it was heard. But *Levi Pearson v. Clarendon County and School District No. 26* never went to trial. Rev. De Laine was left with empty pockets. The people were disappointed, but my father felt personally responsible for not knowing about the tax line and for disillusioning them. He believed his credibility as their torchbearer had been eroded. To him it seemed that all of his work had gone for naught.

Early in July the NAACP sued officials of the South Carolina Democratic Party/Club, seeking both temporary and permanent injunctions against the oath requirement. Annoyed about what had happened after his last ruling on the issue, Judge Waring heard the motions immediately and signaled his displeasure with the Democrats by scheduling trial for July 16, less than two weeks later and one day after the National Democratic Convention ended. The judge promptly refused the request for a delay.

The 1948 National Democratic Convention is historically notable for the nomination of the party's presidential candidate, Harry S. Truman, on the first ballot and for the southern delegates' expressing their displeasure concerning an antisegregation proposal by walking out of the convention en masse. Judge Waring's scheduling of the trial undoubtedly infuriated the already angry group, adding fuel to their subsequent decision to leave the Democratic Party and form the Dixiecrat Party.

During the trial Judge Waring minced no words in castigating party/club leaders. No time was wasted before he issued an opinion that explicitly spelled out his orders:

> Enrollment books for party membership had to be opened immediately and kept open six hours daily, from 10 A.M. to 1 P.M. and from 3 to 6 P.M., until the end of July.
>
> No prospective registrant could be required to swear to support any belief, tenet, or opinion.
>
> If party members did not obey the announced orders, they would be imprisoned.

In spite of the judge's directive, Clarendon black people had difficulty finding the enrollment book. In desperation Rev. De Laine and ten others traveled to nearby Sumter County to have statements concerning the unavailability of the book notarized by William James, a black attorney. There they found that the Sumter folks had encountered the same thing. Mr. James called Judge Waring who, in turn, gave the Democrats' county chairman one hour to make the enrollment book available. The man immediately announced that black people could register at the courthouse, adding (according to my father), "All of them can enroll. I'm not going to jail for this foolishness."

In the following weeks Rev. Seals and Rev. De Laine attended several meetings in Sumter to learn how to make new voters aware of the issues and the mechanics of voting. Despite the obstacles many Clarendon people succeeded in registering, with my father and others helping with transportation.

Some white people still tried to obstruct justice. One of the registrars reportedly began to turn the waiting black people away, telling some of them, "Too —— many niggers from Summerton are already enrolled." And the county treasurer would keep them standing at the window three or four hours when they came to pay taxes or cash claims. In this way he prevented many from registering. Nevertheless my father was pleased with his own efforts.

A blistering hot July gave way to an even hotter August. With the heat of summer, came the fervor of revival meetings that should have brought more than enough religion to cause the "river of divine grace to flow deep and full" and "corrupt and degenerated hearts to be made anew." But the spirit of holiness, love, and truth did not find its way into the hearts of Clarendon officials. If it did, it was a holiness, love, and truth unknown to the God of the long-suffering black people.

Two years had passed since the Society Hill drowning, and nothing had been done for those schoolchildren. More than a year had passed since the formal submission of Mr. Levi's complaint, but his children still walked to school. Clarendon County was pretty much the same as it had always been. However, on the second Tuesday of August 1948, J. A. De Laine—at the age of fifty years, one month, and eight days—would cast a meaningful vote, for the first time in his life, as a citizen of the United States of America.

The night before the election, my uncle Lewis and two other Manning men came to Summerton. They wanted to find out how Rev. De Laine, now the recognized leader of the county's black people, and the rest of the Summerton group planned to vote. My uncle informed the group that Mr. Jackson, a highway patrolman and a candidate for sheriff, had asked for his support. The Summerton people were surprised. They had heard that all county candidates had promised they would not solicit black votes. But, as my father liked to observe, promises and pie crusts both tend to fall apart under a little pressure.

Uncle Lewis confessed, "I told him I would vote for him."

The others must have been exceedingly surprised and not known why my uncle would do such a thing. According to my father, he and the rest of the men "didn't want Mr. Jackson—stewed, broiled, boiled, baked, nor fried." The patrolman had been too "indiscreet against Negroes on the highway." He once participated in the brutal beating of a black soldier before throwing the injured serviceman into the county jail. Not until the black ministerial alliance sent charges against the patrolman to Fort Bragg did the military police know where the soldier was. Rev. De Laine was aware of that because, as secretary of the alliance, he had written and signed the letter.

Perhaps the new voters weren't aware that one's vote was a personal matter or that a change of mind was permitted anytime until the vote was cast. However, they were honest men, and each of them firmly believed a person's word was an unbreakable bond. As they saw it, my uncle's vote had been unconditionally committed. They decided he should not break his promise, but no one else would vote for Mr. Jackson.

At close to ten A.M. on election day, several voters met at our house. Others assembled at St. Mark Church. As they excitedly continued planning and discussing, Edward "Bubba" Ragin reported having heard that the incumbent sheriff, Mr. Shorter, didn't want black votes. Stunned, but dead set against voting for Mr. Jackson, they didn't know what to do.

My father defined the course of action. "The best thing is to call Mr. Shorter and see what he has to say." He and Mr. Bubba went to the nearby black-owned King's Funeral Home to use one of the town's few telephones. When the sheriff answered, Rev. De Laine identified himself and explained the dilemma. He said, "I've been trying to get as many of the colored people as possible to vote for you. But they say you don't want Negro votes. And they don't want to vote for you unless you want their votes."

The astonished sheriff asked his caller to again identify himself. Once he understood the situation, he said, "Reverend, go back and tell them that is a wholly unfounded lie. I want every vote I can get, white or black."

Wanting a witness, Rev. De Laine responded, "Around thirty-five people are at my home now and they sent Mr. Edward Ragin and me to get the facts. Will you tell him what you said to me?" The sheriff repeated the words to Mr. Bubba.

The men were satisfied they had chosen wisely. Although the established power structure in Summerton was against him, the sheriff was reelected by a narrow margin, thanks to the black vote. On its first foray into county politics, the small voting bloc had shown its power. And Rev. De Laine had once more been the leader.

The year moved on to September with still no indication of what would happen with the *Pearson* bus transportation case and no compensation for the money my father had spent. Despite his activities and his prediction of being fired, his contract as principal of Silver Elementary School, in Clarendon District 30, was renewed for the 1948–49 school term. However, Principal Maceo Anderson at Summerton's Scott's Branch hadn't been as lucky. He was let go. The school officials had suspected him of encouraging black unrest.

The reason for Mr. Anderson's dismissal is of no importance to what happened subsequently. The important thing is that, when Scott's Branch opened in September 1948, Maceo Anderson was no longer principal—after more than eleven years. His ouster came at a critical time. In addition to approving a new schedule for teacher salaries in 1944–45, the South Carolina state legislature had also approved the reintroduction of a twelfth grade for public school students. The law affected all students who began ninth grade in or after 1945. So when the ten-room Scott's Branch School opened for the 1948–49 school year, it had a new principal and its first twelfth-grade class. There were also some new ways of doing things.

With the mounting evidence that black demands were not going to disappear and that the NAACP was getting stronger, Summerton's local school officials didn't sit idly after the *Pearson* lawsuit was withdrawn. Instead they did the most effective things they could think of. That is, they found a way to make black families pay for the things they demanded, creating yet another barrier to education for the black families.

Scott's Branch parents learned only in late September of the changes—after H. B. Betchman, superintendent of Summerton schools, mentioned them to a Davis Station parent. Mr. Betchman told the man that school officials would have to follow the law since someone had sued the schools. Out-of-district children would need to make a formal application to their home school districts before they could attend Scott's Branch.

The new system could have easily trapped the poorly educated parents, losing the opportunity for their children to attend high school. However, Rev. De Laine made an application form and gave copies to parents in several Scott's Branch feeder districts. For some reason Mr. Levi took his forms to Vander Stukes, superintendent of District 26, rather than to the superintendent of the district where it was said his taxes were paid.

Knowing Mr. Levi didn't have the skills to prepare the forms, Mr. Stukes asked who did. The response must have caused the superintendent a good deal of concern because he made a surprising offer, directing the farmer to go to the auditor's office and have his tax changed from District 5 to District 26 because he (Mr. Stukes) knew that was correct. He promised to make proper arrangements with the auditor. He added, "If it would be agreeable with the people . . . , they would furnish a bus to take all of the children to high school from both districts."

Undoubtedly Mr. Stukes was thinking of a different bus from that which transported the white children. On the other hand, it wasn't clear whether the "people" to whom he referred were black or white, or both. But, at one point, Mr. Stukes did ask Mr. Levi if the black parents' "bus was in shape to run."

Rev. De Laine advised Mr. Levi not to go to the auditor's office, and his friend declared that he would "send his children to school and let them be turned down but [he would not go to anyone] for any change or compromise."

A letter went to Mr. Hinton and Mr. Boulware, telling them what had happened. The last paragraph constituted a clear cry for assistance. After lamenting, "We are getting knocks on every side," my father went on to plead, "We surely do want to hear from you what to do." Although he was a daring and seemingly fearless leader, my father recognized his limitations. He emphasized, "We are short of legal advice here." He summed up the situation with what almost sounded like a drowning man's words, "I am trying to hold everything together as best I can."

That November my father would end his eighth year at the Pine Grove / Society Hill circuit. The AME Church's policy was to transfer pastors at the end of eight years. Unless my father took the equivalent of a demotion, only two assignments in the county were possible for him. He didn't want one of them because it was a "city church" and he was a country man at heart. The other, Liberty Hill, was being reserved for an exceptionally well-qualified native son of the county, the Reverend E. E. Richburg. A church outside Clarendon County would be unsatisfactory because Rev. De Laine would have to severely curtail his civic efforts and neglect his farm. Furthermore he had risen to a position of power in the AME Church's Central Conference of South Carolina. Because of that, he wielded considerable influence in the church at the state level. A transfer out of the Central Conference would deprive him of his strong voice in the hierarchy of the church.

The bishop refused to honor my father's and his parishioners' petitions to waive the eight-year rule and reassign him to the Pine Grove / Society Hill circuit. Perhaps the refusal was because my stubborn father had become a thorn in the side of certain churchmen as he used his power to discourage their questionable activities. More disturbingly, it is conceivable that he was becoming a nuisance to local authorities and external pressure had been put on church officials.

Determined to not desert his flock, Rev. De Laine opted to be assigned to a small country circuit he had pastored nineteen years earlier, when he had only two years of pastoral experience and no college degree.

5. *Transition*

Come and follow me . . .
Mark 1:17

E ven if Vander Stukes had been able to get Mr. Levi's tax receipts altered and to provide financial aid for the parents' bus, the Pearsons and the other country folk were no longer in the mood to accept such crumbs. Emboldened, they now wanted free and unconditional school bus transportation for their children. Rev. De Laine and the Pearsons made an effort to get the bus issue back on the NAACP's agenda.

Meanwhile Scott's Branch was having its difficulties. The new principal, S. Isaiah Benson, did not respect the teachers, parents, or students. Nor was he skillful in judging the feelings and intelligence of others. This was unfortunate because he had to deal with two major problems: that of out-of-district students and that of accommodating twelve grades in ten classrooms. Some teachers— like my gentle, compassionate mother—already had more than fifty children in one room.

Even so, Mr. Benson gave no evidence of wanting to promote teamwork. Instead, from the time he arrived, he began alienating various segments of the community. According to some, including teacher Albert Fuller, he was a boastful loudmouth who belittled people and talked down to them. He was disorganized, as well as unable and unwilling to ensure proper supervision of students. As a result of this, a discipline problem developed. During Maceo Anderson's tenure, children who misbehaved were sent out into the long hall to wait for punishment. Only on cold days, when coats were shed and hung in the hall (because there were no cloakrooms or lockers), could they find hiding places. With too few nails and too many children, coats often fell to the floor, lying in piles like autumn leaves ready for a bonfire.

Children banished to the hall burrowed under the coats, simultaneously trying to keep warm and to avoid being seen. Mr. Anderson had patrolled the unheated corridor frequently, giving a whack to every mountain of coats with a sturdy cane. A too-resistant pile got an extra two or three whacks and the message, "Come on out. No use trying to hide." Principal and culprit then had marched to the office where, behind closed doors, Mr. Anderson had addressed the child's transgression and meted out appropriate punishment, fairly and efficiently. Everyone accepted the procedure.

The new principal, however, seemed to have no idea of what to do with children who caused problems. When he found a child cowering in the hall, he steered the student—without reprimand or punishment—back to the harried teacher and a room sheltering up to one hundred other pupils. The resourceful teachers, often having less than two years of college education, generally managed to keep order, but the energetic children taxed the ingenuity and patience of even the most experienced instructors. Sooner or later some child accidentally, or intentionally, poked another, and an argument started. With no classroom assistant, it was difficult for the teacher to attend to a recalcitrant or wronged child at the expense of so many others. It was the principal's job to resolve discipline issues. But Principal Benson reneged on his duty. With the child safely back in the classroom, he took no further interest. Student behavior at Scott's Branch degenerated.

Mr. Benson further undermined discipline by his approach to teacher absences. In Clarendon's black schools, six dollars per day was deducted from an absent teacher's paycheck and used to pay the substitute teacher. Often Mr. Benson didn't hire substitute teachers. Instead he drafted older girls to cover classes, a practice common in small rural schools. Scott's Branch, however, was not small, and individual classes were unduly large. Under the inexperienced teenagers, student behavior worsened.

Frequently away from the campus during school hours, the new principal not infrequently failed to meet his ninth- , tenth- , eleventh- , and twelfth-grade students for mathematics. After his first month at Scott's Branch, he taught only three or four classes per month, hiring a substitute teacher to cover the rest. If high school students at Scott's Branch learned any mathematics that year, it was a miracle. The substitute was neither a college graduate nor a student of mathematics, and some pupils had no mathematics textbooks for the entire school year.

Not all complaints against the new principal were about educational materials or teaching commitments. According to Reverdy Wells, president of the Scott's Branch Class of 1949, by the time winter came, whispers about other activities of the principal was open conversation. Things at Scott's Branch were in a mess and getting worse.

Meanwhile Mr. Levi was experiencing retaliation by white residents of the county. When he sought a loan to buy fertilizer for spring planting, he found that his credit had been cut off at every white-owned store and bank in the county. Even so, the lawyers at the NAACP's New York headquarters had turned their attention to other injustices in other places. There were too few of them to squelch all of the fires sparked by discrimination. The problem of Levi Pearson and school buses for a few children in backwater Clarendon County was left in a state of limbo.

But the Pearsons, Daddy, and their supporters were not willing to let the matter drop. At a statewide NAACP meeting in January 1949, they took advantage of a chance to confer with Mr. Boulware, questioning him about how they could proceed with the transportation case. Even though he knew the state NAACP could do nothing without full support from the national organization, the lawyer listened sympathetically. Then, swayed by their fervor, he consented to try to get things moving again.

On March 8, Mr. Boulware wrote to Rev. De Laine, saying that Thurgood Marshall would be holding a meeting four days later to "map out plans for our school action." The letter instructed my father to "come to this meeting so that you can help us with all the information regarding Clarendon County. Bring whoever you can." Assuming the lawyer had successfully refocused attention on the *Pearson* bus case, my father took Rev. Seals and six others on the seventy-mile trip to Columbia. By 1948 the feisty Rev. Seals had become Rev. De Laine's right-hand man and perhaps his staunchest supporter. Although not as charismatic as my father, he was just as dedicated and resolute.

Various people associated with the NAACP—lawyers, state officers, and representatives from some of the local branches—as well as officers of the teachers' association also attended the meeting. Mr. Marshall reported on the national organization's recent activities and thrusts, and he informed the group that the NAACP's efforts were being redirected. That was when he dropped the bombshell. He and his colleagues had decided not to argue any more school bus cases; they wanted to pursue the broader goal of equalizing schools. The *Pearson* bus transportation case was dead. "We will pull up from Clarendon County."

Those words were like a stab in my father's heart. Normally self-controlled and patient, he was exasperated. For almost a year he had paid all travel and boarding expenses related to the bus transportation case, altruistically dreaming of a time when Clarendon's black children could ride to school. Although he expected reimbursement for the money, what he was doing was neither for himself nor for us, his own children. His "flock" looked to him for "deliverance," and he was trying to be a good shepherd. To justify their faith, he had put Mr. Levi in an uncomfortable position and jeopardized his own teaching job.

The stunned Clarendon group objected that the decision was unfair. Normally mild mannered, the unpretentious people from the backward county in one of America's most benighted states refused to accept the verdict of the important lawyer from New York. They told him he had to help because, if the terrible educational conditions in their county were not corrected, their children would be just as shackled and deprived of opportunities as they and their slave forebears had been.

Mr. Marshall was not fazed. He had been in circumstances far more intimidating. Calmly he elaborated on the NAACP's decision and explained that school bus transportation was only an isolated part of the unfair separate-but-equal system. What was needed, he said, was an attack on the entire system, and that was the approach the NAACP's Legal Defense Fund had decided to take. The Clarendon group refused to be either dismissed or mollified. They offered to broaden Mr. Levi's demands and ask for equal school opportunities and facilities, not just school buses. Mr. Marshall wouldn't accept the offer. How could he, when Mr. Levi was only one person and "the race haters may liquidate him at any time?"

Exasperated, Rev. De Laine responded that he had only been asked to find one plaintiff and that Mr. Hammett would take over if something happened to his brother. Mr. Marshall was unmoved, countering that the money needed for a lawsuit would have to be raised. Poor, unknown, and remote, Clarendon County could never capture enough of the public's attention to raise the needed funds.

The contingent still refused to cede their case. They were painfully aware of their schools' deficiencies. At Scott's Branch the students held dances to raise money to buy heating coal. The entire school population obtained drinking water from a single row of faucets in the schoolyard. As a principal, Rev. De Laine could remember having taken money from his teachers' meager salaries of less than fifty dollars per month to buy materials to repair his school building—and the school's official trustees had refused to reimburse him.

Mr. Marshall had not expected the unsophisticated country people to be so adamant. Finally he made a concession, agreeing to prepare a class-action lawsuit for the Clarendon County contingent—*if* his colleagues in New York approved and *if* the group "got twenty families to sue jointly." Without twenty families, the NAACP could "not risk the money for the lawsuit."

My father wondered how, with a good conscience, he could put twenty families in jeopardy. He was dubious there were that many black families in Clarendon who could survive retaliation. Remembering the energy he had put into the failed bus transportation effort, Daddy doubted his physical stamina to meet the new challenge. The others, however, were determined to forge ahead. Rev. Seals, who strengthened my father's spirit more than anyone except my mother, reassured him. "Don't get weak, Rev. De Laine. If Hammett will run for Levi when he cannot run for himself, I will run for you. Take courage [for] I will do everything in my power to make the effort a success." The short, determined man reminded my father that, as the leader of Clarendon's black community, he couldn't give up. The others echoed Rev. Seals's encouragement and promised to help find plaintiffs. Convinced of the need to persist, Rev. De Laine accepted Mr. Marshall's condition.

The bus transportation lawsuit was no longer a relevant issue. On March 12, 1949, the quest turned toward a greater goal, that of equalization of educational opportunities. Even so, two important things had to happen before a lawsuit could be filed. Mr. Marshall had to persuade his New York associates to take the case. And the Clarendon group had to find twenty families courageous enough to challenge the establishment.

Rev. Seals and Rev. De Laine plunged ahead, confident that precise instructions from the NAACP would soon be forthcoming. Their technique would be to alert people of the planned effort and to have interested individuals sign up. Since their base of power was in the southern part of Clarendon County—mainly in the area between River Road and U.S. Route 301—that was where they looked for places to hold meetings.

Although numerous black churches were in the area, most were not suitable for their cause. Some had pastors who could clearly see a heavenly life of white robes, golden honey, and flaky manna, but whose vision of earthly life failed to extend beyond the end of the shortest cotton row. They were what my father called spineless men, fearful of all white people and any figures of authority, in that order. The only things they advocated were unceasing prayer, blind obedience, and acceptance of the black man's lot of second-class citizenship and subservience as God's will. Other churches had pastors who had sold their independence for "thirty pieces of silver"—special favors or loans to buy cars, clothes, and other material things. They were the ones who feared a knock would come in the night, demanding that they turn against their brothers. Even if they sympathized, they dared not speak out. And—like people of all races and from all walks of life—there were church leaders who simply weren't going to rock the boat. They were the most pitiful of all, the leaders who would not lead, who had no convictions, no commitments, no compassion, and who wouldn't even follow.

Only a few of the churches were led by shepherds who believed that God makes change happen by working through the hands, heads, and hearts of humans. Theirs were the only churches where activist meetings could be held. But even among those churches, not every one was suitable.

Eighteen days after the trip to Columbia, the first meeting was held at Mount Zion AME Church. The Pearson family had belonged to that church ever since it was organized after the emancipation of slaves. Both Mr. Levi and Mr. Hammett were church officers. It seemed natural to start the new initiative at the home church of the original plaintiff.

A second meeting was held the following evening at Union Cypress AME Church, near the village of Jordan. The children of Union Cypress's members attended high school in Manning, not Summerton, and some of their parents had also bought a school bus. The list of signatures of people who wanted "Mr. Boulware to go in court and defend their rights" grew, and it soon included names from more than twenty families. NAACP officials were informed that the Clarendon County parents were ready.

Neither of the information meetings had been held in a town, a fact that caused some concern among NAACP officials in Columbia. Therefore two town meetings were arranged. The first was to be held on April 19 at St. Mark AME Church in Summerton, the site of Clarendon's first NAACP meeting in 1943. Its pastor was still Rev. Frazier, an extremely supportive pastor although not a county resident.

The executive secretary of the South Carolina Conference of NAACP Branches, Eugene A. R. Montgomery, came from Columbia to attend the meeting. Accompanying him was Lester Banks, his counterpart in Virginia where the NAACP was working to eliminate public school segregation by making school boards face the expense of equalizing every school. With his experience in recruiting petitioners, Mr. Banks was a valuable resource for Mr. Montgomery.

In front of an overflowing audience, the two executive secretaries explained that they were looking for the best place in Clarendon County for a lawsuit to originate. Then they told the audience frankly of the dire things that could happen to anyone who dared to sue a school board. Mortgages might be foreclosed, jobs lost, or someone killed. Most attendees seemed to want a case to be prosecuted, but the possible consequences were terrifying. Tenant farmers understood they could be tossed off the land they rented. They might become heroes, but they would be homeless heroes. Land-owning farmers already knew what had happened to Mr. Levi. Teachers didn't doubt for an instant that they would be fired. With such depressing scenarios, only three individuals signed. One was a woman whose husband insisted—even before the meeting was over—that she rescind her action.

After spending the night at our house, the NAACP men surveyed conditions at various county schools. In the evening they made a presentation in Manning's Ebenezer Baptist Church where a few attendees signed the interest list. Before leaving, the men told Daddy to try to get the town people from either Summerton or Manning aroused to the same extent as the rural people were.

A follow-up communication from Mr. Montgomery bore both good and bad news. The good news was that the NAACP would accept a case from Clarendon County. The bad news was threefold: (1) only one school district could be involved; (2) the district chosen had to have both white and black high schools for direct comparisons; and (3) the plaintiffs had to be residents of the selected school district.

That meant only Manning's District 9 and Summerton's District 22 were eligible. Except for its smaller number of students, the Summerton district was ideal. It had three black schools (one in "town" and two in rural areas) and two white schools (both in town). The stand-alone white Summerton High School had been built in 1935 using forty thousand dollars of federal money. The black Scott's Branch School was also built in 1935, although at a cost of only six thousand dollars. It served more than 600 elementary and high school students. Furthermore the black school's twelve grades were taught in ten classrooms by eleven teachers. Its first-grade teacher had 117 pupils, and the second-grade teacher 111. Seventh- and eighth-grade classes were combined, with one teacher in charge of 103 pupils. At the white Summerton Elementary School and Summerton High School, things were far different. A total of fourteen teachers were said to serve a total of 279 white students.

The push for getting the schools equalized had come from parents who lived outside of School District 22 and whose children needed bus transportation. Rev. De Laine and Rev. Seals would have to start all over to recruit people from in and around Summerton who, until that time, had shown little interest in the quest for equality in spite of the astounding inequities between the schools. The rural people so desperately wanted the effort to continue that they willingly assumed supporting roles. As disqualified J. L. Miller explained, "We made a vow—Mr. Levi, Mr. 'Flutie,' Joe Lemmon, Rev. De Laine and myself—we locked hands and took a vow that we would fight to the bitter end—even if every one of us had to die."

Another disqualified activist was Thelmar Bethune, who had only finished second grade. His explanation probably summed up what most of the rural people thought. In his youth he had attended a one-room school along with 136 other students. School was in session for only three months. Yet, before the boys could even enter the schoolhouse, they had to go to the forest and find firewood. "By the time you got back from the woods," he recalled bitterly, "it was time for recess. Sometimes, you wouldn't get but one subject a day. In other words, we would get reading about two times a week. You had to go [to school] about three years before you could even make one grade."

In spite of the "townspeople's" reluctance, my father and Rev. Seals were confident of getting the needed support since our house was "in" Summerton and my father had developed a small support base during the voting initiative. They notified the NAACP people in Columbia that the group had chosen Summerton District 22 to become the focal point for an equalization lawsuit.

As Rev. De Laine and Rev. Seals worked to get parents from Scott's Branch and the other two schools in District 22 to join the school equalization effort, they didn't know things had almost reached a boiling point at Scott's Branch. Although my father knew the principal was a source of student unhappiness, discontent caused by an inept black man wasn't something that demanded his attention. His goal was to help change the system, not to trap individuals, and the only way to change the system was to take it to court. A bad principal wasn't caused by unfair legislation, and a court of law couldn't correct the situation if a principal was a scoundrel.

What he needed was plaintiffs. More than a month had passed since the Summerton information meeting and about three months since the meeting with

Thurgood Marshall. Nonetheless only two Summerton people had signed the interest paper. Eighteen more families had to be found, and Rev. De Laine was focused almost single-mindedly on that.

Dissatisfaction was pervasive at Scott's Branch, especially among the older students. The quality of the already dismally poor school plummeted. By February any parents who could afford to do so had withdrawn their high school children and sent them to boarding schools—or to the public school in Manning. Even my brother Jay, an eleventh grader, had been enrolled in private school.

At the start of the school year, Mr. Benson had collected book rental money as usual. However, by the end of April, many textbooks still had not been distributed, and the money hadn't been returned. It was almost the end of the school year, and some high school students still had no mathematics books. Fourth-grade students had no arithmetic books, and reading classes were held for fifth-grade pupils without a reading book. Nevertheless the docile parents did nothing.

The breaking point came at the very end of the school year when seniors who didn't live in District 22 were informed they wouldn't be allowed to graduate because they hadn't paid a twenty-seven-dollar tuition fee, levied for the first time that year. When students asked their parents for the money, the financially strapped adults were incensed. The amount of money being demanded equaled a week's earnings for some. The parents grumbled and groused, declaring in one way or another, "Those people in Columbia know there ain't no black high school in every district. How come they tell us to send our children to another district if they gonna make us pay?"

It was a good question. Practically all students at Scott's Branch had paid the materials fee for the school year. They had brought the money to school tied in the corners of handkerchiefs and carefully pinned in pockets to keep the hard-earned cash from being lost. Teachers diligently recorded each payment and put the money in envelopes that were passed on to Mr. Benson. Since the materials fees were paid, no one understood why out-of-district students were being subjected to an additional tax.

There was also the matter of money that had been raised to defray senior-class expenses. Admission fees for several events had netted well over $135. Additionally the students had raised money by begging church members, shopkeepers, and neighbors for donations. The effort brought in more than $800, which was placed in Mr. Benson's care. No one knew what happened to the money after it was given to the principal. More than enough had been raised to cover any extra student assessments. When students queried Mr. Benson about the money, Reverdy Wells said he replied, "When you raise money and it comes up short, it must be gone in the rat hole."

Mr. Benson also collected the book rental money and money from selling snacks. In total more than $5,000 was unaccounted for. As far as the Scott's Branch School community could ascertain, it had simply disappeared. Another shock came at the time of graduation. The seniors were told if they didn't pay $2.50 for covers for their high school certificates, they wouldn't receive the certificates. Incensed, the seniors formed a class committee to confront the principal. According to Reverdy, when the class representatives asked Mr. Benson what happened to the money they had raised, they were told, "It's none of your business."

My mother brought the news to my father, who until then had avoided any involvement in the school's affairs, determined that his activities would not affect my mother's job. He understood that Mr. Benson was a figurehead who occupied a position that encouraged swindling and promoted fraudulence. As a principal himself, Rev. De Laine had experienced the pressures a superintendent or trustee board could put on a man, so he did not concern himself with the affairs at Scott's Branch.

The day after graduation, a big uproar took place. Members of Scott's Branch's Class of 1949 who "owed" money had been "awarded" blank sheets of paper. The graduates were mutinous, angry about the certificates, the money, the books, and every other injustice for which Mr. Benson was responsible. They confronted the principal. He, in response, threatened to void their transcripts.

My mother observed, "If those children had anybody to lead them, they would straighten up some of the injustices going on in Scott's Branch." Whether she intended them to do so or not, the words "If they had a leader" found the precise place in Daddy's fertile mind to stimulate a new approach to his problem.

He started thinking. No, he told himself. If he stepped in, as soon as the end was accomplished, people would claim, "Rev. De Laine was the one fighting the principal."

As he mulled over the situation, my father began to see a connection between the young people's dilemma and what he wanted to achieve. The Summerton people needed to be roused from their apathy before they would think of asking for equal facilities. They wouldn't rock the boat unless they understood and cared how existing conditions had created their current problem. The high school graduates could be the key to reaching the parents. But they needed a leader.

In Rev. De Laine's mind, God had provided him an answer to his dilemma. Taking a lesson from one of his frequent sermon themes, he would "start at the point where he was" and begin to "go forward." The battle cry would come from the children. They would initiate the fight to "straighten up some of the injustices." His job would be to get the students organized, without showing his hand, and to make sure certain people knew enough to support the moves that he planned.

Reared by his grandparents after the death of his father, a distinguished AME clergyman, Reverdy Wells had been one of the most respected students at Scott's Branch. The strikingly handsome youth's code of ethics had been molded by his grandfather, an honest, independent farmer with the color and features of a Caucasian. Before the old man's death in 1942, he taught the boy not to lie about anything and not to back down when he knew he was right. Josie Ragin, his grandmother and the former first-grade teacher at Scott's Branch, made sure he excelled in school.

Reverdy had already decided he would not let the Benson matter drop, and he eagerly told Rev. De Laine what the senior-class committee had done. Sharing part of his plan with the young man, my father suggested Reverdy mobilize the committee members and send their grievances to the school officials. The young man had no reservations about accepting my father's advice. As another recent graduate, Robert "Buster" Georgia, Jr., put it, "Everybody trusted Rev. De Laine. He always seemed to give the right advice."

The graduates met and wrote a letter that summarized their grievances. As class president, Reverdy signed it, and copies were sent by registered mail to the county superintendent of education; School District 22's superintendent, H. B. Betchman; each trustee of School District 22; and Principal Benson.

No response came, so Rev. De Laine put his typewriter and mimeograph machine at the young people's disposal, and he instructed them to call a meeting of school officials, parents, and the rest of the Class of 1949. They collected the addresses of Scott's Branch parents that they knew and added other addresses that my father kept as secretary of the local NAACP branch. More than three hundred postcards were written and mailed with an invitation to come to a meeting at St. Mark AME Church on June 8. At less than a quarter mile from the school building, the little church was very conveniently located.

Mr. Benson must have received his copy of the letter on June 3, the day before he was to leave for the summer. It was said he immediately went to Mr. Betchman's office. The next day, June 4, instead of leaving town as planned, he went from house to house, offering students refunds of three dollars each. As the "instigator" who signed the letter, Reverdy required special consideration. To appease him, Mr. Benson—or one of his bosses—identified a carrot they thought no new high school graduate would refuse. Mr. Benson offered, "If you take that letter back and shut up, I'll make sure you get a full scholarship to any South Carolina college you want to go to."

Offers of college scholarships were typically not sent until after the end of the academic year. Scott's Branch had such a poor academic rating that its graduates were among the last selected to fill college classes and the last to be offered scholarships. As a highly promising student and valedictorian of his class, Reverdy would most likely have gotten a scholarship. Exactly where he would enroll depended on how much he was offered.

Any other student might have eagerly taken Mr. Benson's carrot, but Reverdy lived by his deceased grandfather's philosophy of not backing down when you know you're right. As far as the youth was concerned, there were no grounds for bargaining. After politely listening, Reverdy replied, "I can't do that."

Word of what happened spread rapidly. By June 8 the flame of anger that had been smoldering among the parents, teachers, and students was ready to burst into a full-fledged fire.

6. *June 8*

Promise to stand with me to the very end,
then—and only then—I'll be your leader.

J. A. De Laine

The children called and the people came. More than three hundred people heeded the call. Sharecroppers, renters, and landowners came; and maids, farmhands and housewives. Journeymen and handymen came, as well as seven schoolteachers and five ministers. St. Mark's plain, unvarnished pews were full. As many as could crowded inside the little church, standing along the walls after all the seats were taken. Those forced to remain outside peered in through the open windows and front door.

They were all ages and shapes and sizes. A few with straight—almost blond—hair and whitish skin, ruddy from years in the sun, moved familiarly among the surrounding sea of light brown, medium brown, dark brown, and almost black faces. The white faces belonged to Edward "Bubba" Ragin and other members of the black community. Neither the color of a person's skin nor the texture of one's hair determined one's race. No matter how many white men there were in one's lineage, one ancestor from Africa—a single great-grandmother—was all it took to make a person black and, thus, relegated to second-class citizenship.

Despite the large crowd, there was no cause for optimism. The officials responsible for the welfare of the school and the education of the area's school-age population had not even acknowledged the students' letter. Their complete absence was a slap in the face to the young people and their parents.

Wearing a tie and his Sunday suit, Reverdy stood in the altar area and opened the meeting. Watching him in eager anticipation, the audience was ready to believe anything the tall youth with the authoritative bearing said. After thanking the people for coming, Reverdy called for selected graduates to detail their complaints against Mr. Benson. Their itemized complaints consisted of the following:

1. We paid for equipment to work in Algebra and Geometry and did not get the equipment, neither was the money returned.

2. Our class which should have been taught by Mr. I. S. Benson, the Principal, was neglected 9/10 of the time.
3. He is holding some of the Senior Class' Certificates, trying to collect $27.00 for tuition.
4. We have had two school rallies and raised over $800.00 to help the school and no results have been seen or mentioned.
5. There were about eight programs in May, with an admission fee at each program. He has put it in his pocket but made no mention of how much has been raised or what will be done with it.
6. Last but not least, he charged us $2.50 for state certificates and, when we questioned him, he threatened [to withhold] our transcripts. Which means to us that he will pretend that they were not made out right before he came here or he means to give us some kind of trouble before our credits are sent to another school. We were willing to work for our credits and transcripts but we will not be silent if any of our transcripts are maliciously confused.

The litany of Mr. Benson's offenses enraged the throng. As each point was read, a wave of comments rippled around the sanctuary and the reader had to pause before continuing. Reverdy told the crowd they had tried to talk to Mr. Benson, and they had sent a written petition to the trustees, the district superintendent, and the county superintendent. "Everybody ignored us," he stated. "We wanted to discuss our grievances face-to-face with the school officials so we asked them to come tonight. But they didn't." In a tone of defeat, he finished, "We did all we can. Now we got to leave it in your hands."

Walking away from the pulpit and its threadbare velvet covering, he returned to his seat, surrendering responsibility to the adults, a group with no spokesperson and no plan. Perhaps failing to understand that their children were asking them to find a solution, both farmers and teachers sat motionless. Journeymen and laborers waited for someone to tell them what to do. Even the normally loquacious preachers were mute, everyone waiting for something to happen.

Before the audience noticed, a man was speaking—his voice so soft he had to repeat himself to get their attention. Slowly all eyes turned to the slight man who seemed even smaller in comparison to the youth who had just spoken. He was saying, "Y'all heard what the children told us. Now they done left it in our hands. What we go do?"

Robert Georgia, father of the graduate called "Buster," stood calmly waiting for a response, his pleasant face somber and his concern evident. Once the crowd focused on him, they heard him clearly. Understanding what he said, but having no answers, the group sat mute, offering no course of action.

Henry Scott, a church deacon and a sharecropper, finally spoke. Although the system had denied him a formal education, it couldn't take away his sharp brain.

Rising from his seat, majestic and unapologetic in his anger, he got to the point, speaking in the region's patois and wasting no time with preliminaries. The words he spoke and the way in which he expressed his sentiments were galvanizing. "It's a dety shame. It's jes' a dety shame. The chillen have to call we parents to meet instead of we parents calling the chillen. It's a dety shame. We must do somp'en. We must get ognis NOW."

Yes, it was a dirty shame. Mr. Scott's meaning could not have been clearer if his words had been delivered with the most precise enunciation by the world's greatest orator. His language might have been the language of an illiterate person, but his words expressed the thoughts of an efficient and focused man of action, and he put them forth in no uncertain terms. His brief message was like flipping the "on" switch for an entire power plant. A clarion call for action had been made, and the people knew they had to get organized without delay. Mr. Scott's forceful words had rolled aside the boulder that had blocked the windows of people's minds, and suddenly they could see beyond their tradition of not questioning those in authority. Perhaps for the first time in their lives, many of them realized the need to be organized if they were to have any effect on the forces that battered them daily. The audience was ready to take action.

Unopposed, Mr. Georgia continued in his role of acting chairman, clearly cognizant of the course that had to be taken. He asked, "Who we gonna have for president?"

A voice immediately called out, "I nominate Mis' Josie."

Reverdy's grandmother quickly declined, claiming, "My arthritis is too bad."

Another voice chimed in, naming Mr. Georgia. He also declined, saying, "I'm a farmer. I ain't educated and I don't know how to talk to educated white people. Get somebody else. Get Rev. De Laine. He a teacher and he know how to talk to them."

My father was at the back of the church, sitting beside a local clergyman who had no children and Amy Ragin, a Scott's Branch teacher and mother of one of the graduates. BB and I were students at Scott's Branch, so my father's interest in the meeting was valid. Like Mis' Amy's or any other teacher's, his teaching job would be at stake if he spoke out.

The crowd immediately realized that Rev. De Laine—already well known as an honest, trustworthy, and accessible "NAACP man" who gave solid advice—would be the perfect leader. Mr. Georgia's motion was quickly seconded. However, Rev. De Laine declined, explaining that school officials might not receive him kindly because of his involvement with the *Pearson* transportation case. Adding that he had sent my brother to Mather Academy in an effort to avoid becoming involved in Scott's Branch affairs, he said, "I think you ought to get somebody else." Before he sat down, he nominated Mr. Bubba, making the observation, "Mr. Edward Ragin is a good man. And he has children in the school."

Looking incredulous, Mr. Bubba responded, "Me? If you tell me to drive a mule, I could do that. I know how to say 'gee' and I know how to say 'haw' but I don't know how to talk to these white folks." The last words seemed completely incongruous because Mr. Bubba looked exactly like one of those "white folks." He continued, "We need to get somebody who know what to do. We need a educated person to do the talking for us."

From the packed church came the cry, "Yeah, Rev. De Laine educated. Rev., we need you."

Pressure was brought from all directions. A chorus of "You can't decline" echoed around the room, followed by, "You have to take the lead."

Mr. Georgia declared, "The motion still stands."

For almost two years my father had focused on the need for bus transportation. During the past two months, he had diligently tried to get parents from Clarendon School District 22 to join the quest for equalization of school facilities. More recently he had helped the graduates arrange that night's meeting. Yet, in spite of all of that, he was refusing to take the leadership as the people demanded.

Stubbornly and inexplicably, he continued to reject the position, offering one reason after another. With poor health and other duties already overtaxing his strength, he said, "I don't know if I could carry through. Especially if something goes wrong. The minute something goes wrong, y'all would quickly put all the blame on me and say you didn't know anything about it." Continuing, he stated, "I don't want to lose friendship and I don't want to jeopardize my wife's standing in the school."

Henry Scott had made the people know that they needed to be organized and that they needed a leader. Once Rev. De Laine's name was mentioned, the group realized that, with his reputation as a "straight shooter who couldn't be pushed around," he was the very person they needed. So more voices joined the chorus that called for him to be their leader.

Still not acquiescing, Rev. De Laine rose, standing as tall, erect, and commanding as an Indian chief whose eyes could interpret every expression, whose ears could decipher every sound, and who knew his people's every thought. With all eyes glued to him, he delivered a short, fiery speech, telling the group, "people will call you to fight their battles and then run away and lay the blame on you." Declaring he would not let himself be caught in such a situation, he said there were others he would support as leader. As he talked, he noticed a man of a certain importance in the community looking through a window. Although he doubted the man would openly fight for justice, Rev. De Laine nominated him. Almost three hundred voices roared with disapproval, "No! We need you, Rev." Some went further, shouting, "We don't want nobody who gonna sell us out. We want action. We want you."

Things are not always as they seem. The sequence of the night's events and the outcome of the leadership position had been meticulously planned by a few

NAACP members at a preliminary meeting the night before. Mr. Georgia and Mr. Bubba were there, but most attendees were from Davis Station and other rural areas. The group had agreed that Rev. De Laine should be the students' spokesperson. Then they planned how it would happen. My father had made it plain he would not accept the leadership position until all attempts to get someone else were exhausted. The people had to conclude for themselves that there was no one else who could lead the group successfully. An astute observer of human nature, my father knew the ways of his fellow humans. Time and again he had seen people desert a cause at the first sign of difficulty—like rats from a sinking ship. If he took the leadership, he knew he would readily be blamed whenever problems arose. For that reason he emphasized to the small group that he would accept the position only with a guarantee of shared responsibility.

The meeting on June 8 was flawlessly orchestrated. Only after much persuasion, and with seeming reluctance, did Rev. De Laine accept the nomination. Even then he didn't accept unconditionally. Still speaking from the rear of the church, my father said, "Y'all are putting me in this position and I know y'all are gonna fight me when the going gets hard. When the whites plot against me and when my life is in jeopardy and even when everything I own might be destroyed, y'all will be ready to turn your backs on me." He looked around, staring into the eyes of first one individual and then another until their souls burned with shame.

Using his preaching voice, he exhorted the assembled crowd, telling them that it wasn't only the principal they needed to worry about because the inequities between the black and white schools weren't Mr. Benson's fault. He stated, "The price will be dear for what you want. The trustee board and the superintendent are going to ignore me. And when they do, we'll have to appeal to the county board because I won't be satisfied to stop. And when that fails, we'll have to appeal to the State Board of Education."

Pausing for effect, he looked around before continuing. His eyes strafed the crowd sitting in the dim room that was barely brightened by sixty-watt bulbs suspended from the ceiling by twisted electric cords. Ominously his voice rang out, "And I'm confident we won't get equal treatment even then. Every time, they're going to turn us down."

Normally possessing a straight-backed posture, he pulled himself even more erect until he looked like a chiseled giant of caramel-covered steel—compelling, strong, and invincible—as he seamlessly wove together the need for redress for what Mr. Benson had done with the need for better school facilities. His voice continued, still vibrant and strong, but lower and more ominous. "Then we'll have to fight the battle in court with the NAACP's help. We'll have to appeal to the State Court and then to the Federal Court and from there to the Supreme Court before we can get justice." Again his voice rose as he proclaimed, "If I take the leadership, you have to stick with me and fight all the way to the United States Supreme Court."

Shifting to a more confidential tone, he declared, "Unless y'all are willing to stand with me through it all, I won't take this position. But if . . . if y'all are willing to insist that your children be provided with the decent schools and the schooling they're entitled to, if y'all promise to stand with me to the very end, then—and only then—I'll be your leader."

Years later my father said that, although the thoughts coming out of his mouth arose from the depth of his heart, the way they were expressed was beyond his control. He declared that the Lord gave him the command of extraordinary words, as well as the gift to use them.

That passionate little sermon from the rear of the church mobilized the people. It directed their purpose, gave them strength, and took away all fear. They were shouting their support by the time my father declared, "Until we reach the Supreme Court." With religious fervor, the church resounded with encouragement: "We'll back you every step, Rev." "Yes sir. We'll stand with you, Rev." "You telling us what we wanna hear." In a revival mood, they yelled, "Amen," "Come on, Rev," and "We ready to follow."

He didn't leave the back pew until the crowd unanimously promised to support him to the end, regardless of the cost or the degree of humiliation. Only when he was satisfied that he would have their support—and after he had made it plain that he was not going to finance their fight—did Rev. De Laine agree to be their leader and advance to the front of the church.

Just before he passed the end of the semicircular chancel rail, his eye fell on E. E. Richburg, the relatively new pastor of Liberty Hill AME Church. Rev. Richburg was a Clarendon native whom my father had known since they were youths. The thought came to Daddy that he needed the man's cooperation and assistance. In a split second he made a decision and, turning to the people, said, "I started to take charge but I can't. Nobody knows what will be the result of this night's meeting. It's possible somebody might try to frame me or damage my reputation. The only way I'll go further is if I have a competent secretary."

Of the seven teachers and other preachers at the church that night, Rev. De Laine wanted Rev. Richburg and no one else. Despite being a country boy who hailed from out by Spring Hill, Rev. Richburg was suave and well spoken with a polish my father never acquired. He also had good experience in keeping records. To my father, however, the most important thing was that he pastored the county's largest AME church. With the ears of so many people—far more than the entire population that lived inside Summerton's town limits—Rev. Richburg could wield considerable influence.

Speaking to the assembled group, Rev. De Laine continued, "I need a good secretary to take the minutes of what we do and say. I will only risk my reputation with one person in this building. That person has served efficiently as the secretary of the AME Church's Central Conference. He is in the person of Rev.

E. E. Richburg, pastor of Liberty Hill. If you elect him as your secretary, I'll be ready to do what I can."

Almost before my father finished talking, Rev. Richburg declined, claiming he was unqualified because he had no children attending school in the district. Rev. De Laine countered, "A secretary needs to be unbiased. We don't want a secretary who will write only one side of the minutes. We need a secretary who, like a clerk in the courts, keeps the records for both the plaintiffs and the defendants."

Then Rev. Richburg's own church members put the heat on him, saying, "Come on, Rev. You can't back out on us like that. You can't 'crawfish' now."

Ultimately he surrendered, immediately assuming the duties of secretary. The people also approved when Rev. De Laine picked Mr. Georgia and Mr. Bubba to work with him. Their committee of three was to be called the Committee on Action. My father would be the chairman and sole spokesperson, needing only the committee members' approval to take any action.

When the meeting adjourned, the parents were confident they had put their problems in the correct hands. Before heading home, they joined their voices in song, intoning the words of the old hymn, "Together let us sweetly live. Together let us die."

7. *Across the Rubicon*

Be strong and of good courage . . .
for the Lord your God is with you.
Joshua 1:9

In the year 49 B.C.E., Julius Caesar and his army crossed the Rubicon, a little river that marked the northern boundary of Italy proper. Since Roman law forbade any general to lead an army across the Rubicon, Caesar's action made armed conflict inevitable. Although it is said that General Caesar was unsure what he would do once he crossed, he went ahead and did it anyway. Then, it is said, he declared, "The die is cast."

Two thousand years later, on the night of June 8, 1949, another die was cast. In the little town of Summerton, a small band of NAACP supporters succeeded in making the town's black community look to Rev. J. A. De Laine, my father, for deliverance. Although the parents in School District 22 were now ready to fight for justice, his acceptance of the role as their spokesperson almost guaranteed that he would lose his teaching job. But there could be no turning back.

Charged with doing whatever was necessary to obtain relief for the young people's grievances, the Committee on Action—Rev. De Laine, Mr. Georgia, and Mr. Bubba—began to work the very next morning. Bearing a letter with the condensed charges made by students, a date of June 9, and the signatures of all three of them, the men went to see Superintendent Betchman. He was on vacation, so they went then to see J. D. Carson, the trustee who served as the school board's clerk.

Mr. Carson took his time before granting the committee an audience. When he did deign to see them, he was as angry as if his three visitors had done him some personal harm. Apparently he had heard about the parents' meeting. Instead of being attentive and alert for any merit to the allegations, the man heaped abuse on each visitor, trying to humiliate them in every way he could. My father, the parent of two students at Scott's Branch, was told, "You have no business in this. You have nothing to do with that school." Then the trustee began to vilify a young woman who lived on his property and had signed the grievance.

On June 8, 1949, Scott's Branch School parents elected J. A. De Laine (center) as their leader. With the parents' approval, he chose Robert Georgia (left) and Edward "Bubba" Ragin (right) to serve with him as members of the Committee on Action. Photograph by E. C. Jones. Courtesy of the De Laine Family Collection

Rev. De Laine had repeatedly taught those who worked with him "to outclass anybody who tries to insult you." However, his own resolve was sorely tried as Mr. Carson ranted. Nevertheless he and the others managed to maintain their dignity. At a break in the tirade, my father asked for a hearing where formal charges could be presented. Reluctantly the fuming man promised to call a board meeting. Then he added spitefully, "Don't bring nobody else. I'm not gonna hear no children trying to speak against the principal, so don't bring them." He emphasized the hearing would be to hear the Committee on Action—and "only the committee." The three parent representatives would have to act as proxy witnesses for the young people.

Due to leave soon for summer school at Allen University, Rev. De Laine had brought a stamped envelope bearing his name and a Columbia address to facilitate being contacted for the hearing. He handed the stamped envelope to Mr. Carson as he left.

The die had indeed been cast. Two days after visiting the trustee, Rev. De Laine received a registered letter from the chairman of the Board of Trustees of Clarendon School District 30. Dated June 11, it informed my father that his service as principal of Silver School was terminated as of that day. Although he was not surprised, my father did confront the man. The trustee, who wouldn't look directly at my father, confessed, "It ain't me, preacher. It's them big fellows that's over me."

When he informed the parents of what happened, Rev. De Laine gave proof of his mettle. "That's not going to stop me," he told them. "Nothing's going to stop me as long as you continue to back me." Refusing to compromise, he said the firing only served to remove his shackles. With a strength engendered, in part, from the independence afforded by having a productive and unmortgaged farm, he was ready to pursue the fight until the victorious end.

Nine days passed with no word from District 22's school board, so the committee made a second request on June 18. That request did receive a response. In spite of Rev. De Laine having left an envelope bearing his name and a Columbia address, the communication was sent to Mr. Georgia at his Summerton RFD address. Dated June 23, it bore a postmark of June 24, the same day as its delivery. It announced a hearing would be held that very evening.

Aware that Rev. De Laine was in Columbia, the trustees had deliberately planned to hold the hearing in his absence, probably believing they could easily scare Mr. Bubba and Mr. Georgia. The trustees knew that a letter sent to a Columbia address wouldn't arrive until the next day, but a letter mailed in early morning would be delivered locally on the same day. Mr. Carson and his associates must have been sure they had outfoxed Rev. De Laine. They could hold a kangaroo court, and that would be the end of the matter.

In Columbia, Rev. De Laine was in a seminary class where the topic of discussion was the Christian doctrine of redemption. His mind may have been considering whether it was possible for a modern man to pay a redemption price to "purchase" the freedom of others. Whatever his thoughts, he had no time to share them with others. In an era before cellular phones and when personal telephone calls to students marked true emergencies, the dean of the seminary interrupted the class, which was being taught by the president of the university, to say Rev. De Laine had a telephone call.

Picking up the phone, my father heard the voice of one of his committee members. The school authorities had underestimated the almost illiterate farmers who, despite their limited schooling, were very smart men. Determined that the meeting wouldn't be held without their leader, they had made a long-distance call from King's Funeral Home. The message may have been in code because there were likely to be listeners on the shared party line. Whatever words were spoken, Rev. De Laine understood his presence was urgently needed.

To the great surprise of the trustees, Rev. De Laine was at Summerton High School's library before the appointed time. In addition to the two committee members, Grant Oliver and "Big" William Ragin were there. Having taken Mr. Carson's caveat seriously, none of the young people had been asked to come, and wanting things to go as smoothly as possible, Rev. De Laine asked Mr. Oliver and Big William to not enter the room.

The three trustees of School District 22, the district superintendent, and the county superintendent joined the three members of the Committee on Action.

Two other men were also there. According to the restrictions set by Mr. Carson on June 9, their presence was forbidden. Daddy had seen Mr. Mills, the white agriculture teacher, enter the room and take a prominent seat. However, he was surprised by the presence of Gabriel Tindal, one of the Scott's Branch people, who had somehow entered the library unseen by Rev. De Laine. Nobody asked him to leave.

Mr. McCord, as county superintendent, presided, and Roderick W. Elliott, the school board chairman, read the charges. Immediately one board member opined that "these here Nigras" are trying to "stir things up," to cause problems when nothing was wrong. Others echoed his words. "The Nigras and whites have been getting along together just fine and some of y'all just trying to stir up trouble." My father agreed that the races had been getting along and denied that anyone was trying to stir up trouble. They were not there about a race problem, he said. They were there to present grievances of the school's Class of 1949 and their parents concerning the principal of Scott's Branch.

Mr. Mills, the agriculture teacher, who had no official position on the school board, asked a pointed question. He demanded that Daddy explain where he got authority to represent schoolchildren and their parents. My father answered, "We were elected by the Negro patrons of the school."

A member of the board tried to deny that authority with the declaration, "A church meeting has nothing to do with school affairs."

Neither afraid of white men nor shy, the black farmers remained silent because, as they had said on the night of June 8, they didn't know how to counter the arguments of educated men. In essence my father was alone against six white men who were determined to deny black people the right to question their authority. In their world black men were not supposed to be "arrogant" enough to seek justice and had to be kept in "their place" if the status quo were to be preserved.

The trustees told the committee members that the sum of twenty-seven dollars had been approved by the board as a tuition fee and the principal had a right to charge pupils who didn't live in District 22 that amount. Furthermore the twenty-seven dollars was in addition to the seven dollar materials fee levied on all students. According to the trustees, the money included book rent for twelfth-grade students. The meeting ended with the Committee on Action being told there were no grounds for the students' complaints. Additionally they were belittled because they hadn't presented witnesses. How, the trustees asked, could there be any substance to "grievances" if there were no witnesses? One of the white men suggested, "Someone who wanted to be principal is stirring up trouble." The ordeal was harrowing, almost wrecking Rev. De Laine's normally steely nerves. That night, for one of the few times in his life, he was unable to sleep.

The Committee on Action's report to the parents can be summed up by a single statement. The trustees said Mr. Benson had a right to charge out-of-district pupils twenty-seven dollars.

Rev. De Laine was not one to give up easily. Once he began a task, he doggedly pursued it to completion. As far as he was concerned, the graduates' grievances had not been satisfactorily addressed, and therefore the matter had not been completed. The young people had to be allowed to bear witness to their charges. At this point my father sought guidance from Mr. McCord.

The county superintendent listened, seemingly disgusted with the way Scott's Branch was being run. Although he might have been annoyed that he was being bothered, he assured Rev. De Laine that he wanted the errors corrected. However, the power to change conditions in the school rested with the trustees of District 22. Only they had the authority to hire and fire school employees. Even Mr. Betchman, as superintendent of District 22, held his position at the pleasure of the local trustees. Furthermore those same trustees had helped put Mr. McCord into his office as county superintendent.

Although Mr. McCord claimed he could do nothing directly to help, he said it sounded as though the graduates had just cause for grievance and promised to lend the weight of his office on their behalf. He instructed my father to refile the charges and ask for a rehearing. When asked if a lawyer were needed, Mr. McCord replied, "You can make the charges out yourselves. I'll tell you what to do." With the superintendent's advice, Rev. De Laine knew who should receive the charges and how the copies should be delivered. My father had the impression that the superintendent was happy to see Scott's Branch parents taking an interest in their school and trying to correct the way it was operated.

Rev. De Laine wrote a letter, dated July 9, requesting a hearing concerning the charges against Mr. Benson to be held at the earliest convenience. In one version of the letter, he stated that, although a hearing had been held before District 22's Board of Education in Summerton on June 24, 1949, "the explanations given by the Board to our complaints are unsatisfactory, not in writing, and we appeal to you for a hearing." An enclosure gave relevant information, including a list of charges against the principal of Scott's Branch. The charges included the following:

1. The children paid for equipment to be used in Algebra and Geometry classes, but they neither received the equipment nor had their money returned.
2. Mr. Benson failed to teach his mathematics classes nine-tenths of the time.
3. Two school rallies resulted in over $800 being raised to help the school, but no results had been seen or mentioned.
4. Admission fees were charged for about eight programs but Mr. Benson had not revealed how much was raised or what would be done with the money.
5. Mr. Benson charged $2.50 for state certificates and, when questioned by the students, threatened their transcripts.

Additionally a request was made for an investigation to determine if records at Scott's Branch schools were being kept properly. All three members of the Committee on Action signed the letter. Although addressed to the County Board of Education, the only names listed as recipients were those of Mr. McCord, Mr. Betchman, Mr. Elliott, and Mr. Benson. Rev. De Laine made two handwritten notations on the letter, one of which asked, "Please notify us in time to have notice sent to witnesses."

The prompt reply from Mr. McCord, dated July 13, read:

The Request of your committee for a hearing in the Benson matter before the County Board [has been] received.

It seems to me that the proper procedure in this matter is to ask for a hearing before the local Board of Trustees, District #22, at which hearing you may summon your witnesses to furnish proof of the charges made. Then if the finding of the local Board of Trustees is not satisfactory to your Committee, you can appeal to the County Board of Education and it will be our responsibility to examine and pass upon the testimony offered and the decision rendered.

When an appeal is made from a lower to a higher body we will have to base our opinion on the testimony furnished. I do not feel that the County Board will be justifiable in trying this case and examining witnesses unless and until the local Board of Trustees refuse to give you a hearing.

I would suggest, therefore, that you ask the local Board of Trustees, District #22, for a hearing to examine the witnesses and to determine the issue. So far as I know, the local Board of Trustees has rendered no decision. Therefore you have no ground to appeal until some decision is made or a refusal by the local Board of Trustees to give your Committee a hearing.

Time passed, but the Committee on Action received no reply from the Summerton school board.

Other firings of teachers had followed Rev. De Laine's. It seemed that any teacher who was thought to be a sympathizer of the effort, or who Principal Benson claimed was against him, was fired. Henry Ragin, accused of wanting Mr. Benson's job, was one of the first to be let go. That enraged the community, my father's determination and persistence being contagious. On the evening of July 25, more than forty-four parents—including four who made their marks because they could not write—signed a petition that was sent to Mr. Betchman and the district trustees. The petition requested that no teachers be dismissed if they had not been terminated before June 9.

Rev. De Laine wasn't in town when the petition was sent although he probably wrote the letter. Early that morning, hours before the parents met at St. Mark, he had left for Columbia, taking delegates from his churches to the AME Church's Youth Congress at Allen University. Two women who were not affiliated with his churches rode with him. Lucrisher Richardson, a farmer's wife, and Theola Brown, the wife of the janitor of the white Summerton High School, were accompanying my father on a mission unrelated to church.

After the delegates were dropped off, the adults went to see Mr. Martin, the agent for black schools at the South Carolina Department of Education. After explaining why they had come, Rev. De Laine pulled out a bundle of documents that included minutes of the June 8 meeting, a copy of the students' letter listing the irregularities, and affidavits from seven Scott's Branch teachers.

Mr. Martin took the papers, offered his visitors a seat, and began to read. As he read, he turned redder and redder. Finally he asked, "May I take these around to the State Superintendent of Education's Office?"

That was exactly what Rev. De Laine wanted. Before Mr. Martin left, my father asked, "While you're gone, may we go out to find some dinner?"

Almost two hours passed before they got back, but Mr. Martin still had not returned. To my anxious father, it seemed as though they waited yet another two hours. The man took so long to return that Rev. De Laine assumed the documents were being copied. That was in 1949, the same year the first Xerox machine made its debut. It would be several years before the technology of photocopying came to South Carolina's Department of Education. In order for Mr. Martin to make copies of documents, typists would have had to do the work manually, striking typewriter keys letter by letter. Or photographs would have had to be taken.

Finally Mr. Martin returned. Giving the documents back, he asked Rev. De Laine to meet him in Summerton on Friday, July 29. The request caught my father off guard. He had not expected that. Thinking fast, he demurred. For a man like Rev. De Laine, whose word could unconditionally be relied upon, the half truth that came out stung his lips. "No sir," he said. "I can't. I'm in summer school and I'll be in class Friday."

Mr. Martin then wanted to know if he could be there on Saturday. Another half truth was required. Rev. De Laine said he had to do some library research and couldn't get to Summerton before night. The whole truth was that he could have missed the class and postponed the research, but he didn't want to go to Summerton with Mr. Martin. More than July's summer heat was making it uncomfortably hot in Summerton. The extra heat was generated by the anger of white men. And it was being stoked by their arrogant belief in racial superiority, by spite, and—perhaps—even by hatred. When the school trustees received the parents' petition for reinstatement of the fired teachers, the climate would become even hotter. My father was trying to force a rehearing, but he would do everything in his power to avoid being seen with the enforcer.

Mr. Martin accepted the excuse but asked, "Who is there that I can see?"

Rev. De Laine directed him to Robert Georgia. Having no time to waste on a black farmer, on Friday, Mr. Martin drove directly to the county superintendent's office. There he picked up Mr. McCord, and the two of them went on to Summerton.

Concerning that day, my father said, "I don't know what transpired but something happened." Men who had watched from the sidelines reported that the trustees were bitter and that Mr. Carson called my father a "smart aleck." They also said the clerk of the board ranted that the state's education department was trying to make the district refund the state aid that had been paid as salary to Mr. Benson. Belligerent and furious, he is said to have asserted that no change would be made at Scott's Branch School and that, "Benson will stay there as long as we are the trustees."

The only information Daddy's committee got directly from the trustee board was an undated report of the June 24 meeting on a sheet of plain paper. It read:

> THE BOARD OF TRUSTEES of School District No. 22 met in special session in Summerton High School Library at 8:00 o'clock P.M., on the 24 day of June, 1949, for the purpose of considering the Complaints and charges filed by J. A. Delaine, Edward Ragin, and Robert Georgia against I. S. Benson as principal of the Scott's Branch School. All of the members of the Board were present. The charges were read by the Chairman of the Board. J. A. Delaine, Edward Ragin, and Robert Georgia made statements, but made no attempt to prove any of the allegations, offered no witnesses, and introduced no testimony or exhibits relative to the charges. I. S. Benson presented an audit of his books, which the Trustees reviewed. After due consideration, the Board of Trustees unanimously found that the charges were unsupported and dismissed the same.

The report—signed by R. M. Elliott, chairman; G. S. Kennedy; and J. D. Carson, clerk, trustees of School District No. 22 Clarendon County—didn't state when Mr. Benson had presented the audit of his books.

The Committee on Action sent another letter asking for a rehearing. On August 24, Mr. Carson refused to receive the registered letter. It was a stalemate. The local board refused to acknowledge the request for a rehearing, and the County Board of Education would not grant an appeal until the local board made a decision.

Although the committee members were in a quandary, there was no thought of conceding defeat. The goal was to get equal school facilities. For that effort to proceed, twenty signatures of people from the Summerton school district were needed. The people had to be kept incensed about conditions at Scott's Branch until enough of them consented to sign the NAACP petition.

8. *An Offer That Was Refused*

Trust not their presents.
Virgil

For three months every request for a rehearing was rebuffed. Even the visit by the man from the state's Department of Education failed to trigger a meeting. Apparently determined not to be pushed around, the school board members dug their heels in deeper. At the end of August, Mr. Benson was still principal and the graduates' grievances still had not been addressed. The parents were getting impatient. So, on September 2, the Committee on Action submitted a second formal request for an appeal hearing to the county superintendent.

Soon it would be time to pay the coming year's school fees. Determined to prevent a repeat of the previous year's swindle, the committee sent the following notice to parents:

> The Committee on Action request that no parent or child pay any more to any teacher or school official until an understanding and agreement is reached between the Parents Committee and those . . . in Authority. This applies to the parents and children of Scott's Branch School . . . alone. Money paid to a school should be used for the benefit of the children of the school, and the parents should know how it is spent; especially when it is coming out of the parents' pockets. A principal who receives his salary from monies appropriated for public instruction should be glad to let the parents know what is being done with the monies they give, unless it is going in the "Rat Hole" or the "Private Sinking FUND."
>
> Seemingly, an effort is being made at Summerton to keep the parents ignorant of the school affairs and also to keep them divided, one group against the other. By such methods the past practices may be continued in the future or made worse. Little gifts and nice talk should be carefully watched and proved.
>
> If parents want a Better Deal and assurance over a long period of time, they must stand together. The good of their children and future

generations is at stake in the grievances of this community, as well as many others. This is not aimed after any one man, it is to slow down the evil practices which have existed for so many years.

Around the middle of the month, my father was in the courthouse in Manning on personal business. As he passed the open door of Mr. McCord's office, the superintendent hailed him, saying, "I see those fellows still haven't given you another hearing."

Rev. De Laine agreed, "No sir. And I reckon they don't intend to."

It was Mr. McCord's turn to agree. "I guess I'm going to need to give your folks a hearing."

Pleased, Rev. De Laine responded that would be good. But he was taken aback when Mr. McCord immediately set the date for Wednesday of the following week. In one breath the hearing for which they had fought so long was finally granted. In the next the opportunity to present the case properly was being denied because the witnesses would not be able to attend. The May high school graduates who had so effectively raised their parents' hackles were now enrolled as September's college freshmen.

My father replied that the timing was very bad. The college students couldn't be taken out of classes during the week, and the committee needed time to call a meeting to ask the parents to send for their children. Mr. McCord was accommodating. The two men agreed on a date two weeks from then—Saturday, October 1—and the superintendent subsequently mailed formal confirmation to each committee member. It read, in part,

> Your appeal to the County Board of Education of Clarendon County for a hearing on charges against I. S. Benson has been received.
>
> We are calling a meeting of the County Board of Education in connection with the local board of Trustees of Summerton, School District, No. 22, to hear this case on Saturday, October 1, 1949—(nine-thirty) 9:30 A.M., in the Manning Court House.
>
> You are at liberty to present witnesses to prove the charges made against said I. S. Benson.

A separate letter was sent to Mr. Benson, informing him that he could appear to defend himself against the charges, if he so wished.

Determined that nothing would go wrong, the Committee on Action got busy planning. Rev. De Laine met almost daily with Rev. Richburg, Rev. Seals, and others. Meanwhile reports began coming in that some families were being pressured to boycott the hearing.

Back in June the trustees hadn't exaggerated when they said relations were good between the two races. Interracial encounters on the street were invariably civil and usually cordial. A black person always addressed a white one by name, with the added honorific of Mister or Mis'. In turn the black person would also be addressed by name, first or last, but pointedly denied a title of respect. If a black individual went to the home of a white person, everyone knew the back door was to be used. On the other hand, a white person was expected to come straight to the front door of a black home, and no one expected a white man to take off his hat. Everybody obeyed the strict rules, and life was calm.

There were no glitches in race relations in Summerton. Or so the white people thought. Not one of them could remember a racially inspired incident happening in their town. They even pretended not to remember that, only five years earlier, Clarendon County had the ignominious distinction of executing the youngest person in the history of the United States. That was when a fourteen-year-old black boy who lived five miles north of Manning was accused, tried, and executed—all in a period of less than three months—for the murder of two white girls.

The white people were adept at putting unpleasant racial events into a perspective that fit with the myth of good race relations. Mistreatment of black sharecroppers and household help was not considered as such. It was merely a way of reminding subordinates of their proper place in southern society.

Except for a few poor white people such as Mood Corbett and his family, who lived in a miserable shack in the black section of town, life was good for Summerton's white people. On the whole they were benevolent, and some even genuinely cared about the welfare of their servants, employees, and tenants. Somehow they had adjusted to the fact that some white men had black mistresses and that there were black children who lived in town very close to their white relations. Some white men even acknowledged the existence of their black children, siblings, and cousins. As long as no one with one drop or more of black blood dared claim the rights that went with a white birthright, the white people continued believing race relations in Summerton were just fine.

They also believed the black people were happy. They were always smiling and agreeable. Didn't that show they were happy? When black people stayed in their place, accepting without question the actions of white people, things went smoothly. From the white vantage point, things were as close to perfect as they could be.

Things were not perfect. They were not even close to perfect. Black folks, even the illiterate ones, knew they were often cheated. They resented it when white folks took advantage of them. But they feared for their jobs, their credit, their homes, and even their lives. The white people mistook the black people's desire to get along peaceably for being satisfied with the ugly conditions thrust upon them. When their white "masters" expressed displeasure, black people had almost every reason to take note and institute corrective actions. That was why parents who ardently supported the Committee on Action in the church meetings were deathly afraid of speaking out while in the presence of white folks.

As has often been noted, all that is necessary for evil to triumph is for good people to do nothing. What better reason is there for speaking out than that? Perhaps none. But the decision is tough when the choice is between letting evil triumph and having the necessities of life. Although Summerton's African Americans should have been willing to state what they knew to be the truth, Rev. De Laine and his committee understood that people could get cold feet and back out at anytime.

The steering group had a big job ahead if the hearing was to be successful. Therefore a preliminary meeting was held to persuade the witnesses that the sky would not fall if they spoke in the presence of a white person. The steering group would have to wheedle and cajole, coddle and coax, and do everything they could possibly think of to bolster the resolve of the witnesses.

Friday, September 30, 1949

About three hundred people came to the meeting. Some of the young people who had filed the complaint and a few of their former teachers were there. Rev. De Laine, Rev. Richburg, Rev. Seals, and others practiced with them for the next day's performance, their procedure being based on advice given by Mr. Boulware.

But more than rehearsing testimony was necessary for some. The people were thoroughly brainwashed and convinced they had no self-worth when in the presence of a white person. In the 1857 *Dred Scott* decision, the Supreme Court had ruled that any person descended from black Africans, whether slave or free, could never be a citizen of the United States. Despite the emancipation of slaves, more than eighty years earlier and despite subsequent Constitutional amendments intended to guarantee the rights of black men and women, daily experience reinforced the lesson that black people were not citizens of the United States of America. They had been taught—in every possible way—that the doctrine set forth by the *Dred Scott* decision was still true in Clarendon County.

That mindset had to be overcome in a single evening. Witnesses had to be encouraged to have faith in themselves, to know that what they were doing was right, and to believe that the U.S. Constitution protected them. To this end, copies of the Declaration of Independence and U.S. Constitution were handed out. Rev. De Laine read portions of the Declaration of Independence aloud, emphasizing and explaining certain words. "*All* men are created *equal*, . . . endowed by their Creator with *certain unalienable rights*, . . . Life, Liberty, and the pursuit of Happiness."

Likewise he read the Constitution's first amendment, repeating it over and over until most of the assembled group could recite the words verbatim. "Congress shall make *no law* . . . *abridging* the *freedom* of speech, or of the press;

or the right of people to *peaceably assemble,* and to petition the Government for a *redress* of grievances."

At last my father thought the people were ready. However, he didn't think that he was.

Unsure of himself and not wanting to lose this chance to go forward, he shared his concern. "Y'all want me to represent you, and I'll do it if I have to. But I'm not a lawyer and I don't know anything about law. What we need is a real lawyer." Helplessly he looked around the audience, challenging them: "If you mean business, give me fifty dollars and I'll call Attorney Boulware tonight. I think he can be there by ten o'clock in the morning." In less than five minutes, an amount of fifty-six dollars was on the collection table.

SATURDAY, OCTOBER 1, 1949

At nine o'clock the next morning, the Summerton people were at the Clarendon County Court House in Manning, en masse and in high spirits. Perhaps even more came than had attended the previous night's meeting. A frightened few did stay home, but most were there—parents, some teachers, interested supporters, and curiosity seekers. With the help of supporters, the young witnesses had gotten there from colleges in Columbia, Orangeburg, and Sumter.

Several cars came in a caravan, carrying placards that read, "The Principal must go" and "A change must be made." The placards surprised Rev. De Laine. If he had known of the plan, he would have discouraged the sign makers. His objective was to get a fair ruling for the grievances, not to infuriate the officials or to appear arrogant. But what was done was done, and he smiled at the confidence of the sign makers.

Not long after Rev. De Laine got there, Mr. Boulware also drove up. The two of them went into a huddle, rapidly strategizing. The lawyer knew nothing about the case or the witnesses other than what my father had told him. It was agreed that Mr. Boulware would open the case and lay the premises for the appeal. The lead would then be turned over to Rev. De Laine, with the lawyer's guidance only when an error was made. Ironically the man the education officials had caused to be fired from his teaching job would be their interrogator.

With the bearing of one confident of victory, my father entered the courthouse. Mr. Boulware took a detour to go by the segregated men's room. When he emerged, Mr. McCord saw him and groaned, "Do I have to be bothered with you today, Boulware?"

Grinning, the big, likable charmer replied, "I ain't no trouble, Mr. McCord."

Turning to Mr. Benson, the superintendent inquired, "Where's your lawyer?"

"I don't have one."

Visibly annoyed about the presence of the NAACP lawyer, Mr. McCord advised the principal, "You'd better get one quick."

The hearing was delayed while Mr. Benson went in search of a lawyer. Four lawyers lived in Manning, and it is said that Mr. Benson sought the help of each, one after the other. Each refused, one after the other. One, a member of the state senate, reportedly told Mr. Benson, "If you wanted me, you should have retained me three months ago. I refuse to be embarrassed by letting De Laine beat me. And he could do it by himself, even without an attorney."

When the trustees from Summerton's District 22 arrived, they peered into the courtroom. The black people had filled the seats and were standing around the walls on both sides of the normally segregated room. Whether intimidated or infuriated, not a single district trustee entered. Only Mr. Betchman, the district superintendent, and Mr. Mills, the agriculture teacher who was apparently also acting as the assistant superintendent, remained to represent Summerton. The two members of the County Board of Education were also there, along with Mr. McCord. Finally the accused principal returned alone to face his accusers. Mr. McCord opened the proceedings with the statement, "Since the defendant cannot get a lawyer, I will have to preside, as well as to act as his lawyer."

One by one, the witnesses were presented. One adult was too frightened to speak, but the others presented their testimony clearly. The questioning centered on the previously filed grievances, and witnesses kept to the point. Mr. McCord granted Mr. Benson the privilege of presenting a financial accounting at a later time. Since the Committee on Action was not interested in damaging the principal personally, Rev. De Laine and Mr. Boulware trustingly consented that Mr. Benson could account for the funds later. That, they would discover, was a *big* mistake.

Nevertheless that day would be etched in the minds of the attendees. For the first time in their lives, they saw friends, relatives, and acquaintances stand up to make their voices heard in the presence of white men. They saw Rev. De Laine, one of their own, filling the place of a lawyer. They saw Harold Boulware, another member of their race, become master of the Clarendon County courthouse. It was the first time a black lawyer had stood in those halls in more than a generation.

The Summerton people had seen the trustees of District 22 shrink from defending their decision. They had also seen the district superintendent and his assistant fail to come to the rescue of the "lackey" principal. The people were proud. Fear of their "masters" had been conquered—at least temporarily. Had the school officials foreseen the future, they would have immediately listened to the students' grievances and worked then and there to appease them.

Some petitioners returned to Summerton in an exuberant caravan, feeling as if they—like the biblical Elijah on Mount Carmel—had triumphed over false prophets of Baal. Occasionally honking their horns, they waved their defiant placards during the ten miles of the homeward journey, deliberately staying in front of cars driven by white people by slowing down and speeding up. It didn't occur to the elated black people that, even as they felt triumphant, the opposition was retrenching, looking for new ways to defeat or persecute them.

Although no verdict was issued at the end of the hearing, my father left the courtroom feeling very pleased and exhilarated. Things seemed to have gone in his people's favor. The witnesses had done a good job, and his soul rejoiced. Light in spirit, he started down the outside steps of the courthouse.

Mr. Betchman was waiting for him and called out, "De Laine, come over here. I want to talk to you."

Many of the people still stood around in groups, rehashing the proceedings, so my father had no fear. Although the people had been drilled on how to "out-class the opposition," the rank and file might have let passion overpower better judgment if there had been any hint of threat to him. Unintimidated, my distin-guished-looking father—his back straight and his step light as always—approached Summerton's superintendent of schools, whose thin face was lined with worry. Wasting no time on preliminaries, Mr. Betchman asked, "De Laine, what can we do to stop this?"

Evenly, with no rancor or impatience, my father regarded the white man. The time had passed for bargaining. He replied, "Nothing. But the principal must go. And those teachers must be put back to work." That wasn't an answer Mr. Betchman was prepared to hear. Hearing no anger in my father's voice, he refused to accept the mild reply as uncompromisingly serious. He began to describe how effective Mr. Benson was as principal. Coaxingly, as if talking to a child, he parroted comments like, "Principal Benson is a well-qualified man. He's turned that school around. You know, one of the first things he did was to start a lunch program."

Rev. De Laine was not one to mince words when he knew he was right. And he was almost always right. Unceremoniously he contradicted Mr. Betchman, saying the school was a "hellhole," a "rat trap," and a place "so raggedy that I took my son out of it and sent him to Mather Academy."

His annoyance rising as he remembered Jay's difficulties, he continued. "Ever since then, since January," he said, emphasizing the length of time, "my son hasn't been able to get his transcript. The people at Mather keep asking him for it, but the only things we have are his monthly report cards." My father didn't pause as he shifted to a preaching mode. Rhetorically he asked what kind of school was unable to send a student's transcript in nine months, emphasizing the length of time.

Etiquette didn't permit him to make the analogy openly, but both men knew that even babies were conceived and born in nine months. "We've exhausted every effort we know of to get my son straight in that school. And still he can't get his transcript. Probably he won't even be permitted to graduate next year if he can't present the greater part of his high school record."

That was the opening the superintendent needed. He said, "Come to my office Monday and I'll look into the matter."

MONDAY, OCTOBER 3, 1949

When Rev. De Laine arrived at Mr. Betchman's office, he was invited to sit down and, in due time, asked about the transcript problem. My father again related that he and my mother were so dissatisfied with the academic program at Scott's Branch that they had put my fifteen-year-old brother in private school. However, the school still had not received his transcript from Scott's Branch. My father also added that the same problem confronted the members of the Class of 1949, who were now in college.

Mr. Betchman ignored the reference to the entire class and asked specific questions about Jay. He was shown my brother's monthly report cards from Scott's Branch, almost entirely filled with As. When the school superintendent commented that it looked like my brother was smart, Daddy didn't swell with parental pride. He was well aware of the deficiencies of the system that gave Jay those grades, and he wasn't going to let Mr. Betchman's "sweet talk" divert his attention. Almost spitting out his retort, he told the superintendent that Jay was probably no smarter than most other children at Scott's Branch. "His grades are too high. He has had the benefit of travel, and he was reared in a home sur-rounded with schoolteachers and preachers. My opinion is that he should give more time to his studies."

Eyes piercing into his guest's, the superintendent said it was not the teachers' fault if the boy was ahead of his classmates. After asserting that teachers shouldn't penalize students for their knowledge, he continued talking, preparing the ground to present what he undoubtedly thought was the plum that would mol-lify the black leader, the thing that would turn him into a grateful lackey and yes man. After more than twenty years of dealing with students, their parents, and the general public, as well as a lifetime of dealing with black folks, Mr. Betchman knew human nature well—at least he thought he did.

He instructed his secretary to write up a transcript for Jay, based on the infor-mation my father presented. With the transcript signed and in his possession, Rev. De Laine uttered the proper words of thanks and reached for his hat, ready to depart without saying anything more about the remaining problems. How-ever, the superintendent wasn't finished. He asked, almost as if he were simply musing, "You said the principal must go?"

The precious transcript tucked safely in his coat pocket, Rev. De Laine answered, "Yes. Nothing will be settled until he's gone."

Mr. Betchman pulled a folded piece of paper from his desk drawer. Thrusting it toward my father, the superintendent commanded him to read it. It was a let-ter, signed by Mr. Benson. Silently Rev. De Laine read the words, "I am resign-ing because of the evil influence in the community."

Snorting in disgust, my father returned the letter. He looked the superintendent squarely in the eye and dryly observed, "It seems mighty funny that the influence just got evil enough for him to resign." Mr. Betchman ignored the comment. As far as he was concerned, the exact wording of the letter was unimportant. What mattered was that Mr. Benson was no longer principal. And wasn't that the condition my father had set for ending the "rebellion"?

Glaring at the black man who refused to grovel, Mr. Betchman declared that the black people were doing what my father told them to do. With that he gave a blunt command, "You must stop this fight." Pausing only for effect, he added, "The Scott's Branch principalship is open and school has to start next Monday."

Rev. De Laine opened his mouth to speak, but Mr. Betchman wasn't finished. "I'll have you made principal of the school. But you got to stop the fight."

There it was. The plum. The pièce de résistance.

It was an offer no unemployed man with seventeen years experience in little country schools could be expected to refuse. The position was better than any my father had ever held. The location was perfect. In fact one had to wonder if he had chosen the location of our house with this outcome in mind. As principal of Scott's Branch, his name would be affixed to every letter sent to parents. Every fee levied on students would have his stamp of approval. He would hire the teachers, set the standards, enforce the disciplinary measures, and make sure students earned the grades they were given. Transcripts would be sent out when they were requested, and it would be in my father's power to provide the kind of education he wanted for us, his own children, as well as for other children of the community.

But that wasn't what Rev. De Laine wanted. He had seen the comfortable buses and schools that public funds provided for white children. He had watched the effect that floodwaters had on the education of children at Society Hill. He was privy to the hardships suffered by the Davis Station parents. The principalship of Scott's Branch meant nothing to him.

My normally mild-mannered father, whose tongue could lash out at injustice as quickly and cruelly as a scorpion's sting, regarded the white man without blinking as his steady voice answered, "Mr. Betchman, I was elected to get parents' and class' grievances adjusted. I am ready to resign as chairman of the Committee on Action on Wednesday if you guarantee me that all of the grievances will be adjusted." He paused. His eyes still locked on the white man's, he continued, "When we get that guarantee, my part will have been played." Turning to leave, he added, "If you have the trustees elect me as principal, expecting me to stop the parents, . . . well now, that's a little too big."

From his own experiences, my father knew that the principal in a black school had few freedoms. In fact the bigger the school, the fewer the freedoms. The principal served at the pleasure of the "big fellas." They were the ones who levied fees and taxes on black students. It was they who decided which, if any, textbooks came to black schools. No black person had any say-so about bus transportation for students or fuel for school buses. And if a trustee didn't like one of the black teachers, the principal was powerless to retain the teacher.

The head of Scott's Branch School would have to be both a yes man and a hatchet man. Daddy had never been a yes man or a hatchet man, and he never would be. He had stated his price, and his next words indicated a complete understanding of what acceptance of the superintendent's offer would have meant. "These parents are grown people. If they refuse to follow my lead, you will reverse yourself and have me fired—just as you can have me hired. That price is too much for me to pay."

Mr. Betchman was astonished. He knew of Rev. De Laine's reputation for unassailable ethics, but he had been positive my father would grab the opportunity to become principal of the county's second largest school. Yet the black man hadn't considered the offer for even an instant.

Rev. De Laine's action made it clear he was not an ordinary man. It also revealed that he did not aspire to power or make deals "with the devil." The only covenants my father made were with his God and with himself. His word was his bond. He had given the people his word that he would see the situation through to the very end, and he intended to do just that.

Disconcerted, but not ready to give up, Mr. Betchman pointed a finger in accusation. "You know very well everything would've been settled a long time ago if you hadn't kept up this fight. You're the one responsible."

Not acknowledging his role and not yielding even one iota, Rev. De Laine replied, "If those parents didn't want to do what was done, they wouldn't have filled the courthouse last Saturday."

Mr. Betchman didn't bother rebutting the logic. Instead he tried "sweet talk," saying, "The Negro people need a better leadership and you can give it to them if you want to."

My father countered with, "Then, how would it look if I open school in October and get fired at Christmas because the parents didn't follow my leadership? They would no longer follow my leadership because they would know I had sold them out. Living in front of the school, I'd be seeing those children and their parents all the time. I could never be happy in my home again. No sir, I won't touch that job."

Before walking out, he pulled a batch of postcards from his pocket and showed one to Mr. Betchman. The card bore two messages: the first announced a meeting, and the second reminded the recipients that no one was to cooperate with officials until a written guarantee was received that grievances would be adjusted and fired teachers rehired.

Mr. Betchman read the card and then asked, "What does this mean?"

"Just what it says," Rev. De Laine replied matter-of-factly.

WEDNESDAY, OCTOBER 5, 1949

The committee finally received a report from the County Board of Trustees. It stated that Mr. Benson was found guilty of failing to teach the required number of periods. He was exonerated on all other charges.

Before the weekly Wednesday evening meeting began, Rev. De Laine mailed another letter to the school officials. The letter, signed by the members of the Committee on Action and several other men, reiterated the parents' prior request that no teachers be discharged. They also asked to be consulted before a new principal was hired.

Rev. De Laine arrived at the meeting with a tactical move planned that he had not discussed with anyone. He wasn't taking a chance that the "handkerchief head reporter" who took messages to the white authorities could foil his next move. The meeting opened as usual, with singing and prayer. Then my father recounted what had happened at Mr. Betchman's office. Relating that he had seen the letter of resignation, he told the people they were finally rid of the hated principal.

"Mr. Betchman told me I could be principal if I would stop you. I refused the job. The price was too high. I would've had to stop you from your effort to correct the grievances, and I wasn't going to do that. That would've been selling you out."

As carefully as a master carpenter measures his boards and nails them in place, Rev. De Laine arranged the pieces for his tactical move. By the time he finished speaking to the large crowd, he intended to have built a framework that could be completed in only one way. With so many witnesses present, no one could twist the truth about what he said. No one could claim that things happened in any way other than as they actually did. Let the handkerchief head reporter run to his masters as fast as the wings of the wind. Tonight that was exactly what my father wanted.

"Now that the testimony of the Class of 1949 has been presented," he continued, "I think the job I was elected to do is finished. It's up to the school authorities to make the proper decisions. The white folks are angry with me now. So I think it's time for me to resign."

Cries of shock and displeasure arose. Rev. De Laine could not desert them now, the parents said. The whole thing was not finished, they lamented. He had to stay and see it through, they begged. He was their leader and couldn't quit, they asserted.

A member of the steering group took charge, quieting the people while my father stood by, outwardly calm and uninvolved but secretly elated with the way things were progressing. Someone said they needed to elect a new leader. Rev. De Laine was immediately reelected as president and spokesman. He accepted the position, having even more power than before, without giving any hint that he had arrived with exactly this outcome in mind.

Once "reinstalled," my father pointed out that the demands had not been met. Somehow the parents had to force the powers-that-be to meet their demands. To that end a decision was made to strike and delay the opening of school, which was scheduled for the following Monday.

As expected, the handkerchief head reporter was "on duty," and news of what happened reached the "masters" that same night. Even as the people were leaving St. Mark, less than a mile away a small group of white men were probably hard at work trying to identify my father's Achilles' heel as they waited for the report from the handkerchief head. They would spend the evening planning and trying to outthink the black people.

Thursday, October 6, 1949

The next day Mr. Betchman came to our house. Standing beside the road that went back past the houses of Mose Oliver and Harry Briggs, he informed my mother, a good teacher with no administrative experience, that she had been appointed acting principal of the school. She wasn't given a choice. It would be her responsibility to assign teachers to classrooms and open the school year four days from then. The superintendent and his cronies must have thought, "Aha! This is how we can bring the preacher to his knees. He can't fight his own wife. She is his weak spot, his Achilles' heel."

Rev. De Laine knew the strategy—that of divide and conquer. He could easily discourse on the tactic that has defeated many worthy purposes, movements, and even nations. He often told his congregations divide and conquer was a monster that could cause brothers to fight each other and happy homes to be destroyed. He would inform them how, centuries before, petty gifts and nice talk had led to the downfall of African cultures, saying that—like the biblical Esau—Africans had sold their birthright by accepting worthless trinkets while they were being subjugated, exploited, and enslaved. They had destroyed each other to satisfy their own greed—and, in the process, were subjugated by others.

Yes, he could wax eloquent on the subject. Hitler used the technique in his rise to power. In fooling the Germans into believing they were the master race, he pitted neighbor against neighbor and child against parent to put Jews, Gypsies, and others into concentration camps. The result was the perpetration of a horrendous crime against humanity. Not only would Rev. De Laine warn his flock against the technique of divide and conquer, he was ever alert to ways in which it was used. Mr. Betchman's action could not hoodwink him.

Saturday, October 8, 1949

Hearing of Mother's assignment, some people behaved like small children given pieces of candy. They forgot their grievances and became happy, saying, "Now that Mis' De Laine is principal, everything'll be all right." A number of parents took time from their weekly shopping to stop at our house and give their approval.

My mother was my father's jewel beyond price. Of all the things in his world, she was the one thing most precious to him, even more so than his children. Her elevation to the position of acting principal brought him no pleasure. He remembered the story of Samson, in which the lords of the Philistines had used Delilah to entice the strong man so that they could prevail against him. Had the local "lords of the Philistines" thought they could use my mother in a similar manner?

Daddy's forefathers had done a good job of passing down knowledge of the ways of both saints and sinners, of how traps were set for the gullible, and of how to avoid becoming indebted to any man. He had learned street smarts in the alleyways, rickety houses, and noisy mills of Atlanta, Detroit, and Baltimore. He had learned the ways of manipulators from church politicians. And he knew that a gift horse had led to the fall of ancient Troy.

So his reply to those who came to his home to express their happiness never varied, "You put the responsibility in my hand to let you know when everything is all right and that is what I mean to do. Everything is not all right. This is just a stick of candy and I'm not a child to stop for a stick of candy." Wearily he would continue, "Next year she'll be fired. If we quit just because she is appointed as acting principal, we will never again get everything going as good as it is now. We'll just be behind further than ever."

Somewhat abashed, the visitors would concede, "Mis' De Laine is your wife and you should know." Then they always asked if the strike would still go on. And always he answered that he thought it was the best thing to do. But they should wait. "Be ready, but don't do anything until you get word on Monday morning."

Between Wednesday night and Saturday, placards and signs were made for students and their parents to carry. Some teachers pitched in to help the students prepare the signs. By Saturday night our house was an arsenal of signs. When the inner steering group—Rev. Seals, Rev. Richburg, Mr. Georgia, Mr. Bubba, and my father—parted on Saturday evening, they cautiously agreed the strike would still take place.

Sunday, October 9, 1949

Arriving home from his churches on Sunday, Rev. De Laine felt the urge to meet with some of the steering group. It was not a time to proceed without the best plans possible. So, despite an already long day of having preached at both of his churches, he drove to Mr. Bubba's house. Finding the farmer away from home, he went on to Mr. Georgia's place. He, too, was out.

Reluctant to go home without talking to at least one of his advisers, Rev. De Laine drove farther, arriving at Gabriel Tindal's place. There he found an assembly of about seven men—including Mr. Bubba, Mr. Georgia, and Rev. Richburg—discussing recent events and whether there should be a strike. My father joined the discussion. As far as he knew, the meeting was a spontaneous one. Before parting, the men decided to call off the strike. They agreed, however, that no money was to be collected except for book rental fees.

MONDAY — WEDNESDAY, OCTOBER 10–12, 1949

Early the next morning Mr. Betchman again came to our house. That time it was to tell Mother, "Don't ask the children for any money except for book rent."

Rev. De Laine was thunderstruck. How could Mr. Betchman have come to that decision? One of the men at the previous day's meeting had to be a rat. But which one? For many years afterward, my father wondered how that particular meeting had come about and why he didn't know about it in advance. Which man called it? And why? If he had suspicions, he never named a name. And he never identified the other men who were present.

The four schoolteachers who had been fired were invited to participate in the strike. Three of them came on Monday, but only two returned on Tuesday. That proved unfortunate for the two who stayed away. In trying to gain the upper hand and seeking to weaken the growing resistance, Mr. Betchman relented and agreed that the teachers who were there could be put to work. He instructed my mother to give them a place to go and something to do. Since new teachers had already been hired, Scott's Branch now had two more teachers than it had during the previous year. With only ten classrooms, there wasn't enough space to accommodate the rehired teachers. Mr. Betchman had created yet another problem. What was to be done with the extra teachers?

As it happened, an unoccupied building stood about 150 feet from the school. Three or four years earlier, a young man had the prefabricated building put there to be used as a nightclub. But his plans didn't work out. The owner let his dream die and departed from Summerton permanently, leaving my father as executor of the property. Daddy saw no reason the building couldn't be put to a useful purpose, so an agreement was struck for the school to use the building.

Despite the resignation of Mr. Benson and the rehiring of the fired teachers, there was no improvement in the system that shortchanged black children so badly. No school supplies were forthcoming, classroom space had not increased, and the students still had to trek to outhouses—rain or shine. It was almost mid-October, and Daddy still had not received the NAACP papers that, when signed, would become a formal petition for equal educational opportunities and facilities. My father accepted the fact that he would never return to the classroom. He didn't care. He had committed himself, "the Lord being my helper," to get a lawsuit filed for better schools in Clarendon County.

9. *Warnings*

The LORD is on my side; I will not fear:
what can man do unto me?
PSALM 118:6

Armistice Day was the anniversary of the official end of the Great War, the war some people naively thought would end all wars. The armistice was signed on November 11, 1919, and all firing was to cease at 11:00 A.M.—the eleventh hour of the eleventh day of the eleventh month. One year later King George V of England instituted the practice of commemorating the armistice with two minutes of silence at 11:00 A.M. each year on its anniversary.

Predictably the Great War had not ended all wars. The widespread conflict called World War II had been even "greater." Four years had now passed since it ended. To my father the five months since the June 8 meeting seemed to have lasted longer than the Second World War. Each day of those nerve-wracking months had tested his determination. In the face of the school board's belligerence, people urged him to be cautious. But to any who tried to discourage him, Daddy's reply never varied. He would say, "I am committed to do this, the Lord being my helper. I have nothing personally against Benson. He is just a good rallying point. I'm using him and the problems at Scott's Branch to arouse the parents to a sense of opportunity."

Fortified by a strong faith in God, my father had pressed on with unflagging vigor, and the people continued to follow his leadership. More than twenty Summerton people had finally pledged to sign a school equalization petition, but in spite of the group's readiness, the NAACP had not sent the necessary legal forms.

A month had passed since Scott's Branch opened for the 1949–50 school year. For a while the flush of victory felt after the students' hearing had imbued the people with a sense of pride and power, and they were eager to confront the establishment. But Indian summer came and went, then October faded into November. The harvesting of crops was finished, and debts were settled. Yet nothing had happened, and the people were becoming restless. They wanted action.

The same was true for Rev. De Laine. But nothing more could be done until the petition papers arrived. He and his supporters did what they could to keep the people from losing their courage. They helped the parents get more organized, and some people were given the responsibility of visiting the school to make sure everything kept going smoothly. The hiring of a well-qualified principal gave some reason for hope. However, the new man quickly realized he had come into a mare's nest of problems and departed almost as soon as he arrived.

My father didn't venture onto the school premises; the opposition would have eagerly used his presence to construct an airtight complaint against him. But others of the group visited the school often. For the first time in the history of Scott's Branch School, parents actively kept watch on its operations.

One supporter, Gilbert Henry, heard that the picture of a famous African American had been replaced by the picture of a white man in one classroom. Mr. Henry spoke to the young teacher about the change. Although the teacher was not responsible for the switch, Mr. Henry, the grandson of a black woman and a white Summerton physician, bluntly made his disapproval known. He dryly commented, "This is the Negro school. The white school is the place for people who are white."

Friday, November 11, 1949

On Armistice Day all teachers—black or white—dutifully said a few words about the horrors of war and how America stood for liberty and justice for all. Then their students observed King George V's two minutes of silence. If anybody in Summerton was lobbying for the name of the day to be changed to the more inclusive Veterans Day, it would have been white veterans. Black veterans had more pressing concerns. Because it was a federal holiday, Summerton's postmaster, Jack James, was not required to hold regular window hours. However, everyone in Summerton knew the postmaster was on duty almost every day. Even on Sundays and holidays, the faithful public servant was likely to open the post-office window around ten o'clock, making it possible for postal patrons to pick up special delivery and registered mail any day.

In an out-of-the-way place such as Summerton, the postmaster and the telephone operator were important fonts of information. Between them, they knew almost every bit of news that passed into or out of town. So, whenever Mr. James opened his window, someone was usually there, waiting to hear the latest information—and, occasionally, to pick up mail.

My father arrived to check his postal box around 10:15 A.M. on November 11. Pushing the post-office door open, he saw a group of white men inside. Only white men used the post office as a gathering place. Black men knew better than to congregate in a public building for, if they did, "good race relations" would be preserved by removing the men, and perhaps by arresting them. A single glance was sufficient to trigger his sense of danger. In his brain a silent warning flashed, "Caution." Standing there were Mr. Mills—the agriculture teacher—and some other men. Although disconcerted, my father must have said, "Morning."

The men all knew my father, but not one opened his mouth. Before June 8, 1949, they would have cheerfully, although condescendingly, spoken to him. However, on Armistice Day 1949, a day dedicated to world peace, the small lobby of Summerton's United States Post Office was filled with an almost palpable hatred. Icy loathing by the white men made a silence so deep that, with each of Daddy's footsteps, the creak of floorboards seemed to boom like thunderclaps. Too self-controlled to leave, my father stoically made his way to our mailbox.

The men couldn't see him where he stopped, but that didn't matter. He felt as if each of them was mere inches from his body. His fingers twirled the brass combination dial, and the metal mailbox door swung open. Inside was a single item—a notice for registered mail. He pondered whether, under the circumstances, he should try to collect it that day. A few heartbeats later he resolutely lifted his eyes, pulled his shoulders back to his usual erect stance, and walked around the corner, his bearing reflecting none of the quivering that beset his innards. To get to the postmaster's window, he had to pass all of those hostile faces. Thirty feet at most, but thirty feet that seemed more like thirty miles.

Except for their stares from iceberg-cold eyes that stuck with Rev. De Laine as he moved, the men were as still as stone. My father eased by them. An eternity later he reached the window for special deliveries and registered mail. Only one man—the one who was the least familiar to my father—looked the slightest bit friendly. A farmer and cotton buyer from out by Davis Crossroads, Doc Mallett was also closest to the postal window. He nodded, almost imperceptibly, to acknowledge my dad's presence. The rest of the men just stood menacingly by, watching with malevolent eyes and tightly set lips. These men had once pretended—maybe even genuinely felt—a degree of amity toward Rev. De Laine. But in the post-office lobby on that day of peace, there was only unveiled enmity because the black man had done the unthinkable. He had had the temerity to encourage others to challenge white authority.

Uncomfortable and ill at ease, my father felt compelled to do something. Turning to Mr. Mallett and showing the registered letter notice, Rev. De Laine asked, "Do you think I can get this?"

After taking a good look at the piece of paper, Mr. Mallett smiled faintly and answered, "I hope so. I'm waiting on the window to open for the same thing."

Rev. De Laine didn't think—wouldn't let himself think—that Mr. Mallett and the others were literally waiting for the same thing that he was. That they had been told of the arrival of his registered letter. That they knew what he would be picking up and who had sent it. And that they were there to let him know that they knew, and that they didn't like it one bit.

The men waited. Bitter. Angry. Edgy. In the cold, rancorous silence of the post-office foyer, the minutes passed slowly. More than once my father considered leaving. Just as he was losing his resolve, the postmaster pushed up the frosted windowpane and cheerily greeted the men. Mr. Mallett was first in line. Stepping back, seemingly oblivious to the exaggeration of his limp, he politely told Rev. De Laine, "You go ahead."

Relief swept over Daddy. He desperately wanted to get out of the post office, to flee the chilling animosity that crept up his legs all the way to his lungs, working to choke out his breath. Gratefully he stepped to the window. Postmaster James took my father's notice, retrieved a big, bulky envelope, and laid it—face up—inside the window. The bold letters in the return address loomed large, appearing to leap from the paper in defiance of every vestige of racial oppression.

At last the long-awaited papers from the NAACP had come! But the circumstances prevented my father from showing his elation. With the envelope in his possession, he hid the face of the letter as much as he could, trying to keep from aggravating an already tense situation. It was plain now. The men were indeed there because they knew Rev. De Laine had a registered letter and because they knew who had sent it.

During the past seven months of agitation, my father and his close supporters had talked boldly and openly. They could show no reticence or cowardice if they expected others to sign the petition. Because of that openness, every move they had taken to attain justice had been quickly known and reported to the "opposition." But this time common sense told Daddy it was not a handkerchief head who told the opposition of the registered letter. Only one man was in a position to know that a letter from the NAACP was awaiting pickup in Summerton's post office. And that man had just handed the envelope to him.

Outside in the crisp, cool air, the United States flag flapped lazily. A pickup truck turned left from Duke Street onto Main. Near the corner a sparrow pecked at something in the grass. In a few minutes, at precisely 11 A.M., traffic would stop, and two minutes of silence would be observed—a tribute to the dead and to the cause of world peace. Then, at various places along the East Coast, bugles would sound the haunting notes of "Taps."

Looking heavenward and feeling God's presence, my father let a deep sigh of relief escape his lips. Some of the words of "Taps" were correct—God *was* nigh. Daddy knew it. But he also knew that other parts were not correct: all was not well, and he could not safely rest.

As curious as he was about the letter's contents, he wasn't going to let the men see him open it. Knowing from its bulk that the envelope contained the petition papers, he put it on the seat and turned the car toward our house. But he didn't go home. Now that he had the papers, he wanted to encourage everyone to attend the evening's meeting. Not until he finally went home did he study the contents of the envelope. He counted the legal-sized sheets of paper that were to be signed by each parent and "for each one of their children of school age." Then he read the petition.

It was addressed, by individual names, to six individuals—to the trustees of the district and county boards of education, and to the county and district superintendents of education. Fourteen points were listed, with points five through twelve providing utterly damning evidence of the educational inequalities between District 22's racially separate school systems. The accusations ranged from insufficient teachers and inadequate teaching facilities through the lack of running water and poor lighting to the absence of janitorial services and bus transportation. If what was written in the document was true (and it was), one had to conclude black students in District 22 were being discriminated against in every possible respect.

Rev. De Laine looked once more at the volume of papers. The corner of his mouth pulled up into a little smile. He probably thought, "We might not get that many signatures, but we'll get more than they expect."

Laying the petition papers aside, he carefully read the accompanying letter. Toward the bottom he spotted words that stopped his elation. The letter advised him to avoid calling a public meeting. Astonished, he realized he had made a grave error because, as the letter cautioned, "There could be trouble when people begin to sign the petition."

More than one hundred people were expected to attend that night's meeting, and he had already spread word of the papers' arrival. For seven months he and his group had worked for this day, and the people were more than ready for something to be done. The white authorities were beginning to apply more pressure on his sympathizers, so each day that the signing was put off presented the risk of losing signatures. No further delay could be tolerated.

Since it was not advisable to have the papers signed at the open meeting, he would have to find another place for the people to go. Word of the location would also have to be circulated. Frantically he tried to think of a place—nearby, private, and available—that could be used.

He weighed the options. Our house was far too visible. Harry Briggs, a World War II navy veteran, lived a short distance up the lane behind us. The thought came to him to ask Mr. Harry if his living room could be used as a temporary office. My father walked the four hundred or so yards to the Briggs house. Mr. Harry wasn't at home, so Daddy laid the problem out to Mr. Harry's wife, Mis' Eliza. She was amenable and said, "When Harry comes, I'll ask him." She promised to help find another place if her husband was not agreeable.

Rev. De Laine was busy for the rest of the day. As the children went home, he stood near the school telling them to remind their parents of the evening's meeting. Although he still hadn't heard from Mr. Harry when the meeting opened, he told Rev. Seals and Rev. Richburg of the plan to use the young couple's home. The two other pastors took charge and began to redirect prospective signers to the "temporary office." Likewise they guided the state NAACP executive secretary, Eugene Montgomery, to the Briggs place when he arrived.

When Harry Briggs finally got home, he found his dining room set up to serve as an office. In response to the question of whether his house could be used, he wordlessly took one of the papers and wrote two words on the sheet. Harry Briggs. His signature.

His wife also signed. So did their school-aged children and a visiting brother-in-law. Before the evening meeting had even begun, at least fourteen signatures were in place, each person having the tedious task of signing twelve different sheets of paper. By the end of the evening—after months of agitation—adults from more than twenty-four School District 22 families, along with their minor children, had signed the NAACP-drafted petition. Heeding earlier advice from Mr. Boulware, neither Daddy nor anyone else from our family signed. Just above the list of signatures, dated November 11, 1949, and immediately below the fourteen points, the petition concluded with the following request:

> WHEREFORE, Your petitioners request that: (1) the Board of Trustees of School District Number twenty-two, the County Board of Education of Clarendon County and the Superintendent of School District #22 immediately cease discriminating against Negro children of public school age in said district and county and immediately make available to your petitioners and all other Negro children of public school age similarly situated educational advantages and facilities equal in all respects to that which is being provided for whites; (2) That they be permitted to appear before the Board of Trustees of District #22 and before the County Board of Education of Clarendon, by their attorneys, to present their complaint; (3) Immediate action on this request.

One hundred eighteen years earlier, on November 11, 1831, former slave Nat Turner was hanged in Jerusalem, Virginia, for planning an uprising. Only time would tell whether the actions of Rev. De Laine and the rest of his supporters would be regarded as a gesture for peace and justice, or whether one of them was destined to become another black man who was killed because he wanted racial justice.

Three days after the signatures were collected, Mr. Montgomery wrote to Rev. De Laine: "As you probably know by now the petition was mailed Saturday and I am certain that the members of the county and district boards received them today. We are going to wait 30 days for a reply then file for the case to be heard in Federal Court." Altogether 107 adults and children had signed the petition. One person who signed was a college graduate. One or two others could barely write. On the other hand, some eligible supporters had not signed because they were too useful in another role, too vulnerable, or not available that evening.

Members of the core group were ecstatic, confident that nothing could stop them. They hoped the petition would result in things being changed for their children in the not-too-distant future. A rumor my father called "a malicious lie" immediately began to circulate—that the black parents in Summerton wanted to send their children to white schools. It antagonized Summerton's white people, who began to actively persecute any suspected dissenters, even individuals who had given their white employers years of faithful and uncomplaining service.

The men that Rev. De Laine referred to as "boasting" and "blusterous" seem to have interpreted the petition as a sign of treacherous rebellion. They blamed him for making the black people arrogant enough to think they were as good as white people. If what was said in the state's legislative offices was any indication, the white men in Summerton asked themselves, "How dare they think we ought to give them better educational facilities? Do they really believe jobs like picking cotton and tying tobacco pay enough taxes for them to deserve more?" The white men refused to acknowledge how dependent their own incomes and lifestyles were on the sweat, muscles, and diligence of black people. Or that the condition of the black people was a direct result of discriminatory actions by themselves and their forefathers. Or that they were perpetuating an evil system in order to maintain a permanently illiterate labor force.

As owners of large farms, businesses, and motels, Summerton's "boasting" and "blusterous" men—such as school trustee J. D. Carson, businessman David McClary, and lawyer S. E. Rogers—thought about finances a great deal. They understood, in terms of dollars and cents, what they would personally lose if black people became educated enough to keep records of their own earnings and debts. And those men were adamant and outspoken about preserving the racial status quo.

Products of their time, these men vehemently opposed any acceptance of black people as equals. Taught since birth that black people belonged to an inferior race, it was impossible for them to think of their children going to school with the snotty-nosed children of the women who kneaded their biscuits and washed their dishes. It was all right for their offspring to play with black children in backyards and fields but, surely, sitting in the same classroom with a black child would irreparably harm a young Caucasian.

Those white men also "knew" that black men could not control their libidos. They seemed to think that the black men who shined their shoes, repaired their houses, and tended their fields had to be carefully watched lest, at every opportunity, the black men would take advantage of white womanhood, defiling that which was "pure and untainted." Those men, the "boasting," "blusterous" ones, never accepted the words "all men are created equal" or applied them only to people of their own race. In fact some—even some of those who had black siblings or had themselves used black women to satisfy their carnal desires—refused to believe people of African ancestry were human.

Who knows what the silent majority of Summerton's white population thought? Certainly a few sympathized to some degree with the equality movement, but they dared not speak out. The social price was far too high. Only animosity, ridicule, and perhaps persecution would have been gained by voicing their opinions. Furthermore even the sympathizers understood the financial reality that helped make the "boasting," "blusterous" ones so upset by the petition.

Most of the men who ran things in Summerton were basically good men—conscientious family men who went to church on Sundays, provided for their wives, and loved their children. On their farms and at their mills, they took care of "their Nigras," providing basic shelter for their sharecroppers and advancing loans to their renters. They extended credit to their workers, and they took the sick to see Dr. Stukes—at his back door.

The way the system worked, most black people in Clarendon could never acquire the skills that encouraged financial independence. Many were totally illiterate. Others had attended school long enough to learn a little reading and a little arithmetic, but not enough to know how to keep records of their debts. Consequently people lived on borrowed money during much of the year, even though they worked steadily. If their crops were poor, their white bosses let them "carry" their debts over to the next year. Unfortunately, when their crops were good, they might also be "carried over" because they didn't know how much they owed and "the boss man" told them they were "almost, but not quite, paid out." Only a few could confidently say, "I owe this much and no more."

This situation contributed to the strange things that started happening within days after the petition was mailed. Old grocery debts began to spring up. Hardware bills that people didn't even know about were presented. Balances owed on wagons and plows were called due. It was late November, a peculiar time for such requests to be made. "Paying up time" was always right after the crops were sold—in September and October. By November, Summerton's black people were traditionally free from the worry of paying debts until the following year.

But now it was December, and, without warning, people were being told to pay up, even though they had no money coming in. Notifications were given for unpaid doctor bills and back taxes. Outstanding fertilizer bills multiplied overnight. As persecution and reprisals became more acute, Daddy encouraged the parents' group to unite with the NAACP branch. The people responded, and the NAACP's membership mushroomed from fewer than fifty members to more than five hundred.

However, even with the strength that came from the union with the NAACP, Summerton parents were in no position to protect themselves. The white segregationists breathed constant threats, and morale began to fall. The petitioners trembled fearfully. Murmurs against Rev. De Laine were heard, with people complaining about the difficulties he had led them into. Seeds of discontent had been sown, and the seedlings of dissension quickly sprouted.

On the second Sunday of December, one month after the petition was signed, Rev. Richburg stepped up to his pulpit at Liberty Hill. He exuded the confidence of a man who had never known a moment of fear. More than half of the petitioners

were his parishioners, and many of them sat in the audience that morning, looking to him for the religious message of the day. His congregation also included
those black people who were closest to the "boasting" and "blusterous" men.
They too sat in the audience, waiting for news to carry to their white masters.
However, neither they nor the tales they would carry frightened Rev. Richburg,
and he did not intend to disappoint any of his congregation. That morning he
was a man with fire in his belly and vengeance in his mouth.

Refined and smooth, his words cut through the solemn Sunday morning like
a double-edged steel sword, honed razor sharp and wielded with surgical preci-
sion. Mincing no words, his declarations raked across his congregation as he cut
at the underpinnings of their doubts and wavering. His biting accusations pierced
the hearts of any who had a conscience, rebuking the turncoats and chastising the
faint of heart. "I was there when you elected Rev. De Laine," he reminded them.
"With my own ears, I heard him tell you the time would come when you would
lay the blame on him. He told you that, when the going got rough, you would say
he was responsible. He was right. This was what he prophesied. Today is what
Rev. De Laine foresaw when you elected him on June 8."

Dramatically Rev. Richburg pointed at the audience, booming out accusatory
words, reproaching them with words that burned like molten lava. "*You* elected
him against his will. *You* also elected me as the secretary against my will. When I
finally accepted, I took this cause as my own. And now, I tell you, I will not desert
it. And I will not desert Rev. De Laine."

In the almost unnatural quiet of the church, he took a breath and then made
a declaration of his own dedication and constancy, "Even if my own brother goes
against Rev. De Laine and this cause, I tell you, 'He did not suck the paps which
I sucked.'"

The declaration that he would disown one nourished by the same breasts as
he had been was truly serious. But the well-spoken, erudite man wasn't finished.
He was on a crusade, fanning the barely glowing embers of courage until flames
leapt up and once more burned. "It's too bad Negroes don't realize their own
strength. We could move *mountains* if we did. You quiver and shake because
you feel an economic pinch. But why? *They* need you just as much as you need
them."

His voice rolled on, the sword swinging and undulled, preaching power to his
people. "If you'd stay out of the stores in Summerton, in ninety days you could
put some of these white folks out of business and bring the others to their senses.
No man is wholly independent. Not even the boasters who vow that they will dry
us up."

He gave an edifying analogy, followed by practical advice on how to survive
until they were victorious. "If a mule knew his strength, he wouldn't let children
beat him and use him as he does. You have strength! Call a boycott and tighten
your belts. Eat your peas and corn bread. Get your gas from somewhere else and

stop riding so much. Go to 'Monkey' Smith's store. He can furnish you enough for your necessities."

The petitioners left church inspired to believe they could hold on, positive they would win equal educational facilities for their children. The "Uncle Toms" closest to the "boasting," "blusterous" men went straightaway to make their report, saying, "Richburg got up preaching the NAACP this morning."

Late that afternoon when my father got home from his own church, he heard the good tidings of how Rev. Richburg had sounded the battle cry at Liberty Hill. Someone else told him that Rev. Seals, who had just replaced Rev. Frazier as pastor at St. Mark, had also done his part to inspire the members there. Less than a mile east of the town limits, Davis McFadden and one of the Witherspoon men had taken the ball at Taw Caw Church, inspiring and encouraging the hundreds of Baptists who sat in that congregation.

His spirits were lifted and refreshed. As resolute and strong as he appeared to others, he was neither impervious to worry nor immune to discouragement. Concerns about the well-being of his flock pressed in on him daily—and what had happened to James McKnight was still fresh in his mind.

Mr. McKnight was one of the many people who signed the papers authorizing the NAACP to prepare a lawsuit. He and his brother—outspoken men who worked hard trying to make their lives better—lived ten miles west of Summerton and were both members of one of Daddy's churches. One day in late October, he was driving on U.S. Route 301, on his way home from Manning. With him were his uncle, another adult, and several children. Unfortunately Mr. McKnight had a weak bladder, and nowhere along the ten-mile stretch of road was there a place for a person, black or white, to "answer nature's call." He pulled the car over to the road's shoulder and did what men have done throughout the ages. He went behind a tree.

Another car immediately drew up, and two white men jumped out. One of them was Skipper, an angry man who operated an icehouse said to be a dangerous place for people of color. Skipper was—from all reports and from what he did to James McKnight—a savage and a poor excuse for a human being. Bearing some kind of object, Skipper confronted Mr. McKnight, accused him of indecency, and proceeded to beat him mercilessly. The car's occupants were told they would also be beaten if they got out. Hearing screams, a man who lived nearby ran to the site and begged Skipper to stop. But it was too late. The unfortunate black man was already dead. And Skipper was still beating the limp, lifeless body.

The brutal murder occurred in full view of family members, yet Skipper was never even charged with a crime. The coroner's jury, an all-white group of "upstanding men, unbiased and fair," reviewed the evidence and found that Mr. McKnight's death had not resulted from any willful or wanton disregard for life by Skipper. The brutal homicide was exonerated, with the killing justified because the white killer said it was.

Rev. De Laine worried how his followers would manage as the going got rougher and more people suffered horrible retribution. He didn't see a way to proceed. Who knew what bad things would happen in the future?

No money was owed on our house, our farm, our car, our horses, or our wagons. Our larder was filled with produce from our own lands and gifts from parishioners. We rarely patronized local stores. Although it would be difficult to destroy my father's independence, the panic-stricken white men—determined to cut his every source of income—might somehow find a way. With the news of the inspirational messages the other preachers and laymen had given, Rev. De Laine became more confident the storm could be weathered. Grateful that Rev. Richburg was on his side, he gave a prayer of thanks.

In his capacity as grand master of his local Prince Hall Masons' lodge, my father was obliged to attend the annual statewide meeting that would be held the next day in Columbia. He and a fellow lodge member left early in the morning for the event and returned to Summerton in time for a Monday evening parents' meeting. Rev. Seals was waiting at our house, spitting mad. As the travelers ate supper, he reported that Mr. Betchman had summoned him to his office and, without preamble, said, "I understand that's your church where De Laine is holding those meetings. That true?"

"Yes, sir," replied Rev. Seals, the newly assigned pastor of St. Mark.

Mr. Betchman audaciously proceeded to tell Rev. Seals that he had to stop allowing meetings to be held at St. Mark. Rev. Seals was outraged. Even in segregated, Jim Crow South Carolina, one of the pillars of American democracy was the separation of church and state. The United States was founded on that principle. Yet the white man called Betchman, a man whose salary was paid by the state, had the presumption to tell the black man called Seals, the pastor of an AME church, how his church could be used. Rev. Seals was more irate than a wet hen. Neither as articulate in speech as Rev. Richburg nor as commanding in bearing as Daddy, the short man could nonetheless more than hold his own in any encounter. "I told him that white folks had no jurisdiction over St. Mark, that it was an AME Church, and that the AME Church was the colored people's church. I told him that Richard Allen organized the AME Church because the white people wouldn't let the Negroes have their freedom in the white church."

Summerton's white people might not want black people to have any freedom, but their wishes were not supposed to have influence on what happened inside the African Methodist Episcopal Church, and Rev. Seals had told Mr. Betchman so in no uncertain terms. Nevertheless Mr. Betchman didn't hear. He held a trump card that he was ready to play. He thought that when he did, Rev. Seals would give in, his farm being too small to provide him with the kind of livelihood to which he was accustomed. Mr. Betchman gave his ultimatum. "You either stop

De Laine from having meetings in St. Mark or I'll take your class register and you won't have a teaching job."

The gutsy Rev. Seals boldly pushed his class register with its list of pupils' names and grades toward Mr. Betchman. Unyielding, he declared, "As far as I am concerned, you can have my register right now."

Mr. Betchman made no move to take the register, and Rev. Seals left in a huff.

Still seething with anger, Rev. Seals assured Rev. De Laine, "As long as I am pastor of St. Mark, meetings can be called there whether I am present or not." His feathers still ruffled, he left and drove to his church. Meanwhile my father and his fellow lodge member walked the two blocks in the cold, invigorating evening air. Near the church Lee Richardson, a petitioner, called Daddy aside.

Hat in hand and clearly worried, Mr. Richardson told him, "Reverend, the man I rent from was out to the farm today and he real mad with you. He say if you don't stop these meetings, they gonna get rid of you. He say you talking too much and they don't like it. He tell me to tell you if you keep your mouth shut, they'll stop everything, all the pressure they putting on us. He told me they got another petition in Lawyer Rogers's office. He say if we sign it, it'll take our names off your petition. I ain't tell him, but I'll die before I sign it." Shaking his head, Mr. Richardson looked first at his feet, then straight into his leader's eye. "Reverend, I don't know, but I advise you not to hold the meeting tonight."

J. A. De Laine wasn't a man who caved in to threats. Believing God and truth were on his side, he usually saw no need to change his course of action. He carefully examined all evidence before coming to a conclusion, then, once he made up his mind, no one could bully him into changing it. Reason and right could persuade him, but threats—like bits of dandelion fuzz—were totally unworthy of his attention. His spirits still buoyed by Rev. Richburg's words on Sunday and by Rev. Seals actions in Mr. Betchman's office, my father soberly commented, "Thank you, Lee." After a moment's consideration, he continued, "So he said if I don't stop these meetings, they're going to get rid of me? Well, I reckon, they better go on and do it, because it's time for me to open the meeting and that's just what I'm going to do."

He resumed his progress, only to be waylaid again. This time Ezekiel Walters sidled up. Taking Daddy's smooth, uncallused hand into his own work-roughened one, he said, "Rev., you know I'm with you." Two dollars were slipped into Daddy's hand. In a confidential tone, Mr. Walters murmured, "You know how I work on the highway. Well, today I heard them talking. They say if you don't shut your mouth, they going to shut it for you."

The laborer laid his hand on Daddy's arm, imploring, "Rev., don't go in there because they mean to get you."

Having faith that his Heavenly Father would provide protection, my intrepid, but down-to-earth, father graciously replied, "Thank you, Ezekiel.

They'll just have to get me because nothing but God can keep me out of St. Mark tonight."

Once more he started toward the church steps, but again he was stopped. This time, it was by a man named Wilder. The man asked gently, "Would you step over here, Rev. De Laine?"

My father knew almost nothing about Mr. Wilder, who seemed to be a hanger-on who always came to meetings but said nothing. Ignorant of Mr. Wilder's motives, Daddy intuitively didn't trust him. Right or wrong, his gut feeling was that the man calling to him was a handkerchief head, and that the reason he came to the meetings was to get something to carry back to his bosses. Warily my dad demanded, "What for?"

"I got something to tell you."

Annoyed with the warnings and eager to get the meeting started, my father snapped, "Then say it. I got a meeting to run."

Mr. Wilder glanced around, as if someone might be watching him. Softly and haltingly he spoke, "I just want to tell you something that happened today. In the hardware store."

Daddy's ears perked up. The hardware store? What had happened there? Was the man really a stool pigeon? Or was he in agreement with the movement, wanting changes to happen, but afraid of getting hurt? Daddy demanded, "Tell it, man. What happened at the hardware store?"

"The KKK met there today. They knowed about the meeting tonight and they say if you open your mouth tonight, they gonna take you for a ride. I heared them talking. They didn't care who heared them."

Instead of frightening him, the news made Rev. De Laine angry and more determined than ever. He had no fear of cowards who hid anonymously behind white sheets, losers who tried to mask their worthlessness by terrorizing honest people. There had never been any previous talk of a Ku Klux Klan chapter in Clarendon County, and the idea that hatemongers from outside had come to stir up trouble made his anger reach a fever pitch. He battled to abide by his own teaching of "outclassing the opposition" and to make reason suppress his anger.

My father felt an irresistible compulsion to defy the KKK. Like the bravest of warriors that ever headed into battle, he left his informant and fearlessly strode into the church as if clothed in impregnable armor. Each footfall was a declaration that he would never be cowed.

A man I will call Mr. Crawler was inside. A big-bellied, quick-tempered man, he belonged to Liberty Hill Church and was perhaps the most reliable stool pigeon in the entire area. Rev. De Laine was not disturbed by seeing him. On the contrary he invited Mr. Crawler to take a seat in the front pew. A place for those in need of special prayer during religious services, that seat served a different purpose during the parents' meetings. As it was the best location to see and hear well, my dad had reserved it for those who owed their souls to the opposition, the ones he called pimps, handkerchief heads, and belly crawlers. Like everyone else, Mr. Crawler knew that. Refusing the invitation, he left the sanctuary to eavesdrop, unseen, from outside.

David Lawson, one of the state's few black policemen and a member of the Liberty Hill congregation, was also inside. Dressed in his uniform, he sat quietly in the back of the church. Ready to take on any and all comers, my father called, "Hey, Chief. You come to arrest me tonight?"

"No, Rev. I been hearing so much, I just thought I'd come by and see for myself what's going on."

Summerton's black people, including Daddy, were proud that one of their own had been hired as a policeman. Nevertheless they thought Mr. Lawson was primarily a flunky, and Rev. De Laine was certain the man's superiors had sent him to the meeting. So, for the second time that night, he issued the invitation, "Come up and take a front seat."

Policeman Lawson also declined the offer. However, he stayed right where he was.

Rev. De Laine opened the meeting, putting up the most pleasant and congenial front he could. He was determined to show no bitterness or anger that might encourage any rowdy element to do something foolish. The meeting's agenda, mainly a review of Sunday's events, was completed. There followed some discussion about the opposing petition in the office of S. E. Rogers, the lawyer.

Everyone knew about the warnings my father had received, and, despite being a little frightened, they waited throughout the meeting for mention of them. Their expectations were disappointed when Rev. De Laine announced that the business was finished. It was time to go home. The fire in the pot-bellied stove was dying, and the chill December air was creeping in. However, despite his pronouncement, their leader didn't end the meeting. He was finally ready to talk about the warnings and the Ku Klux Klan.

Radiating fearlessness and determination, Rev. De Laine suddenly seemed unbelievably tall, his salt and pepper hair taking on the gleam of a halo. The audience listened solemnly as he told them of the warnings. As he talked, his voice rose to a crescendo, reaching the tempo of an old-time revival meeting. The emotional temperature soared. The little church echoed with cries of support. Here is how my father vividly described what happened:

> In a time like that, when the war on your nerves is furious and your psychological reaction is prompted by a stern determination, it's possible to transcend your natural ability. This is especially true when your words are screened by your subconsciousness which has been conditioned by premeditation. Further, when your case is put in God's hand, without selfish strings attached to it, it's possible to use words and thoughts that never occurred to you before. This was the case with me on December

12, 1949. I tried to be calm and unravel the experiences which would probably happen.

I invited the KKK to come on and take me for a ride because "I'm too fat to run." I offered them fifty feet of my front yard to burn their cross on—at whatever hour they choose. I entreated them, "Please, don't come to the front bedroom of my house because it will disturb my daughter." Instead, I invited them, "Come to the back bedroom. I'll be patiently waiting." I admonished them to inform the doctor and undertaker of the time their visit would take place because both would be needed.

I described the funeral processional ceremony of a "night riding KKK that interfered with the peaceful rest of the righteous." I sounded an alarm of the danger that awaited anybody walking on the street near my house after dark. I made it plain that this applied to both colored and white. Any animal that looks like a man must call his name as he approaches the area of my house 'cause I'm gonna shoot first and then ask, "Who's that?"

I waxed more eloquently than has ever been natural to me. Unconsciously, I reached the point where responses were drawn freely from the audience. The group from Davis Station was leading in a dialogue, responding to me, saying, "Talk, De Laine" and "That's a man." Someone yelled out, "Say what you mean, Rev. You know we gonna stand by you."

We reached a point I think may be compared to rabble-rousing. But don't forget, these were not a low class of people. They were church members, devout people. They were not the kind given to cursing and rioting. Injustice had been their part to bear and they had borne it patiently. Now the breaking point had come. Patience had ceased to be a virtue.

An issue was at stake and that issue was a threat on our lives. There were many economic squeezes. There was a war on the Negro's nerve. We, the Negroes, were being driven to the point of desperation or surrender. But the whites' backs were also against the wall. The words that poured from my mouth were a counter defensive war on nerves.

I said to the audience, "You empowered me to speak for all of you and I now declare there will be neither retreat nor surrender. You must agree to sign the opposition's petition ONLY when the opposition gets ME to call a meeting for all of us to sign it together. The KKK or anybody else can take me ten miles beyond hell, and I still won't change."

The audience was almost disorganized by their rallying cries of response. Probably, I may have lost my temper, when I exclaimed, "Tell the Ku Klux Klan that I-SAY-GO-WHERE-DIVES-IS."

With my hand, I slapped the table in front of me vigorously to empha-size what I was saying. "And, if they don't know where Dives is, tell them to read St. Luke 16:23. There, Jesus said, In HELL he lifted up his eyes."

Tell the Ku Klux Klan, "Go where Dives is and there lift up your Ku Klux Klan eyes."

10. *Showdown on Main*

Two types of people are interested in me. The first type
wants to see me live long, happy, and successfully. The
second would like to see me suffering, unhappy, or dead.
It is the second type I intend to disappoint.
J. A. De Laine

B y the end of the fiery Monday night meeting, Daddy was a hero. The
people's spirits were lifted and their determination strengthened. Lee
Richardson, the sharecropper whose boss had sent a message to my father, declared,
"If Rev. can take a stand like that, I sure can keep my name on that petition."

Rev. Richburg took the floor before dismissal, cautioning the people to use
discretion when talking about the night's events. Calmly he also instructed them,
"Let Rev. De Laine, who you elected to speak for you, do the talking. But don't
sign anything unless Rev. De Laine calls all of us together to act in concert."

Tuesday, December 13, 1949

The opposition—men my father accused of hovering "on the border of being
educational and political gangsters"—quickly learned what transpired, and the
very next night they held their own meeting. Although the number of people
attending that meeting and what transpired are unknown, it's clear Daddy's
strong talk had made them furious. They apparently decided my father had gotten too big for his britches. Assembled in one of the most gracious houses in town,
Summerton's guardians of education in School District 22, perhaps along with
other town fathers, devised a horrendous plan to silence the black man who
dared to defy the KKK so boldly.

The plan may have begun to take shape earlier in the day. My father was told
that some white men had tried to recruit a workman at Mr. Carson's lumber mill
to lure him out of the house. Once he was outside in the dark, the dirty work was
to be done by someone else. The worker refused the offer, declaring, "No, sir. Not
me. I ain't going near Rev's house at night. Anybody who go to that house after
dark want to die and I don't want to die like that. I ain't gonna get killed that
way. If he'll shoot the Ku Klux Klan, you know he'll shoot me."

After the failure to find a double-crossing rat at the mill, a diabolical plan was devised in the gracious room.

Thursday, December 15, 1949

With only ten days remaining until Christmas, it was downright cold. Daddy's routine was to work in his study until about ten, then collect the mail from the post office and go to the farm. He needed to clear stumps from a field where he had recently cut trees for timber. Although the temperature inched up a few degrees as the sun rose higher, it was still cold at ten-thirty. Daddy pulled on his coat and gloves, backed the car out of the garage, and headed for the post office.

On Main Street the traffic moved along as usual. A car or two waited for a green light at the town's single traffic signal. Truckers who had slept upstairs at Godwin's Hotel were, by this time, miles and miles away from Summerton, their bed linens already being laundered by women whose children went to Scott's Branch School. Farther along a few cars were parked, one close to the entrance of S. E. Rogers's law office.

Stores had been open for business since nine, but the cold street was almost deserted. A couple of people walked briskly along, intent on reaching their destinations and getting inside. Across the street from the post office, six white men stood, smoking and talking, coat collars turned up and shoulders hunched against the cold.

A vehicle rolled past the post office and Carrigan's Sinclair station, headed west toward the "colored" side of town. To strangers whose cars passed along the sleepy street, Summerton was only an interruption in their driving speed, a place where something of importance had never happened—and never would.

My father pulled into the angled parking space, barely noticing the men on the street. His mind was busy planning the rest of his day; even the cold had stopped commanding his attention. His pistol lay on the seat beside him. It was always there nowadays, ready to be used if needed. He wasn't breaking any laws. South Carolina allowed anyone—even black people—to carry an unconcealed weapon. Everybody in town, even the police, knew he carried it.

Automatically covering the firearm with work clothes, he left the pistol where it was. Mounting the curb, he turned toward the post-office door. Suddenly, seemingly out of nowhere, a man loomed in front of him. Engrossed in thought, Daddy hadn't seen him until that instant. Inches away hovered Mr. Crawler, the quick-tempered man from Liberty Hill Church. Having inherited the straight hair and reddish coloration of his Caucasian paternal ancestors, Mr. Crawler looked like a white man. He also seemed to have a general hatred for black men, especially the educated ones or those who achieved a degree of success. On more than one occasion, he was heard to declare, "Ain't no Negro any good. All my friends white."

Mr. Crawler had been the first to act in opposition to the Committee on Action when it was organized. At the time he was having trouble with other members of his church. During a church meeting in May, he had initiated an argument during which he pulled a knife on a younger relative, a teacher. The younger man remembered the defensive training he learned in the armed services and drove his fist into his attacker's face. Still bearing a grudge, the big-bellied man brought that animosity to the June 8 meeting. He knew Scott's Branch would need a new principal if Mr. Benson were ousted, and the idea of his young relative being a prospect for the job at Scott's Branch sorely galled him. Mr. Crawler gave a report of the parents' meeting to the school trustees—his white "friends"—and he accused his relative and several others of starting trouble because they wanted the principal's job.

On that chilly December morning, the big bully blurted, "Rev., either me or you gotta go to hell today." That was when the presence of the six men standing across the street in the winter chill registered with my father. They weren't there by coincidence. In spite of his normal wariness, he had allowed his sharp mind to be lulled into complacency by expectations. Mr. Crawler's fighting words made him instantly recall the message that had warned of the encounter. But he hadn't expected anything to happen at ten-thirty in the morning. And certainly not on Main Street, out in the open where all could see.

The previous day he had been at the farm, working on the tree stumps. The fuse for a stick of dynamite was already lit, and he had stepped away from the coming explosion when a car rolled to a stop. The two women in the car waited until the charge went off before getting out. Daddy was surprised to see them—and perplexed as to why they were at our farm, six miles from town.

The ladies were clearly worried. Their mission was urgent, and their message distressed them. They had brought a warning from a white woman.

My father remembered the woman well. She had been a supervisor for the Summerton school district when he was principal of Liberty Hill School. One afternoon, while she was at his school, a group of black farmers and two white agriculture agents assembled for a meeting. In those days almost every type of meeting began with a religious devotional service. Rev. De Laine was asked to conduct the devotion.

Having once been an agriculture teacher, he knew an appropriate scripture reading. Taking a Bible from his desk, he turned to Luke 8 and began reading verses 5–15. Almost without looking, he repeated the words, "A sower went out to sow his seed." The entire group immediately became alert, listening closely as he read the parable of the sower. Then he closed the Bible and gave a lesson on the reading. In the process he referred to Hosea 10:12. "Sow to yourselves in righteousness, reap in mercy; break up your fallow ground: for it is time to seek the Lord, till he come and rain righteousness upon you."

He didn't threaten the group with hellfire and damnation. That wasn't his style. At that moment the group was interested in farming, not in entering the pearly gates. And he didn't hoot and holler. The white men were astounded that a black principal of a four-room country school could, on the spur of the moment, read appropriate scripture, interpret the scriptures in the light of farmwork, and hold the attention of both educated white men and almost illiterate black men.

The education supervisor observed the entire episode. It was probably the first time she had ever really noticed Rev. De Laine, the first time she thought of him as anything other than a source of school attendance numbers. She was a good woman, but the social chasm was so wide that surely it never occurred to her that a black man was anything other than an animate fixture. But from that day forward, she made it clear that she considered Daddy and our family to be "as fine as" any other people in Summerton. And now she had sent a warning that he was in mortal danger.

The previous night's meeting of the white men had been at her house. There they had devised their diabolic scheme. They laid out detailed plans and identified the perfect hatchet man, having thought of a way to get rid of my father without any white man getting his hands dirty. The strategy was for a black man, known to be inimical to Rev. De Laine, to pick a fight with him and, in the heat of battle, either kill or wound him. By prearrangement, witnesses would be on hand to attest that the preacher started the fight and that the attacker had acted in self-defense. No matter what happened, the rebellious leader of the "Nigras" would be ruined. If he survived the encounter, he would be physically maimed. Blamed for the fight, he would be charged with criminal assault. With so many white witnesses agreeing that he was the attacker, no court in South Carolina would let him go free. The thug would be exonerated, but my father's trouble would be unending. He would surely be convicted and jailed, having to pay a defense lawyer and court costs. In addition the "pillars of the community" who thought up the plan would help the thug mount a damage suit. Our family would be financially destroyed. And Rev. De Laine would be silenced. The insubordinate black people in Summerton would be taught a lesson they would never forget.

The plan seemed foolproof. The hatchet man would be Mr. Crawler. His large size and combative nature, combined with his almost single-minded dislike of black men, made Mr. Crawler perfect for the part. Even without asking, the white men knew he would do it.

Perhaps it is true that God works in mysterious ways. As the men perfected their plan, a silent witness heard every word they spoke and saw every movement they made. And she was horrified. The woman of the house, the supervisor who had come to Liberty Hill School, was disgusted. She knew my father could not deserve the fate that had been planned for him. Ashamed of her husband's being part of such a plan, she decided to sow her own seeds of righteousness. So she sent the warning by way of the two black women. "Don't stay out after it gets dark." The visitors also told Daddy that the woman berated her husband, demanding that he "get out of that dirty mess."

It was clear this was no idle gossip from an overwrought woman. It was dangerous for a white woman to send a cautionary warning to a black man—dangerous for the sender, dangerous for the messengers, and dangerous for the recipient. The message—which named names, suggested conditions, and specified expected outcomes—gave real cause for concern.

Departing, the messengers again cautioned Daddy not to stay out at night. "If you do, Mr. Crawler will get you and they'll have him exonerated. They got people who will go to court as eyewitnesses."

The Bible verse Luke 8:8 admonishes, "He that hath ears to hear, let him hear." Daddy intended to heed the warning. He would make sure he was in the house before sundown every day. And he wouldn't let anyone leave his house for any purpose before daybreak. It was the nighttime—with its shadows and hiding places—that provided invisibility and gave a cloak of anonymity to dangerous men. In the dark the "snakes" and "belly crawlers" ventured out to inflict their evil on innocent people. Daytime, however, was safe. Honest men were up and about, their presence acting as a deterrent to those bent on mischief.

But the unimaginable had happened. At ten-thirty in the morning, in the open on Summerton's Main Street, Mr. Crawler stood, threatening Rev. De Laine's life. His mind racing and his heart beating even faster, my father knew he had to bluff. Outwardly his handsome face appeared to be completely confident and unafraid. Inwardly he trembled, asking, "My God, my God! Hast thou forsaken me?"

Frantically trying to think of a way to defend himself, he pushed his right hand deep into the pocket of his overcoat, touching the pocketknife he always carried as a tool. Lacking a better strategy, he grasped the knife, then pointed his index finger, knife, and overlying cloth toward his would-be attacker. The coat draped as if over the barrel of a pistol.

With his right finger and the knife jutting outward, he jabbed his free left forefinger to within an inch of Mr. Crawler's face, challenging, "What you want to go to hell for? Because it's sure not me who's going."

Terror stricken, perhaps thinking he had already been shot, Mr. Crawler swayed and practically keeled over on the spot.

Surely God works in mysterious ways! Before the big man had recovered from his shock, Summerton's only Esso gasoline truck came to a stop, blocking the white men from view. The driver—a man who had signed the equalization petition—called out, "Come here, Rev. De Laine."

Never had Daddy been so glad to see a person. James Brown seemed like an angel descended from heaven in a cylindrical chariot of deliverance borne on

James Brown, a plaintiff in the withdrawn equalization petition, was the man who saved Rev. De Laine on November 11, 1949. Although he was still driving the Esso truck when he interrupted the attack on Rev. De Laine, he already knew his job would end that day. Courtesy of the De Laine Family Collection

rubber wheels. Before Mr. Brown had time to say anything more, my father moved backward and cried out, asking him to wait until he got in his car. "This thug is trying to pick a fight out of me and those skunks across the street are his witnesses. Let me get away from here and I will meet you near your home."

Practically before Mr. Brown could change gears in the truck, Rev. De Laine was driving off. Mr. Brown followed in the Esso truck. After reaching a safe place, they parked and the story of what happened poured out of my father. Mr. Brown listened with alarm. Finally Daddy remembered that Mr. Brown wanted to talk to him. Although he had just saved my father from physical harm, James Brown had his own bad news. He soberly related that Sprott's Esso Fuel Service would no longer employ him.

From the beginning the people had been told that the price for equality would be steep. That prediction was proving to be correct. Levi Pearson had dared to sue, and "they" had gotten back at him by refusing to loan him money. Teachers—including Daddy—had been fired. But for James Brown to lose his job? That was inconceivable. As a youth he had run errands for the first owner of Sprott's and formed a close friendship with Buck, the owner's son. As he grew older, he helped unload fuel tanks from the train that ran through Summerton in the 1930s. When he grew up, Mr. Brown became the truck driver for the company, delivering gasoline, kerosene, and oil to service stations, farms, businesses, and industries throughout the region.

The "educational and political gangsters" of Summerton were starting to play dirty. If they were able to coerce Buck Sprott into letting James Brown go, the outlook was truly dire. My father's head ached, his lungs hurt, his gut boiled, and his will to continue was severely undermined. The encounter with Mr. Crawler, combined with the news from Mr. Brown, had distressed him more than anything else had ever done.

He didn't go to the farm that day. Instead he went home and reviewed the week's events. First there was Rev. Richburg's sermon on Sunday. Then Mr. Betchman threatened Rev. Seals on Monday. He had sent his rebellious message to the KKK on Monday night after getting so many warnings. The white men had met on Tuesday, and the woman sent him a message on Wednesday. Now, on Thursday morning, two horrible things. He would have to protect himself. But how? The pistol wasn't enough. If he shot someone, his opponents would provide at least one "reliable witness" against him and he would be doomed. He considered the options.

There was no one in Summerton to whom he could turn. No black man in town had the means to help, and common sense showed the fallacy of looking to any of the white residents. If Buck Sprott could be induced to relieve James Brown of his job, any white man in town could be intimidated. The incident with Mr. Crawler needed to be reported, but seeking help from the town's police chief or magistrate didn't seem wise. Both held their jobs at the pleasure of the very men responsible for his dilemma. The lawmen in Summerton offered no protection for my father. They might listen to him, but, most likely, neither of them would give any help.

After Mother got home, my parents drove to Manning to report the incident to the county sheriff. Sheriff Shorter wasn't in his office when they arrived, so they went to see the magistrate, who had the promising name of Eden. My father explained that he wanted to place a restraining order on the culprit by taking out a peace warrant. Enforceable throughout the county, a restraining order would keep Mr. Crawler away.

In response to the query about why he hadn't gone to the Summerton magistrate, Rev. De Laine replied, "Mr. Medlin's sick." Although Mr. Medlin was sick, Daddy mused to himself that the man also was either afraid of Summerton's "gangsters" or was one of them himself.

After hearing Rev. De Laine's complaint, Mr. Eden said, "I believe in giving a man a second chance. Sometimes dogs bark but don't do nothing else." A moment later he added, "That's the way some men do, too."

My dad was not to be put off so easily, and when the magistrate became convinced of the legitimacy of the request, he began to write. Finished, he read aloud, "It has come to my attention that you have been threatening Rev. J. A. De Laine. This is a warning to you. If anything at all happens to him, you will be the first to go to jail. It is best for you to attend to your own business."

He put the letter, addressed to Mr. Crawler, in an envelope, stamped it, and passed it to my father, drawling, "Drop this in the mailbox." As my parents were walking out, he added, "Make sure y'all see the sheriff before y'all leave town."

Surprised, Rev. De Laine turned. "I went there before I came here, but he wasn't in."

Looking directly at him, Mr. Eden firmly repeated, "Y'all make sure y'all see him before y'all leave this town." The pause was brief before he added, "It's better to have him on your side than against you."

My parents left, obeying both of the magistrate's commands. They mailed the letter, and then went back to the sheriff's office. That time the sheriff was in. When the secretary announced them, Sheriff Shorter rushed to the door. He grabbed my father's hand and greeted him effusively. "De Laine! I'm so glad to meet you. Why didn't you drop by my office before? How've things been?" The sheriff ran on and on.

My parents were startled by the sheriff's behavior. But the man continued, telling how lies had been spread about him when he was in bed asleep. It took a little while before my father realized the sheriff was referring to the previous year's election. The sheriff had instantly recalled the pivotal role the small black voting bloc played in his reelection.

It had never occurred to Rev. De Laine that he should take advantage of the goodwill he had created, so he had never visited the sheriff before. Fortunately the sheriff had a good memory and recognized that my father wielded considerable power in the black community. His willingness to accept support from black people showed that, unlike many of his peers and associates, he didn't have a small mind. His attitude reflected his political savvy: the sheriff recognized that if you had helped him once, he needed to return the favor—if only because he might need your help again.

Eventually, his gratitude duly expressed, Sheriff Shorter exhibited an openness to assist a supporter. He congenially asked, "Now, what can I do for you?"

The sheriff seemed aware that something was afoot in Summerton, but he held his tongue as my father reviewed the morning's incident. Ready to pay his debt, the man instructed him, "Go back home and let me know if anything else happens to you. As far as old Crawler is concerned, I'll be at his house before the sun goes down. I'm going to let him know that I'll mellow his head if I hear anything else."

11. *A Not-So-Merry Christmas*

> With strong determination, people can
> make a way out of no way.
> J. A. DE LAINE

Rev. De Laine stopped walking Summerton's streets alone. "Hellhounds" and "hyenas" were after him during that awful period of terror—the worst, the hardest year of his life. The colorlessness of winter brought with it an equal drabness in the soul. In the little three-room houses where sharecroppers lived, chilly winds pushed at the flimsy newspapers that covered cracks between the wallboards. On individual hearths, burning logs struggled to keep the frigid air at bay. But as far as the petitioners, their supporters, and the "blusterous" men were concerned, a boiling pot of fury was keeping the temperature high.

Just beyond Summerton's southern town limits, the dirt road called Gipp Street joined U.S. Route 15/301. Barely half a mile long, Gipp Street was part of what was once a large tract owned by Thomas "Gipp" Ragin. A successful farmer and businessman, Mr. Gipp planted orchards and built houses for his family and his workers. By 1949 he had passed on, the farm was diminished, and most of the houses sheltered various relatives.

Although poor, the people on Gipp Street lived well compared to many other black folks. The men, and some of the women, held steady and secure jobs. Zinnias and marigolds grew in front yards, cowpeas and tomatoes in the back. In the winter the chickens pecked among the collard plants that, along with banked sweet potatoes, ensured a supply of vegetables throughout the season.

James Brown, the Esso truck driver, lived on Gipp Street. His wife, Mis' Theola, was Mr. Gipp's daughter. Barely out of their teens when they married, the Browns were model citizens and excellent parents. Their three children excelled in school, and the couple felt financially secure. Life was good, but, like parents everywhere, they dreamed of a better life for their children. Believing that equal educational opportunities would help them reach that goal, the Brown family was among those who had gone to Harry Briggs's house on the evening of November 11 and signed the petition.

For the nineteen years that Mr. Brown worked for Sprott's Fuel Service, he and Buck Sprott had been like brothers. Unlike some brothers, they were actually friends. Their interracial, but close, relationship was unusual in the segregated South—even though a stranger might have found it hard to believe Mr. Brown was an African American. Friendship notwithstanding, his employment at Sprott's came to an end exactly one month and eight days after he signed the school equalization petition. Technically he wasn't fired. Deftly applied economic and social pressures had squeezed Buck Sprott between a rock and a very hard place, leaving the man with almost no choice. He could either fire his friend and, by doing so, support his white compatriots in their effort to quell the black rebellion—or retain his employee and suffer severe economic consequences by losing business. Mr. Brown recalled telling Mr. Sprott, "If that's the way it is, I'll quit. No sense in both of us suffering."

Mr. Brown's son, Thomas, also lost his job. The eleventh-grade Scott's Branch student worked at the drugstore after school. His boss was reluctant to let the exceptionally intelligent and reliable sixteen-year-old go, but the peer pressure was too great.

Other petitioners were beleaguered as well. Willie Mood "Bo" Stukes, a handsome navy veteran, and his attractive wife, Gardenia Martin Stukes, had once been neighbors of the Browns and two other petitioners. They and their children signed the school equalization petition. Born around 1917, Mr. Bo was the son of a black teenage girl and a prominent white Summerton businessman. He was reared by his mother's aunt and her husband. Already adept at fixing things by his early teens, he became a mechanic and started working at "Juicy" Davis's garage.

Able to get any engine to run, Mr. Bo started a side job repairing cars at home. That activity was especially lucrative during the summers when many tourists used the Florida route that passed through Summerton. By the time he joined the navy, he and Mis' Gardenia were the parents of three children. Upon his discharge in October 1945, he went right back to work for Juicy Davis. To make it easier for their children to get to school, the family moved away from Gipp Street in August 1948. The elder Stukeses were determined that their children would not be stunted in their academic development. They signed the equalization petition because they felt things would only get worse if they didn't take a stand. Like other supporters, the couple took their children along when they went to the meetings at St. Mark. The little children slept on the back pews while the older ones used a flashlight to do homework. Juicy Davis fired Bo Stukes—perhaps the best mechanic in town—on the same day James Brown lost his job.

With Christmas approaching, some of the "pious" white Christians of Summerton seemed to be working overtime to make the season a memorable one for the black people. Apparently the meaner they could be, the better. What happened to Harry Briggs was a good example of their cold, cruel, and calculating maliciousness.

Except for a short stint in the navy, Mr. Harry never lived more than a mile from where he was born. When he married Eliza Gamble in 1940, he was already working at Carrigan's—Summerton's Sinclair gasoline station. The newlyweds set up housekeeping on Gipp Street, a few doors from James and Theola Brown.

A few months before the end of the war, Mr. Harry joined the navy. When he returned, he was welcomed back to his old job as a gas station attendant. Using a GI loan, he and Mis' Liza (as most people called his sweet-tempered wife) were able to build a frame house on a parcel of land not far behind our house. It was there that, on the evening of November 11, Mr. Harry became the first person to put his name on the equalization petition.

A month and a half later, on Christmas Eve 1949, at closing time, Mr. Carrigan offered Mr. Harry his good wishes for a merry Christmas and, in the spirit of the season, gave him a carton of cigarettes as a Christmas bonus. Then he fired Mr. Harry.

Hazel Ragin, one of Mr. Gipp's sons, also lived on Gipp Street with his family. Although he worked regularly as Summerton's only housepainter, Mr. Hazel lived for the hours when he could hunt or fish. The profusion of game and fish that he brought home kept the families of Gipp Street more than adequately fed. Making the most of his avocation, he regularly supplemented his income by acting as a guide for out-of-towners who came to take advantage of nature's bounty. With his hunter's instinct and sure aim, Mr. Hazel wasn't intimidated by anything. He and his family signed the petition at the Briggs house without any fear. No one asked him to paint after that.

The Windsor Motel, owned by David McClary, was close to the point where Gipp Street veered off from U.S. Highway 15/301. One of several places in the Summerton area where weary travelers could rest, the motel also provided lodging for the men—white men—who came to hunt in the state forest or to fish in the water of the new Lake Marion. Many hired Hazel Ragin as a guide. Thanks to the labors of black women who washed the sheets, scrubbed the floors, and made the beds, the two-story inn was a desirable place to stay—always clean and neat.

Mazie Solomon and Annie Martin Gibson worked at the Windsor Motel. Although Mis' Mazie was a strong supporter of the equalization movement, her name does not appear among the petitioners who signed the November 11 petition. Neither is her name on any of the lists from the four interest meetings. Nevertheless, one day in late December, Mr. McClary told her he heard that she signed the petition. When she didn't deny it, he accused her of having been persuaded to sign something she didn't understand, saying she didn't know what she was doing because she didn't have a mind for "stuff like that." The woman defiantly retorted, "I might do wash, but ain't nothing wrong with my mind. If I don't know what I'm doing, how come I can make your laundry come out right?"

They weren't "slapping words," but Mr. McClary reacted as if they were. He turned red and walked away, telling her to take her name off the petition immediately, or she would be fired. A spunky woman who didn't take kindly to threats, Mis' Mazie replied, "In that case, I guess I'll be leaving."

Leaving her work unfinished, she located her co-worker, Mis' Annie, who had signed the November petition. When told what Mr. McClary said, Mis' Annie mildly replied, "Then I guess I'll be leaving too." Together the two women went to the desk to inform the "house lady" and to get their pay. Surprised by the suddenness of their decision, the white woman asked the reason and told them, "If all y'all leave, I'm gonna leave, too." But Mr. McClary didn't threaten any of the other women, and although they knew what was going on, they weren't willing to leave their jobs. The house lady changed her mind.

Mis' Mazie went home. Soon afterward, the owner of their rented house told her family they would have to move if she let her name stay on the petition. He said that if he let them stay, he'd lose all of his privileges—privileges like getting his cotton ginned or selling his farm produce. He kept saying he was real sorry and that if it were up to him, they wouldn't have to move. The pressure being put on him was too great. He gave the family a month to get out. Mr. Gabriel Tindal, another petitioner, saved the Solomons from homelessness by letting them move into a small house on his property.

In spite of their "divide and conquer" approach, the white men failed to cow the petitioners and their supporters. Nevertheless, with Christmas fast approaching, a mood of despair began to creep over the people. Everything indicated there would be no treats for the holidays. The threat of "not being carried" meant no money would be advanced to them during the coming year. The petitioners wouldn't be able to buy fertilizer or seeds come spring. Christmas would be very slim. Toys, new clothes, and feasting were out of the question.

The educational and political gangsters were determined to destroy the financial bases of the dissidents, including those who were semi-independent of white people. One "blusterous" man boasted, "We're going to starve you, and dry up 'Big' William Ragin and De Laine." It wasn't clear how they would do that, for my frugal father lived within his means and had always refused to depend on local white sources for financial assistance. As a teacher, he tried to encourage his followers to be independent, telling them they should not be "like children who want to be grown and do as they please but, at the same time, want to lean on their parents for help." The way he lived, Daddy didn't have to lean on anyone.

An advantage of being a property owner was that one could neither be fired nor evicted. Several petitioners and supporters enjoyed that luxury. Like Daddy, Big William had succeeded in becoming semi-independent of local white businessmen. He operated a reasonably large farm and owned most of the acreage he used. Something else, however, contributed to his independence. He had a rather volatile temper and he didn't tolerate fools, being more than ready to let his gun do his talking in any disagreement. People—black or white—who were acquainted with him knew it was best to avoid his wrath.

Big William's neighbor, the gentle and mild-mannered Robert Georgia (the man who was a member of the Committee on Action) also owned his farm. However, he had not yet reached Big William's degree of independence. When he was told to remove his name from the petition, Mr. Georgia refused. Determined to destroy the insurgency, the white men looked until they found his weak spot. Then they attacked.

David McClary, the man who fired Mis' Mazie, the motel maid, also sold wagons. Mr. Georgia had bought a wagon from him and was due to finish paying for it when settling time came in 1950. But he had signed the petition, so the loan was called due in 1949, and Mr. McClary sent a policeman to collect the money owed on the wagon. That was very bad, for a farmer without a wagon or mules was virtually helpless.

Big William happened to be at Mr. Georgia's house at the time. He laconically advised the policeman, "I wouldn't carry [it] if I were you." The implied threat was enough. The policeman left without the wagon, with Big William promising to pay Mr. McClary within a month—which he did.

Over the years since it opened, Senn's Mill and Blacksmith Shop had variously been home to a blacksmith shop, a gristmill, and a bottling plant. In 1949 its founder, John G. Senn, had been dead seven years, and his seventy-seven-year-old son-in-law, Frank W. Josey, was in the process of passing the ownership to Walter B. Senn, Jr., the thirty-two-year-old grandson of the founder. John Hazel Richburg was the blacksmith at Senn's Mill. He was also the person who actually sold the corn, the hog and chicken feed, the grits, and everything else at Senn's. Both Old Man Josey and the young Senn seemed completely satisfied with the way Mr. John Hazel managed the shop, and over the years they had given him free rein in its operation.

The blacksmith lived with his wife, Mis' Rebecca, in a house inherited from his grandmother. Mis' Rebecca tended the house, cooked, and cared for their children. Her happy disposition brought a ray of sunshine wherever she went, reflecting the confidence and independence of a woman who knew her own mind. On November 11, she and her daughter signed the petition. Her husband didn't attend the meeting that night, but his absence didn't matter. Mis' Rebecca signed because she thought it was right to do so and because she wanted to.

Over the next few weeks, the young owner of Senn's attempted to get his shop manager, Mr. John Hazel, to make his wife remove her name from the petition. But he was wasting his breath. The blacksmith told his boss, "My wife's got a mind of her own. You better talk to her."

Mr. Senn never did talk with Mis' Rebecca. And he never threatened to fire her husband. Instead he told the man to stop selling to black customers. The store

The four AME pastors in Clarendon County whose teamwork was vital to the genesis of the Briggs lawsuit: (from the left) E. E. Richburg, J. W. Seals, J. A. De Laine, and Edward Frazier. Rev. Frazier, who was not a resident of the county, preceded Rev. Seals as pastor of St. Mark AME Church in Summerton. He continued to work with the Clarendon group even after his pastorate was changed. Here Rev. De Laine is receiving a check for four hundred dollars to help with his legal fees for the Benson slander case. Photograph by E. C. Jones, circa 1952. Courtesy of the De Laine Family Collection

manager replied, "I can't do that. Not as long as I'm a Negro, too." So the boss tried another approach. He told Mr. John Hazel to stop extending credit to black people. To this the confident and highly ethical black man, replied, "If I give credit to white people, I got to do the same for colored people." And he did.

The family of Bennie Parson lived on a parcel of more than eighty acres of inherited land. By working diligently, he and his wife, Mis' Plummie, earned a reasonably good living. After they signed the petition on behalf of their only child, life became very trying. One night some men came to their house and asked for Mr. Parson, who was not at home. Mis' Plummie asked what they wanted. The men said they were looking for a lost boy and left without asking the women any questions. The next day the Parsons asked the neighbors if the men had come to any of their houses. The men had not inquired at any other houses. If a boy was lost, the men were not looking for him very hard. If Mr. Parson had been at home, he might have been taken out and flogged—or worse.

With Christmas 1949 at hand, Summerton's terrorists were intimidating every black person that they could. They called my father, Rev. Seals, Rev. Richburg, and Rev. Frazier "Communists." Some white farmers told their sharecroppers the four AME ministers were being paid by Russia to stir up strife. Others told the black people that their leaders were getting rich from the money they gave to the NAACP.

People were told, "You got to get a resignation from Rev. De Laine and prove you are out of the NAACP." Most of them had never joined the NAACP, but so many years of being denied their rights had left them ignorant of many things. They didn't know they couldn't resign from an organization to which they did not belong. Nevertheless they came to our house on Christmas Eve and Christmas Day to ask my father "for their resignation."

These people were not plaintiffs, nor were they people who attended the meetings. My father knew some of them, and others he didn't. But they all came with the same story. They wouldn't be able to get anyone to lend them money or furnish provisions for the next year unless they got their resignation from the NAACP. After the first one or two came, Daddy devised a way to deal with their requests. "I learned to politely tell them to go to Lawyer Rogers and get him to draw up the kind of papers they needed."

Black people, who normally constituted a large percentage of the business in Summerton's stores, were not shopping. They had no spare money. The Summerton stores were sleepy. Trade was down. Only a few people could withstand the pressure being applied, and all were feeling the pinch. In describing conditions, my father wrote, "The merry Christmas was not so merry. The plaintiffs had been suffering since before Christmas. But when misery is accompanied by a strong determination, people can make a way out of no way. Our meetings had conditioned many to eat their peas, bread, and water if they didn't have a pig to kill."

By the time revelers across the country were singing "Auld Lang Syne," a concerted attack was being leveled against supporters of the equalization petition. For the second time, Mr. Betchman called Rev. Seals in. He asked, "Are you ready to play ball?" Rev. Seals snappily replied, "Mr. Betchman, if what I've been playing isn't ball, I don't know the game." This time Summerton's superintendent of schools took the class register and fired the preacher who had, under the GI Bill, taught veterans for the last two years.

The year headed crazily into 1950. When Mr. Harry's cow somehow got loose, she went into the nearby white cemetery. The creature must have stepped on Old Man McClary's grave—or eaten the grass around some of the gravestones—because the police arrested the cow, imprisoning her in the town's jailhouse.

3

Outcomes
1951–1955

12. *Liar, Liar*

Shall we suffer endless persecution?
J. A. DE LAINE

T he sudden loss of jobs and homes by plaintiffs and supporters made life
  onerous. With home mortgages and growing families, the now unemployed Harry Briggs and Bo Stukes desperately needed incomes. Somehow both
were able to secure enough land to qualify as farmers. That made them eligible,
under the GI Bill, for monthly stipends of ninety-two dollars each—provided
they were enrolled as students. When the two navy veterans tried to enroll in
agriculture classes at Scott's Branch, they were refused places. To get their
stipends, they would have to travel to Manning for classes. White men with
whom they had played as children were now eager to keep them in "their place."
Taunting the two petitioners, their former "friends" told them the only way they
could make things better for themselves was to take their names off the petition.

In spite of the hardships of that awful winter, neither man yielded to the pressure. Nor did any other plaintiff. Some were even adamant about keeping their
names on the petition. Mis' Liza and Mis' Gardenia, for example, went so far as
to threaten to leave Mr. Harry and Mr. Bo if they removed their names.

JANUARY 1950

The situation worsened, with terror messages being sent to people whom the
"bosses" had not found a way to control. By early January things were alarming
enough for Rev. De Laine to write an open letter. In it he asked the rhetorical
question, "Doesn't it indicate something is really wrong when cruel intimidation
tactics are used to weaken parents in their desires for American privileges for
American children?"

A series of other thought-provoking questions followed. "Is this the price free
men must pay for wanting their children trained as capable and respectable
American citizens? Isn't it the right of parents to petition school officials when
they think it necessary? Shouldn't officials employ dignity, foresight, and intelligence in at least the honest effort to correct outstanding evils? If the trustees place
the authority in the hands of a superintendent, shouldn't he adjust matters—or

advise the trustees to do so—when grave conditions arise? Shall we suffer end-less persecution just because we want our children reared in a wholesome atmos-phere?"

At one point in October or November 1949, some building materials were brought to the school on flatbed trucks. Three or more weeks passed before the prefabricated supplies were assembled into an ugly, barrackslike structure, then covered with brick-patterned tarpaper siding. The monstrosity became a class-room building that—according to a later allegation by District 22's trustees—converted Scott's Branch into a "new and modern school."

Plywood panels, hinged to the ceiling, separated the interior space into three rooms, each of which opened directly to the schoolyard. When desired, the pan-els could be lifted and their bottoms fastened to the ceiling by lightweight hooks, transforming the space into an "auditorium." (Fortunately the structure was dis-mantled before a raised wall fell on someone.)

By February the entire seventh-grade class occupied the "room" of the build-ing that was equipped with permanently attached auditorium seats. My brother BB was in that class. Now that there was sufficient seating for the entire class, he and his classmates no longer jockeyed for places to sit. However, there was a price to be paid. With no desktops, they had to rest notebooks, pencils, and textbooks on their knees. BB dryly observed, "I reckon they didn't want to make things too easy for us."

The entire third grade, as well as half of the first grade, also moved into the "new and modern" addition. Before January was over, the structure housed more than 150 pupils. Nevertheless the relief from crowding was not a signal that the trustees were ready to work with the parents. To the contrary, they were digging in their heels, preparing for a battle they were confident of winning. The dyed-in-the-wool segregationist who served as the school district's lawyer, S. E. Rogers, had begun bolstering the school board's resistance with his ingenious deceptions, half truths, and barefaced lies, turning the board's response to the requests from black parents into a fight as dirty and deceitful as the lawyer was able to devise.

It had to be the short, self-important Mr. Rogers, with his store of legal knowledge, who thought of a way to attack my father after December's planned treachery was thwarted. Shifting their tactics from violence to legal robbery, they vowed to make my father pay all costs incurred because of the petition. They per-suaded Mr. Benson, the deposed principal, to sue for slander and accuse my father of making the statements that were used in the young people's complaints. In his lawsuit, *Benson v. De Laine,* he asked for twenty thousand dollars in damages.

Since Rev. De Laine didn't have enough money to pay a monetary judgment if the verdict were unfavorable, his property would be confiscated, and we would lose everything. Fortunately he got wind of what was happening well before the legal papers were served. To keep our property out of the clutches of the "educa-tional gangsters," it had to be taken out of his name.

The task of transferring property titles could have been quickly completed with the help of a lawyer, but there were no black lawyers in Clarendon, and Rev. De Laine couldn't trust the white ones. Harold Boulware, the NAACP's attorney, couldn't take the case because of conflict of interest. William James and Esau A. Parker, who practiced twenty-three miles away in Sumter, were among the very few black lawyers who had been admitted to the South Carolina bar during the first half of the twentieth century. Daddy approached them for assistance, but neither was available.

A white Sumter lawyer consented to take the case if given a retainer of one thousand dollars. The amount was more than three months' salary for a teacher, and without a salaried job Rev. De Laine would have been hard put to pay him. When someone discovered the man was a close relative of one of School District 22's trustees, my father resumed his search.

For a black man in Clarendon County, Daddy owned a substantial amount of land. In addition to 316 acres of farmland and several other properties, he had bought thirty-four lots near our house on which he intended to build houses. A woman had contracted to buy the one house already erected. It was most fortuitous for our family that she paid cash for it the same day my father received the *Benson* summons. Regarding that sale, Daddy said, "The opposition always thought the NAACP was financing me, but the sale of that house was a God-sent blessing."

The plan to build more houses was interrupted, and there was no time to sell the empty lots. It was imperative that titles for all of his holdings to be immediately transferred to others. Dr. Adams, Daddy's staunch friend from Columbia, had a real-estate license, and he began the process of transferring property ownership. The two overworked lawyers from Sumter realized just in time the seriousness of my father's predicament and took the case.

My dad gave Harry Briggs outright a long, narrow lot that adjoined his home but didn't open to a street. The rest of the property was distributed among seven other people, including my mother's brother who lived in Columbia. The property where our home stood, along with our farm, was put in Dr. Adams's name. J. A. De Laine was left financially at the mercy of others—for the first time since shortly after he left home at fourteen years old.

Even though Mr. Parker, the attorney, personally drove from Sumter to the Manning courthouse to deliver documents and facilitate things, the paperwork had not been entirely finished when Rev. De Laine was served with the *Benson v. De Laine* papers on January 24.

FEBRUARY 1950

After the slander lawsuit was filed, the school board's trustees turned their attention to other issues. They finally granted Mr. Boulware a hearing regarding the parents' petition. It was held in the white Summerton High School. Eleven days

Liberty Hill Elementary School was one of three black schools in Clarendon School District 22 in 1949. The four-room building, which stood about one hundred feet from Liberty Hill AME Church, was erected in 1935 with funds raised primarily by parents. Courtesy of South Carolina Department of Archives and History

The ten-room Scott's Branch School was built in 1935 by parents. Serving the black community of the Summerton area, it housed eleven grades until the end of 1948. For the 1948–49 school year and the first part of the following year, the same structure housed twelve grades and more than six hundred students. Courtesy of the De Laine Family Collection

later the board formally responded to the charges with a document that was a masterpiece of double-talk, arrogance, and outright untruths.

The parents' petition had claimed poor "facilities, physical condition, sanitation and protection from elements" at the district's three black schools—Rambay, Liberty Hill, and Scott's Branch—collectively describing them as "inadequate and unhealthy, old, overcrowded, and in dilapidated condition." In contrast it described the town's two white schools—Summerton High School and

In late 1949, more than a year after a twelfth grade was added at Scott's Branch, this three-room prefabricated building was erected on the school's grounds. Equipped with interior partitions that could be raised to the ceiling, the structure was also supposed to serve as an auditorium. Courtesy of the De Laine Family Collection

Summerton Elementary School—as "modern, safe, sanitary, well equipped, lighted and healthy," with buildings that were "new, modern, uncrowded and maintained in first class condition."

Sent from the office of the lawyer S. E. Rogers, and presumably composed by him, the response from District 22's board—signed by all three members and dated February 20, 1950—unequivocally denied the existence of a white high school in the district. Although the consolidated high school (whose principal was Mr. Betchman) must have been in its own district, it shared District 22's school board, District 22's superintendent (Mr. Betchman), and the principal of Summerton Elementary School (Mr. Betchman).

The following sixteen excerpts (punctuation inserted and spelling corrected) are from the trustees' report.

> The Board [of Trustees of Clarendon School District 22] established and maintains three elementary schools for negro children, [all] erected less than 15 years ago, with the advice and cooperation of the State Department of Education. [They] are . . . in all respects . . . properly constructed and maintained and are not in poor physical . . . or . . . dilapidated condition.
>
> The white [Summerton Elementary School], more than 43 years old, is a two-storied structure, contains 8 rooms, is improperly lighted according to modern standards, is antiquated, and its physical condition is such that it has been a source of dissatisfaction to both patrons and trustees. Erected at an original cost of approximately $25,000.00, [it] is now insured . . . for $28,000.00. . . .
>
> Scott's Branch School, less than 15 years old, is built according to approved plans for educational buildings. . . . [It] contains in the main building 10 rooms, and 3 additional rooms have been recently constructed

The building that housed Summerton Grade School was erected in 1907. Until 1966 it served the first eight grades for white children in Summerton. Courtesy of South Carolina Department of Archives and History.

Summerton High School. Constructed in 1935, this building served as the white high school for students from Summerton and the surrounding areas until the end of the 1965–66 school year. The building was later renovated and now serves as offices for Clarendon School District 1, one of the three school districts in the county. Courtesy of South Carolina Department of Archives and History

by the Trustees, making a total of 13 rooms available. Its original cost was approximately $18,000.00 and the building is now insured for $24,000.00.

Neither of the schools has a central heating system. . . .

The white school is . . . in one of the lowest areas in the Town, and . . . on a Street over which passes the traffic of two main North-South Highways. . . . The Scott's Branch High School is erected on a site selected with advice of the patrons with due regard for the safety of the children and the convenience of the patrons.

. . . all of the negro schools are provided with sanitary toilet facilities erected according to the specifications of the State Health Department. These same facilities were in use in the white schools until the Town of Summerton installed a municipal water and sewerage system. . . . [After] its installation by the municipal authorities, the Board of Trustees permitted the white Parent-Teacher Association to install sanitary toilet facilities in two of the cloak rooms of the white school. The municipal sewerage system does not serve the area in which the Scott's Branch School is situated, and no such request has been received from the Patrons' organization of the Scott's Branch School. . . .

. . . although the municipal water system does not serve the area in which the negro school is located, the Board, at a great expense to itself, laid a water line from the municipal system to the Scott's Branch School . . . which . . . was installed . . . under the direction of the colored school authorities.

The patrons of the white school, not the school board, furnished drinking fountains for the white school. There are no inside drinking fountains in the Scott's Branch School, but if the patrons desire to install them, there certainly would be no objections to their being installed. The School Board . . . installed the outside drinking fountains at the Scott's Branch School, although they did not do so at the white school.

The Scott's Branch School Library contains 1678 books, containing 56 encyclopedias, 21 progressive reference sets, 3 dictionaries, and other books of suitable material for a school library. The white school library contains only 642 volumes with 9 reference sets. . . . [The] libraries . . . have been donated by various individuals and organizations.

The janitorial services of the white school are furnished by one janitor. [At] the request of the principal of the Scott's Branch School, the janitorial services there are performed by various students selected by the principal. . . . The cost of janitorial services for the white school . . . is $18.00 per month, while the cost of the janitorial services to the colored school is $16.00 per month. If the method of using students as janitors is not satisfactory to the patrons of the colored school, we feel sure that the principal would be glad to discontinue the same.

The school operated for whites has . . . 7 teachers. The Scott's Branch School has . . . 14 teachers. The average attendance in the white school is 190. The average attendance in the Scott's Branch School is 468.

Fuel for all schools in the District, both white and colored, is furnished by the Board on request of the principal of the school, and it appears that all such fuel has been furnished for the present school year by the Board.

Facilities are furnished in Scott's Branch High School for the teaching of general science, chemistry, and agriculture. No such facilities are furnished by the District at the white High School, inasmuch as the district maintains no high school for whites. . . .

School District No. 22 provided no transportation by bus or otherwise for any students, white or colored.

A cursory inspection only will reveal that the facilities, physical condition, equipment, safety, and protection from the elements are accordingly better with the negro schools than the whites, although the Trustees are of the opinion that they are in all respects substantially equal.

In conclusion, the Board finds that the negro children . . . in school district No. 22 are not being discriminated against, . . . that there is no violation of the rights to equal protection of the laws as provided by the Constitution of the United States, [and] that the facilities afforded to the white and negro children of District No. 22 . . . are substantially equal.

Is equality in the eyes of the beholder, or is it built on half truths, omissions, and outright lies of those in power? The board's audacious claim of equality was made even though Scott's Branch School served more than three times as many children with fewer than twice the number of classrooms as Summerton Elementary School. The black school, constructed more recently, cost far less to build and was insured for less than the white school. More money was spent for janitorial services at the white school than at the black school. The report mentioned neither that black parents, unlike white parents, had raised the money to build their school nor that there were no cloakrooms in Scott's Branch—a school "built according to approved plans for educational buildings"—to convert for use as sanitary toilet facilities.

The board's report includes a statement that Summerton Elementary School was constructed of sand dug from the premises. The description brings to my mind visions of a pre–Industrial Age mud hut, precariously standing in a low-lying swamp. The mental image is totally incongruent with what I know to be fact. The Summerton Elementary School building (that looked like it was stone) was hardly a hut. Furthermore the maximum difference in elevation between the lowest and highest points in Summerton is less than thirty feet and the school building was no lower than the street; the implication that it might be swamplike (and therefore malarial) was unfounded.

Anyone familiar with the Scott's Branch of those days would wonder where the school stored the "1678 books, including 56 encyclopedias, 21 progressive reference sets, 3 dictionaries, and other books." I was in ninth grade at Scott's

Branch the year the report was written, and the ninth-grade homeroom was supposed to double as a library. Three dictionaries may have been on the mostly empty shelves, but, as far the other books were concerned, they definitely were not in the "library." The count must have included all student textbooks, the school's entire supply of outdated magazines that had not yet been confiscated for use as toilet paper, and photographs of encyclopedias and "progressive reference sets" (whatever they are).

The portrayal of the school board as a compassionate entity, one that laid— "at a great expense to itself"—a water line to the Scott's Branch School and that magnanimously installed drinking fountains outside the black school, is completely at odds with its refusal to hear student complaints and its belief that parents of students were not entitled to be involved in affairs of the school.

One thing that stood out in the farcical report was the "apples-and-oranges" comparison of a single black school—the one that accommodated twelve grades— to the district's white elementary school that housed only eight grades.

Near the end of the board's report was a list of items said to be needed at Scott's Branch. Allegedly the list was submitted by the principal on October 25, 1949, in response to the board's request. Since the school had no principal on October 9, the person preparing the list had a maximum of fifteen days to determine the needs of the school—and did so at the beginning of the school year in the midst of chaos. The exact list of requested items follows:

Wood and coal
Twelve scuttles and shovels
Six boxes of crayon and 12 erasers
11 doors and window locks
Material (lumber and nails) to repair windows and sashes
Three additional classrooms
Three additional teachers
One teacher for the 7th grade, one for the second grade,
A music teacher for eighth grade, through twelfth grade
Sanitary material, toilet paper, soap, powder, etc.
A janitor for the school which is very essential to good health;
    who will keep the plant in good condition

One has to wonder why so many doors and window locks were needed for a building that was "not in poor physical condition." What had happened to the scuttles and shovels from the previous year? Either the building had been severely vandalized or, more likely, severely neglected. Regardless "the Board granted every request listed and all of the things requested have been furnished, except a music teacher." The white elementary school had no music teacher, so it must have seemed reasonable that high school students at Scott's Branch School should not have one as requested.

NAACP lawyers apparently didn't agree with the report's conclusion because they prepared to file a lawsuit for equalizing school facilities. Meanwhile, with the *Benson v. De Laine* slander lawsuit scheduled to begin two weeks later, on March 6, the school board and its lawyer turned their focus to another way to wreak havoc.

MARCH 1950

My father had another health crisis soon after the board submitted its response. Not trusting the Clarendon County doctors, he went to Columbia where he remained for the two weeks before the slander trial was to begin. Three nights before the trial's set date, Robert Georgia's son Buster was driving home from a basketball tournament. He had dropped off the last of his passengers when the night duty policeman stopped and questioned him about being out so late. Released, Buster continued toward his home. Along the way he noticed scores of white papers strewn beside the road. Curious, he stopped to pick some up, then took a few home to show his father. The next morning the police chief arrived at the Georgia home and accused the young man of distributing the papers.

Each piece of paper, half a letter-sized sheet, bore a crudely composed, type-written message that had been mechanically copied by means of a stencil. Although the first words were "Warning Benson," the message was clearly not directed at the ousted principal. It was a threat, but it wasn't obvious who was being threatened—or who was doing the threatening. One of the papers bore the message that is copied verbatim below.

WARNING BENSON:

YOU HAD BETTER NOT APPEAR IN JUDGEMENT AGAINST ANY PERSON IN SC OR ANYWHERE. AND MAY WE EMPHASIZE THE FORTHCOMING COURT. TOO, YOU BETTER BE TOLD THAT ANY SUBSEQUENCE COURT WILL BE JUST AS PERILOUS AS THIS ONE. THE PEOPLE OF SOUTH CAROLINA WILL NOT ALLOW A CHARACTER LIKE YOU TO SERVE OF HANDLE PUBLIC AFFAIRS. TELL YOUR "DARKY" SUP-PORTERS THAT IF THEY WANT TO DIE WITH YOU COME AND WITNESS FOR YOU.

KU*KLUX KLAN

The papers were on our porch, inside our screen door, and on the Scott's Branch schoolyard. They were also at other places, including the mayor's yard and the white schoolyards. Some people found them amusing, but others were petrified by the thought that the Ku Klux Klan might be in Summerton. On Main Street the "educational and political gangsters" claimed it was the work of De Laine and his followers, an accusation that made other white people truly angry. The town's atmosphere became exceptionally tense.

While the opposition gloated over Rev. De Laine's anticipated fate, my mother and one of my aunts took a couple of copies to Daddy in Columbia. My father had the papers taken to NAACP officials who, in turn, sent Mother and my aunt the seventy miles back to Summerton for more of the papers. By the time they returned to Columbia, the NAACP people had already swung into action. Before the day was over, copies of the paper had been delivered or sent to a large number of law enforcement officers, ranging from Summerton's chief of police to the head of the Federal Bureau of Investigation to the president of the United States.

In Summerton there was much speculation about the meaning of the papers. When Monday morning arrived, a gleeful crowd of white people went to Manning to witness the trial, certain of seeing my father convicted. To their surprise his lawyers presented an affidavit that attested he was not well enough to appear in court. The trial was postponed, and the "vultures" were disappointed.

Returning to Summerton, the people found several strange lawmen. They carried a blanket warrant that permitted them to search every house in and around town. The officers had been directed by some white people to the place where two of my aunts lived and to our house. They searched my aunts' small rented rooms, strewing their belongings all around. Not finding anything, the investigators came to our house. Mother asked what they were looking for and was told they wanted to find the kind of equipment that produced the papers.

Saying, "If that is what you want, I'll show you what we have," she showed the officers my father's typewriter and duplicating machine. Deciding the equipment did not produce the papers, the investigators left. Accompanied by a deputy sheriff, they proceeded to visit every black place in town that might have similar pieces of equipment.

When nothing relevant was found in a black home or business, town leaders suggested that black college boys must have done the work at one of their schools. Apparently putting no credence in that explanation, the investigators began to search white establishments.

Rev. De Laine was not in town to see what happened, but his supporters unobtrusively watched and listened to the unfolding drama. Something of interest—the men didn't know exactly what—was found in the office of a school board member. Although it wasn't what was being sought, my father claimed, "The newspaper said the chairman of the board and his partner were fined $9,900 each."

The investigators were ready to give up after futilely searching the white schools. Seeing Henry Brown, the white schools' janitor, they asked about any places in those buildings where there might be typewriters or duplicating machines. Mr. Brown replied, "Other than what's in the office, the only thing I know about is up there in the attic. Couple of them boys took it up the other day."

Inside one of the buildings, an investigator eyed an overhead access hole and asked Superintendent Betchman, "What's up there?"

"Nothing."

"For curiosity, I want to see."

In the dark loft a flashlight revealed a duplicating machine, its circular drum still loaded with a stencil bearing two copies of the same message. When the inked drum was turned, the message could be transferred to a sheet of paper. By cutting the page in half, less paper was needed to produce two copies of a message. On that particular stencil, the two copies were slightly different—just like the papers that Buster had found. The stencil was the same one used to produce the messages my mother and aunt carried to Columbia.

Among black people it was rumored that both the school superintendent and the town were held responsible for the forgery. My father didn't know if that was true, but something must have happened because the ranting "educational and political gangsters" became calm and nothing was heard from them for some time.

Rev. De Laine thought the investigators had come from the Federal Bureau of Investigation, so he wrote a letter of thanks to FBI director J. Edgar Hoover for having "searched my house" to find evidence of the source of the papers. A reply, dated March 16, 1950, came from Mr. Hoover's office denying its involvement. My father was amazed to discover the investigators had come from the South Carolina Bureau of Investigation in response to being contacted by the NAACP officers.

April 1950

The situation had reached a point where people were advising Rev. De Laine to take a pastoral position elsewhere and leave town to insure his safety. Most of the advice givers were genuinely concerned about his welfare, but the interests of some were more selfish. My father had attained an influential position in the statewide organization of the AME Church based on his support in the AME Church's Manning District (almost identical with geographical area of Clarendon County). If he consented to be transferred to a church district where his name was less familiar, he would lose that position. However, he was a little too honest and moral for some of his ministerial colleagues, and they were eager for him to be transferred. On the other hand, my father was determined to stay in Summerton until he finished what he had set out to do with the equalization lawsuit.

His health remained fragile, and he was unable to return to his pastoral duties until well into April. One day when he was finally recovering, he went to Allen University for an important meeting of the Board of Control, of which he was a member. As he walked onto the campus, Dr. Adams hailed him to deliver a message: "Bishop Reid wants to see you in his office."

"I bet he wants to send me to St. James in Lake City where Dr. Jackson just died," Rev. De Laine commented wryly. "Well, I've got news for him. I don't want Lake City in any way—stewed, broiled, baked or fried."

Dr. Adams jovially laughed and said, "We'll tell Bishop Reid that and he'll know how to adjust you." More soberly, he added, "You certainly need to leave Summerton since of all of your property has been taken out of your name."

In his office the bishop told my father, "St. James needs a pastor and I want to send you there."

Rev. De Laine didn't think the transfer was a good idea. Bishop Reid, however, maintained, "God directed me to send you there."

Countering, my father reminded the bishop why he had chosen to take an appointment at the Antioch / Zion Hill circuit the previous year. Despite having served at the small pastoral charge nineteen years earlier, before he graduated from college, he had opted to return, taking a big demotion so he could remain in Summerton and continue the struggle for equality.

Bishop Reid was persuasive. "De Laine, your work at Summerton is well done. You have served your purpose there. Your life now is at stake." Looking my father squarely in the eye, the bishop went on, delivering an ultimatum. "I'll give you from now until 9:00 a.m. tomorrow to decide. The magnitude of the Lake City charge is too great to trust it to local preachers for five more months. If you refuse it, I am appointing somebody there tomorrow."

Rev. De Laine wasn't swayed. He replied, "Lake City is a KKK hole. That's the place where, years ago, the white people killed that black postmaster, Baker."

Grandpa H. C. had told my father of the murder that took place in 1898, the year of my father's birth and two years after South Carolina systematically deprived people of African descent of their legal rights. President McKinley had appointed Frazier Baker postmaster at Lake City. Angry white people didn't like it and tried to scare the postmaster into leaving the position. When they didn't succeed, they stooped to murder in the darkness of night, setting the postmaster's house on fire and shooting him as he tried to escape.

The bishop—who didn't know the story—persisted unfazed, saying, "You've served your purpose at Summerton well, and the equalization case will be filed in a few days. Now that the NAACP has it, you don't have to fear that your efforts will fail."

Bishop Reid saw it as his Godly judgment and a blessing from God to be able to get my father away from the threats on his life and the annoyances caused by the lawsuit. The bishop also saw an excellent opportunity to assign a suitable pastor to the St. James circuit. He envisioned my father going to a place, forty miles from Summerton, where he would be accepted as an ambassador of the Gospel. He anticipated him moving into a comfortable, reasonably well-furnished parsonage. But he didn't see what the future held. He couldn't—even with his Godly judgment.

From his perspective my father saw the choice as being between "the devil and the deep blue sea." Taking the appointment, in his opinion, would be like "leaving torment and going to hell." Although his bishop was giving him a choice, as he saw it, he had no choice. It might have been time to get out of the "frying pan," but he was finding it truly hard to avoid stepping "into the fire."

Needing to discuss his dilemma with someone else, he left the bishop with a "swelling at the heart" and drove almost fifty miles to the home of one of his church elders. The man summoned several other officers, and they unanimously agreed it was probably best for their pastor to obey the bishop. If he didn't, they concurred, he might be killed—or have to kill somebody.

Taking courage, my father drove on to Summerton to talk with my mother. He told her, "You know they're going to fire you." Mother calmly accepted the inevitable with the observation, "You're a good man and it's hard to keep a good man down. If they move you or fire me, we'll make it—somewhere, somehow."

Once more he realized what a strong fortress he had in the wife who stood by him in his hours of crisis. Armed with the advice of the churchmen and confidence buttressed by my mother's words, he was back in Columbia the next morning, tired and sleepy from so much traveling and talk, but on time to inform Bishop Reid, "I've decided to accept your Godly Judgment." My father dutifully mouthed the words, but he really didn't see the bishop's judgment as being very Godly. To him the situation was best described by the saying, "Damned if you do and damned if you don't."

After the meeting of the Board of Control opened and business was completed, Rev. De Laine's new pastoral appointment was announced. Dr. Adams laughed in his usual good-humored way and said, "De Laine, you said Lake City is Hell. Just go on to Hell, and God will bring you out all right."

13. *Moving On*

Things don't just happen, you have
to make them happen.
J. A. De Laine

Once the 1949–50 school year started at Scott's Branch, it went on without interruption—except for the continual change of principals. A couple of days into the term, my mother found the combined responsibility of teaching sixth grade and running the school too much. She asked for assistance and Mis' Amy was assigned to help her. Shortly thereafter a new principal was hired. He stayed perhaps two weeks before leaving in disgust. Mis' Amy was then asked to act as principal, with Mother as her assistant. Then another man was hired as principal. He resigned even before he could be introduced to the staff. The female duo of acting principals once more took the reins. Next in the procession of principals was an alcoholic who kept the position almost as long as anyone else did that school year, probably being too drunk to realize there were problems.

In keeping with the custom of the day, the school board was determined the principal should be a man. Desperate, they turned to the existing staff. All the male teachers had been fired before the school year began, and only one man, a fresh college graduate, had been hired in September. In early February the twenty-four-year-old Albert Fuller—with four months' teaching experience— became the sixth principal of Scott's Branch during that school year.

On one occasion the young principal sent a child home as a disciplinary measure. But before classes were dismissed that day, his superiors had reversed the decision. The Committee on Action protested the administration's lack of support for him, and my father, on behalf of the parents, wrote a letter to the superintendent and the trustees. It read in part:

> As a result of the raggedy way the school ran last term, the children lack the proper respect, [and] without respect there is no way of avoiding further dissatisfaction and unrest. [How] do you think the discipline of the school can be carried out when you make a figurehead of your choice as a principal?
>
> We realize that the present principal is young and inexperienced but you were the ones that put all of the last six principals there. If we [had

been] permitted to help you, this embarrassing situation would never have arisen. You should sustain the principal in his administrative acts when he is right. Even if he is wrong, we think he should be sustained at least one day for the good of future discipline.

The parents did what they could to help the inexperienced young man, and he managed to complete the school year as principal. When the year ended, his contract as agriculture teacher was renewed. However, as Daddy had foretold, Mother's contract was not. Something else happened that my father had never considered. His sisters and niece were also dropped from their teaching jobs in School District 22. Even the wife of my uncle Lewis, who taught in another Clarendon district, lost her teaching job. The authorities were applying pressure in every way they could to destroy the leader of the rebellion.

Rev. De Laine's transfer to Lake City took place slightly more than a month before the school year came to a close. A former pastor of St. James, my father's new church, recommended that he contact Luther Green, a church steward who owned a funeral home. My father immediately wrote to him. Green's Funeral Home and an adjacent barbershop turned out to be centers for black news in Lake City. There one could get information about voting, school irregularities, domestic disputes, or any other local issues that involved black people. Daddy's letter to the churchman immediately became a public relations document, heralding his arrival.

The whole family (except Jay, who was away working for the summer) drove to Lake City with Rev. De Laine on his initial Sunday at St. James. The first church member to introduce himself to my father was Webb Eaddy, a church officer who lived next door to the parsonage. The church was packed, crowded with the devout, the curiosity seekers, the church opposers, and its lukewarm members. The news of his arrival had been broadcast very effectively.

Although we were not going to change our place of residence until August, my father immediately set about establishing himself as a presence in Lake City and drove to Lake City several times a week. One of his early acts was to send a letter to the town's mayor, explaining who he was and why he would be living in Lake City. In the missive he offered his services to help in town affairs in any honorable way.

Undoubtedly both surprised and curious, the mayor responded by visiting the parsonage one day as Daddy was arranging books in his little study. The two men exchanged pleasantries and ended their meeting with mutual pledges of support. Before leaving, the mayor told Daddy of a tragedy that had happened a day or so earlier involving the Ku Klux Klan and a black man who ran a nightclub in the town of Myrtle Beach.

Displeased that white women frequented the club to learn the latest dances, Klan members paraded in front of the club in their vehicles. The nightclub owner responded to the threat boldly, declaring, "They can ride as much as they want—as long as they mind their own business. But when they interfere with my business, I'm going to teach them a lesson."

On hearing the message, Klan members donned their white robes, covered their heads with hoods, and went to the nightclub. They riddled the place with bullets and inflicted many injuries upon the owner. When the smoke cleared, one man had been killed by gunshot. The dead man, who wore a police uniform under his Ku Klux Klan robe, was said to be the magistrate-elect of the nearby town of Conway.

Scornful of the KKK, Lake City's mayor denounced such actions, confiding to my father, "I don't go along with this kind of thing but you ought to know it is also here in Lake City."

Daddy immediately remembered the postmaster's fate. Perhaps he had truly jumped out of the frying pan into the fire.

Welcomed by his new congregation and the mayor, Rev. De Laine put any misgivings behind him and made a point of learning who was who in Lake City and establishing vital contacts. One visit was to the principal of Lake City Colored School. Although Mother had not yet been discharged from Scott's Branch, it was clear she would need to find a new job. The principal of the school in Lake City was himself having a public-relations problem, and he saw a potential benefit for himself if he hired Mother. His response to my father was, "I'd like to get your wife to teach with me. It will help you and it can help me. Since you will be the pastor of St. James Church, you will have the ears of some of the strongest parents in Lake City." So, as school authorities in Lake City were preparing a contract for my mother, Summerton administrators were dropping her from their teaching rolls.

Although things were going well in Lake City, my father's heart was heavy every evening as he returned to Summerton. Almost three years had passed since Mr. Hinton of the NAACP threw his challenge out to the summer school teachers. Ever since then my father had worked unrelentingly to force authorities to provide more equal educational facilities for Clarendon's black schoolchildren. To him, however, it seemed that no real progress had been made.

For two years his small group of activists had struggled. Unfortunately some black people turned a deaf ear to their message, and others talked things over with their oppressors. As a result of his push, many of his followers had lost their homes, jobs, credit, and peace of mind. A man had died. My father's own life had been threatened, and he had been sued. The plagues being visited upon the African Americans of Clarendon County seemed endless. Worried when the NAACP failed to file the equalization lawsuit after the board's response in February, he opined, "It looked like Attorneys Harold Boulware and Thurgood Marshall were playing with us to see how much trouble they could get us into."

That was not true. The NAACP lawyers in New York were working in busy, understaffed, and poorly funded offices. The Clarendon equalization issue was only one of many inequitable situations suffered by people of color in the land that promised liberty for all. Across the nation people wanted help, and NAACP's dedicated staff was trying to address the many wrongs in the right ways.

Finally, not long after school closed for the summer, Mr. Boulware finally walked into the federal court building in Charleston and handed a package to a court clerk. After signing a number of papers, the court clerk gave Mr. Boulware a receipt and the lawyer left. That was all there was to it. The equalization petition had been officially filed as Civil Action No. 2505 in U.S. Eastern District Court of South Carolina, on behalf of twenty-nine adults from Clarendon County. The petition also bore the signatures of seventy-nine minors. The first signature on the list was that of Harry Briggs, the man in whose house the petition was signed. The news broke in newspapers and radio the next day, June 7, 1950. Black people in Summerton were suing Clarendon County officials for equal schools and educational opportunities!

Civil Action No. 2505 was named *Harry Briggs et al. v. The Board of Trustees for School District Number 22, Clarendon County, South Carolina, R. W. Elliott, Chairman, et al.* The defendants—the seven Clarendon County men legally responsible for public school education in District 22—were charged with failure to provide equal schools and educational opportunities for black children.

The tempest in Summerton's teapot had boiled over, and the erupting steam caused storm clouds to gather all across the state. The answers the lawyer Rogers gave to inquiring reporters had the same spin as the school board's response to the parents. According to a June 7 article in the *State* newspaper, Mr. Rogers made the half-true declaration that the black school was newer and more modern than the white school. Overnight Scott's Branch became a site of great public interest. Sightseers came to gape at the school as if it were one of the wonders of the world. Cars loaded with white people poured into Summerton, the occupants wanting to see conditions for themselves. Our house, across the street from Scott's Branch, became a hated object, and Rev. De Laine was truly a marked man.

Unlike my father, many of the plaintiffs and the petition's supporters were hunters. They knew how to move stealthily, hide patiently, and shoot straight. Despite their own troubles, these men had fearlessly organized themselves to guard our house each night, redoubling their vigilance in the last days before our mid-July move to Lake City.

SUMMER 1950

I turned fourteen in the summer of 1950, and for a short time I felt as if I didn't have a single friend. One of my best friends had moved away from Summerton during the school year. Even earlier another good friend had been taken out of the deteriorating Scott's Branch School and sent away to attend a private school. Our move to Lake City meant I had to leave all the other girls and boys that I knew. We would be living across town from most of Lake City's black community, in the very last house on the edge of town. The house itself was on the same piece of property as Daddy's church, which faced Church Street. Across that fairly major street was a smelly sewage treatment site. Beyond both the church and the treatment site lay a swamp, which also often smelled bad. In the opposite direction, entrances to the church's parking lot and to the parsonage were on the unpaved Lake Street. And a poor white family lived directly in front of the place we would call home. I doubted that I would ever be able to make new friends!

My worrying had been needless. Our entire family was warmly welcomed, and by the time school opened, we felt very much at home. In September the four of us began settling in to new academic lives. Jay went away to begin his first year of college. Mother, having graduated from college, took charge of fifth grade at the Lake City Colored School as a fully qualified teacher with years of experience. BB and I enrolled in the same school, which was two miles away, on the other side of town. For the first time in our lives, we often walked a long distance to school—the way other children did.

Daddy still went to Summerton several times a week, often taking BB with him. He was no longer living in Clarendon County, but he had no intention of abandoning the people who had so faithfully followed him into battle.

October 1950

The postponed lawsuit for slander came up for trial in October. The only witnesses were white men affiliated with District 22, including the local superintendent of schools, the county superintendent, one or two members of the school board, and the agriculture teacher from Summerton High School. Except for the agriculture teacher, they were the defendants named in Civil Action No. 2505, *Briggs v. Board.* They were also some of the men who had publicly predicted Mr. Benson would win the case and who had bragged they would make Rev. De Laine pay for the school equalization lawsuit.

An effort to get black people to testify against my father had been unsuccessful. Albert Fuller, the young man who had served as principal of Scott's Branch for part of the previous school year, was asked to witness for the prosecution. He refused because he did not witness any of the events, which happened before he arrived in Summerton. One trustee rebuked him for refusing.

The trial was held in Manning with William James and Esau A. Parker from Sumter representing my father. Daddy wrote that Mr. Benson "went into the back of the courthouse and cried" while the school officials acted as if they were the plaintiffs. One thing that happened during the trial truly bothered my father, who had little tolerance for lying. He had expected most of the witnesses to distort the truth, but he was astounded when the county superintendent, Mr. McCord—a minister of the Gospel and pastor of Manning Presbyterian Church —lied under oath.

Using one of the itemized complaints that the Scott's Branch Class of 1949 had written, the man swore, "De Laine came to my office and told me Benson stole the school money and used it for himself." My father claimed the event never occurred, that he only served as an intermediary for the young people. In my father's eyes, the superintendent had committed a grave offense against both God and man, stooping as low as a man could by bearing false witness when he had sworn "to tell the truth and nothing but the truth." Shaking his head in disappointment and disgust, Rev. De Laine said, "What made it worse with me was to see a preacher do that."

The trial lasted three days. After four hours of deliberation, a verdict of guilty came back on only one charge—the one attested to by Mr. McCord. Undoubtedly the twelve men on the jury knew the pastor had been framed, but they were white and the witnesses were white. The black man had to be found guilty of something, so the jury chose to believe a black man of God would lie under oath, but a white man of God would not.

Despite the sum awarded being less than one-fourth the amount asked for, five thousand dollars was still a substantial amount of money. In 1950 the price of a first-class postage stamp was three cents, and a new car cost about fifteen hundred dollars. Three years earlier Harry Briggs had built a modest five-room house for less than three thousand dollars. The total annual income of a black family with two people working as teachers would probably have been considerably less than the fine that was imposed on my father.

The "legal robbers" had won that round. But getting the money they wanted would be extremely difficult. With Daddy's property tied up in other people's names, it would be a challenge to collect any money.

NOVEMBER 1950

The back-and-forth travel, along with the stress of the lawsuit, began to affect Rev. De Laine's already fragile health. He discussed the situation with the other leaders, and they agreed that Rev. Richburg should take over the effort's leadership. They thought that, if Rev. Richburg and Rev. Seals worked together, they could keep the people's spirits up until the lawsuit was finished. When the opposition learned Rev. Richburg had assumed the mantle of leadership, they began to threaten him. As we were no longer living in our Summerton house, the men who had kept watch over our house shifted their focus and began to guard Rev. Richburg's home.

About that time a date was finally set for the trial of Civil Action No. 2505. The lawsuit claimed not only that the defendants failed to provide equal educational facilities for the black schoolchildren, but that the failure to do so resulted

In his years on the bench, Judge J. Waties Waring made many rulings that contributed to African Americans' progress toward equality in the United States.
Appointed a federal judge in 1942, Judge Waring steadily grew more outspoken
regarding justice for black people. Rev. J. A. De Laine wrote about him, "When
future historians write of the strange state of a society in which standards of conduct and belief were weak and lacking, they cannot help but recognize that there
was a federal district judge—J. Waties Waring—whose decisions meant much in
correcting the evils that political demagogues had imposed upon the society." The
photograph was a gift to Rev. and Mrs. De Laine. The accompanying tag, signed
by the judge, bore the inscription, "To my friends the De Laines with affection and
admiration." Courtesy of the De Laine Family Collection

in violation of their right to equal protection as provided by the Fourteenth
Amendment to the Constitution of the United States.

At the pretrial hearing on November 17, by words that do not seem to have
been recorded, J. Waties Waring, the presiding judge, indicated that the NAACP
would probably win Civil Action No. 2505. However, the outcome would merely

amount to another small skirmish. The central question of whether public school segregation itself violated constitutional rights would still not be addressed. He thought that failure to provide equal schools and educational opportunities could not be translated to mean that the Fourteenth Amendment was being violated. In a move that added to a growing list of actions that made him unpopular with other white people, Judge Waring tacitly let the NAACP lawyers know they were taking the wrong approach to gain equality in public school education. He could have let the case proceed, saying nothing. However, he believed in judicial fairness and was uncomfortably aware of the disadvantages that the biases of southern judicial systems imposed on black people. "Separate" could never be "equal," and he recognized that fact. In his view the doctrine of "separate but equal" had to be directly challenged.

To make such a challenge, a lawsuit directly addressing the constitutionality of segregated public schools would have to be filed, and the U.S. Supreme Court's 1896 *Plessy v. Ferguson* decision would have to be addressed. Furthermore such a lawsuit would involve a conflict between South Carolina's Constitution and that of the United States, thus requiring a panel of three federal judges.

Back in March 1949, Thurgood Marshall consented to take a Clarendon County case partly because he knew J. Waties Waring would be the presiding judge. Having argued cases before him several times previously, he knew Judge Waring was just and fair. But if a three-judge panel were required, the two additional men would, most likely, be hostile to the Clarendon County plaintiffs. With that in mind, Mr. Marshall and his colleagues considered simply trying to amend the equalization case so it would remain in a friendly court.

In the end, however, the NAACP lawyers were swayed by the judge's logic, and Civil Action No. 2505 was withdrawn *without prejudice.* Judge Waring's pretrial actions were the keystone for what subsequently happened.

The Clarendon County plaintiffs were sorely disappointed when the trial was not held as scheduled. They knew the case had to be "refiled," but didn't understand the magnitude of what refiling meant. The NAACP lawyers, however, understood very well. Having overcome their initial reluctance, they were determined to take full advantage of the chance to bring the question of public school segregation before the United States Supreme Court. Although formal withdrawal proceedings for *Briggs v. Board* were not begun until December 26, 1950— and the associated paperwork was not completed until January 5—the NAACP lawyers immediately began to prepare their new thrust.

Public school segregation would be challenged on a national basis. The NAACP's New York office had already received a request from parents in Topeka, Kansas. Some members of the legal staff enthusiastically began to develop the case from Topeka, which was viewed as being very promising. Others, including Thurgood Marshall, set about reworking the case that had come out of Clarendon County.

December 1950

Sometime in mid-December, letters were sent to tell the Clarendon leaders what needed to be done for the new lawsuit. In Summerton, Rev. Seals and Rev. Richburg waited anxiously for Rev. De Laine's opinion before they made any plans. However, the letter to him lay in the Summerton post office, our mailbox unopened for more than a week. Although my father no longer made the trip to Clarendon every day, he still received mail in Summerton. When they were unable to postpone action any longer, his colleagues sent a message that they immediately needed to get signatures for a new petition.

Surprised by the news, my father was unhappy because, yet again, he would have to recruit plaintiffs. There was also the dilemma that, as Daddy recalled, "Richburg, Seals and I had said we were not trying to abolish segregation but we were now asking for just that." They would have to break their word because the new game had different rules. As my father put it, "In the language of Thurgood Marshall, we were asking for Equal Everything." A firm believer in the equality of men, Rev. De Laine appreciated the merit of the new approach and fervently hoped the plaintiffs would not withdraw their support.

The three AME pastors—Rev. Richburg, Rev. Seals, and Rev. De Laine—set December 18 as the day for collecting signatures. The weather was cold, a day for gloves and a heavy coat. Physically weak and battle weary, Daddy would have much preferred to remain inside the warm house in Lake City. Nevertheless he was determined to do his part. So, one year and three days after Mr. Crawler threatened his life on the town's Main Street, my father arrived in Summerton, ready to continue the quest for his people's equality.

The NAACP's guidelines were clear. Every petitioner had to be a bona fide resident of School District 22 as well as the parent (or guardian) of at least one child who attended school in the district. Only one adult per household could sign, and the signatures of children were not permitted. Under these criteria several of the previous plaintiffs were ineligible. Rev. Richburg, for example, was eliminated because, even though he lived in the district, he had no children in the district's schools. The same was true of Esther Singletary and Thomas Gamble. James Brown and his family had moved out of the state. Among themselves the three pastors agreed to avoid getting signatures from certain people—such as Henry Brown, the white schools' janitor—who were particularly vulnerable to retaliation. Rules in hand, they were ready to get signatures.

It was nearing the end of deer-hunting season, and six of the most stalwart supporters—five of whom had signed the equalization petition—were twenty miles away, trying to provision their families with meat for the winter. Rev. De Laine was given the task of finding them. Not a hunter, he was unfamiliar with the forest. But determined that the lawsuit would have enough signatures, he drove to different parking areas until he found their vehicle. Then, in the chill winter air, he set out on foot, not stopping until he found his quarry.

The new petition, suing for desegregation of public schools in School District 22, was signed one year, one month, and seven days after the equalization petition had been signed at Harry Briggs's house on Armistice Day 1949. It was a direct challenge to two of South Carolina's legal directives. The first was Article II, Section 7, of the Constitution of South Carolina, which read, "Separate schools shall be provided for children of white and colored races, and no child of either race shall ever be permitted to attend a school provided for children of the other race." The second was Section 5377 of the Code of Laws, which declared, "It shall be unlawful for pupils of one race to attend the school provided by the Board of Trustees for persons of another race."

Of the twenty-nine families who signed the equalization petition, a few weakened under the economic pressure, but not one name had been removed. When the shift was made to desegregation, the few who weakened had their chance to escape. Of the required twenty signatures, the new petition had eighteen of the original names, and Harry Briggs's name was again first. One of the two new names was that of Gilbert Henry, a member of the hunting party my father located. A longtime supporter of the effort, Mr. Henry was the same man who had questioned the change of photographs in the Scott's Branch School.

The petition struck at the very heart of racial discrimination. If the courts agreed with the plaintiffs, the state would be forever enjoined from requiring schoolchildren to attend racially segregated schools. The way Rev. De Laine put it, "the feed roots of segregation were already being cut. Now the power-saw was starting to work on the taproot of segregation."

Civil Action No. 2657, the lawsuit for desegregation, was filed four days later. An Associated Press article, datelined December 22, announced, "The opening gun in what could be a long, drawn-out court fight, aimed at breaking down the traditional policy of segregation in the South Carolina public school system, was fired today." The article went on to say the "plaintiffs requested that a three-judge Federal Court be convened as soon as possible, and that sections of the state constitution of 1895 and statutes under which children of white and Negro races are segregated, be declared unconstitutional. . . . The action yesterday was not unexpected."

The new case was *Briggs et al. v. Elliott et al.* The same people were being sued, but the name of the lawsuit and the petitioners were slightly different. And the issue now being addressed had implications for American society far more profound and penetrating than any of the petitioners could have ever imagined.

Many black men and women in Clarendon County were instrumental in bringing the quest for equality to the courts, and the contributions of some will never be known. But the ones who signed their names at St. Mark AME Church on December 18, 1950—despite having already been victimized by the white community—are true American heroes whose names should be memorialized.

Susan Ida Oliver Lawson signed both petitions. Abandoned by her husband in 1940, Mis' Lawson was rearing her three children alone. She was a sharecropper, struggling to till the soil, plant the seeds, hoe the weeds, and harvest the crops. As a single mother, it was also her job to cut the wood, cook the meals, and wash the clothes. She eked out a barebones existence with help from loving relatives who lived nearby, but who had to tend their own households first. Mis' Lawson—probably believing that life couldn't get any worse—signed the petition with the hope that her children, or her children's children, would have an easier life than she had.

Her sister Onetha Oliver Bennett and her father, Frederick Oliver, guardian of some of his grandchildren, likewise signed both petitions. The family stuck together to see the lawsuit through to the end. Mr. Frederick's brother Mose "Nutta" Oliver was a handyman who lived rent free in a house on our property in exchange for helping my father with various tasks. Daddy deeded the small house to him when he had to dispose of his property. Like his relatives, Mr. Nutta signed both petitions.

Three more petitioners were members of a different Oliver clan. Lucrisher Oliver Richardson signed both the first and second petitions, as did her sister-in-law Mary Smythe Oliver and her brother-in-law Lee Richardson. The families of Mis' Lucrisher and Mr. Lee were tenants on the land of white men and, like most of the petitioners, earned their livelihood as farmers. Mis' Mary and her husband, on the other hand, owned Oliver's Café, a major node in the local black news grapevine. They were all threatened, and the time would come when each of their families would be "punished," but none of them wavered in the conviction that they had done the right thing.

Landowner Bennie Parson also signed both petitions. After he, his wife, and his daughter signed the equalization petition, Mr. Parson was often pushed to remove their names, but he was a man of strong convictions. Once he made a decision, he usually stuck to it—even in the face of adversity. After he signed, a white man with whom he had regularly played as a child warned Mr. Parson, "The white children'll be dressed better'n your young'un and your young'un'll be wearing shoes with holes in 'em." The farmer's firm reply was that he didn't send his daughter to school to get something on her feet, but to get something in her head.

James Bennett didn't sign the first petition although he had worked closely with the group and was a strong supporter almost from the beginning. Older than most of the other petitioners, he was the father of adult children. However, after the first petition was filed, he learned he was eligible to sign on behalf of grandchildren who lived with him. Delighted to give his support to the battle for equality, Mr. Bennett signed the *Briggs et al. v. Elliott et al.* petition, Civil Action No. 2657, with no hesitation.

Eleven of the Briggs plaintiffs at St. Mark AME Church, along with family members and supporters, 1951. Photographs of five more plaintiffs are inset in the upper left corner, and circles have been placed around the faces of all plaintiffs. Front row (plaintiffs' names are in bold): Maxine Gibson, **Mary Oliver,** Sarah Ragin, Celestine Parson, Katherine Briggs (small child), Eliza Briggs, **Rebecca Richburg,** Ester Fludd, Plummie Parson, **Annie Gibson.** Second row: **Robert Georgia, Edward Ragin,** Jessie Pearson's son (small child), **Gilbert Henry,** Harry Briggs, Jr., **Harry Briggs, James Bennett, Bennie Parson,** B. B. De Laine, **Lee Richardson.** Third row: **Gabriel Tindal,** Hammett Pearson, Levi Pearson, Jessie Pearson, Jessie Pearson's son. Fourth row: Charlotte Pearson, J. W. Seals, J. A. De Laine, E. E. Richburg. Insets, from the top left, are of **Susan Lawson, Hazel Ragin, Lucrisher Richardson, Henry Scott, Willie Stukes.** Plaintiffs not pictured are Onetha Bennett, Frederick Oliver, Mose Oliver, William Ragin. Photograph by E. C. Jones. Courtesy of the De Laine Family Collection

Gilbert H. Henry, a veteran of the First World War, was also older than most of the other petitioners. He was a farmer who supplemented his income by working as a carpenter and a trucker. The outspoken man had supported the effort from the beginning. Perhaps he didn't sign the equalization petition because it was uncertain whether he lived in School District 22. The issue must have been resolved by the time he was found in the forest, for the white physician's grandson was glad to become an official petitioner, like his cousin Edward "Bubba" Ragin and Mr. Bubba's nephew "Big" William Ragin.

Rebecca Richburg, a sister of Big William's wife, never considered having her name removed from the first petition. Perhaps the young boss for whom her husband worked didn't much care about threats from those with power in Summerton. Or perhaps the old boss, Mr. Josey, who had a genuinely warm feeling for the Richburgs, had not completely relinquished control of the blacksmith shop and had reached an age where he didn't fear bullies.

Whatever the case, neither man put any real pressure on Mis' Rebecca's husband. The last instruction that the younger boss gave to her husband on the subject was to keep running the shop as he wanted. However, the blacksmith would have to take responsibility for any bad debts incurred. John Hazel Richburg continued to extend credit. And sometimes he had to cover bad debts. With even more conviction and determination than she had the first time, Mis' Rebecca signed the second petition.

Henry Scott was the man who stirred the group to action on the night of June 8, 1949, a time that now seemed an eternity ago. The hardworking, upright gentleman was sharecropper, a pillar of his church, and, like the others, a United States citizen who wanted the best for his child. Perhaps because he lacked a formal education, Mr. Scott recognized and appreciated the value of education, cooperation, and organization. He steadfastly refused to be intimidated by Summerton's bullies and boldly put his name on the second petition.

Gabriel Tindal, another landowning farmer, had joined the Summerton effort early on. Because of the support he gave to the effort, he was considered one of the stalwarts of the group. Older than most of the petitioners, he signed on behalf of grandchildren who lived with him after their father had been killed in World War II. His signature, along with those of the remaining stalwarts—Robert Georgia and Hazel Ragin—was affixed to the desegregation petition, right along with the names of Annie Gibson, Willie "Bo" Stukes, and Harry Briggs. No amount of pressure would ever force any of this group to forsake their effort.

As with the equalization petition, Harry Briggs's name was first on the list of plaintiffs. R. W. Elliott, chairman of the District 22 school board, was the first of the listed defendants. The other defendants were the same white men named in the earlier equalization case—Messieurs Carson, Kennedy, McCord, Plowden, Baker, and Betchman. Although the name Elliott has been immortalized in a negative way, the man Elliott had every reason to believe in segregation. Born a mere eighteen years after the end of slavery, Mr. Elliott was taught from birth—by word and by example—to believe in the segregated way of life. So were his associates. They may—or may not—have also been taught racial hatred.

Mr. Elliott and the third board member, George Kennedy, probably did what was necessary to survive in Summerton. No mention of the personal negative involvement of either of these men seems to be on record in the effort of the Clarendon parents to achieve equality. The same is true of the two county board members, W. E. Baker and A. J. Plowden. They were probably more like the observers of a drama who suddenly found their names on the list of actors. The same cannot be said of defendants Carson, McCord, and Betchman, who—along with the lawyer Rogers and agriculture teacher Mills—seemed to have actively worked to keep the black people of Clarendon County from gaining educational equality for their children.

14. *Federal District Court*

Future historians cannot help but recognize there was
a judge—J. Waties Waring—whose decisions meant
much in correcting the evils political demagogues
had imposed upon society.
J. A. De Laine

T he plaintiffs and their supporters continued to wait, impatient for the trial
to be held and trying to manage in spite of their difficulties. And there were
difficulties. The worst was Bo Stukes's fate. Unable to find employment, the
dashingly handsome navy veteran had supported his family for more than a year
by using his backyard as a makeshift automobile garage. Then a freak accident
occurred less than a month after he signed the desegregation petition. The inad-
equately supported car on which he was working came loose from its moorings
and fell on him. Mr. Bo was dead when his oldest child found him. With five children and no means of support, Mis' Gardenia left Summerton, taking her children to join relatives in Philadelphia.

As for the lawsuit, Mr. Bo's death didn't change anything. His name, Willie
Stukes, remained on the petition. Even if it had been removed, there would have
still been nineteen others. Thurgood Marshall's insistence on having signatures of
adults from twenty families had ensured that the removal of any one person
would have no effect on the legal proceedings.

May 1951

Nevertheless a heaviness fell on Summerton's black community, and my father
went there as often as he could to help Rev. Richburg and Rev. Seals bolster the
plaintiffs' spirits. Ultimately, five months after the desegregation petition was
signed, the case was set to be heard on May 28, 1951, by the U.S. Eastern District
Court of South Carolina, Charleston Division, Third District. The Summerton
parents had done something truly unique. As a class-action case, the lawsuit did
not seek relief solely for the petitioners. It was the first time that a group of
American citizens had petitioned a United States federal court to abolish segregation in public schools with the claim that it violated the equal protection clause

of the Fourteenth Amendment. A ruling in their favor could apply to all public schools in America and to all children attending them.

Briggs et al. v. Elliott et al. was the third lawsuit my father had caused to be filed in federal court. The two earlier ones, the bus transportation case and the school equalization case, had been withdrawn before being heard. Now, finally, after all the successes and failures, the cooperation and noncooperation, the praise by well-wishers and abuse by enemies, the hopeful anticipation and deep despair, the day had come when the parents were to be represented in the courtroom. My father fervently prayed nothing would go wrong.

Early on the morning of the twenty-eighth, the people—their "heads bloody, but unbowed"—mobilized at St. Mark Church. They lined up where all could see the string of vehicles being loaded, bound for Charleston, seventy miles away, to witness the court proceedings. Instead of being downcast because they had been forced to move from their homes, because their debts had been called in at an unreasonable time, or because their mortgages had been foreclosed, they were bubbling with happiness. It had taken a long time to reach the milestone, but at long last it was happening.

Their action that morning was a stinging slap to their opponents. Although some had been threatened if they did not show up for work, they stubbornly took places in the lineup, more than willing to suffer the consequences of disobedience. The cavalcade formed as if it were a group of people were going to a picnic, although somewhat more sedate.

In battered cars and trucks, hundreds of black people made the pilgrimage. Their zeal and excitement was great, some of them never having been so far from home before. Along the way bystanders watched their progress. Some even joined the caravan. At the federal courthouse at the corner of Charleston's Broad and Meeting streets, ropes had to be used to keep the crowds back. Knowing how small the courtroom was, some Charleston residents who wanted to view the proceedings had arrived in early morning. The seats inside had been filled when the Summerton people arrived, and they weren't allowed to pass the ropes. Fortunately, however, the petitioners were allowed to enter when it was discovered who they were.

Rev. De Laine reported, "Not over twelve white people were in the overcrowded courtroom, but there were so many Negroes that many people couldn't even look in the door."

As people pushed to get a peek, somebody said, "Wait!"

Reflecting the mood and the deepest feelings of the crowd, an impatient voice boomed out, "I've been waiting all of my life."

The presiding judge was North Carolinian John J. Parker, senior judge of the Fourth U.S. Circuit Court of Appeals. Known as a "fair-minded and generous-spirited southerner," he was a fairly progressive man who favored change—but only if it came gradually. The other two judges were George Bell Timmerman,

Sr., and J. Waties Waring. Judge Timmerman presided over another of South Carolina's district courts. As an avowed segregationist and an outspoken advocate of white supremacy, he was the very antithesis of Judge Waring.

The people's anticipation and their lack of familiarity with the courtroom setting were obvious. At one point Judge Parker called for order but failed to get it. The bailiff tried to carry out the order, but he also failed. The judge finally resorted to asking Thurgood Marshall to request that the people be quiet.

People had come from quite far away to witness the trial. A man from Georgia who was sitting beside my uncle Lewis asked, "Show me the people from Clarendon County. I want to see how they look."

My uncle replied, "Why? You think they green? Or blue?"

The man said, "No. But I want to see how they look."

Uncle Lewis said, "They look like any other colored people."

The man responded, "But any niggers who will fight for their schools got to be different."

My uncle looked at the man. "I'm one of them. Half the people here are from Clarendon. Just look at me and any of the rest of these colored people and you will know how Clarendon County people look."

The shocked man said it made him very proud to see a group of black people who were brave enough to bring the white people to court. He offered encouragement with the words, "I sho' hope they win."

A battalion of lawyers from the NAACP's Legal Defense Fund represented the plaintiffs. Besides Mr. Boulware and Mr. Marshall, there were Robert Carter from New York, Spottswood Robinson, III, from Virginia, Arthur Shores from Alabama, and A. T. Walden from Georgia. They, in turn, had recruited an army of social science experts to testify about the adverse effects of segregation on child development.

The three lawyers for the defendants were Robert McC. Figg, Jr., T. C. Callison, and S. E. Rogers. Mr. Figg, the brilliant and thorough Charleston lawyer who had dreamed up the scheme to privatize the state's Democratic Party, headed the team. Mr. Callison was the state attorney general, and Mr. Rogers was the same self-important, little bulldog of a man from Summerton who had crafted the board's response to the plaintiffs' original petition. The defense team brought only three witnesses. One was E. R. Crow, newly appointed head of a recently formed State Educational Finance Commission. The other two witnesses were County Superintendent McCord, and R. W. Elliott, chairman of the District 22 School Board.

Mr. Crow was brought as a witness because of events occurring at the state level. During the previous year, staunch segregationist James F. "Jimmy" Byrnes had come out of semiretirement to run for governor. He was highly qualified for the post, having been a member of the U.S. House of Representatives, a member of the U.S. Senate, a justice of the U.S. Supreme Court, and a U.S. secretary of state. With his formidable political record and wealth of experience, Mr. Byrnes understood how the state's high illiteracy rates and abysmal educational system affected both the state and the entire nation adversely. He knew the state needed to spend more on education but was aware of the financial burden already placed on South Carolina's budget by the equalization of the salaries of black and white teachers.

Mr. Byrnes also recognized that the state's black citizens were becoming more aggressive in their demands for equality. With a degree of foresight and wisdom, he had made school improvement a part of his campaign platform, proposing that improvement of black schools would help preserve the "great institution" of segregation.

In 1948 a special state commission had studied ways of improving South Carolina's schools. The recommendations in its report were rejected as being too costly, but the young Ernest F. Hollings was appointed head of a committee to study ways of increasing tax revenue. The state's politicians then put the issue of school funding on the back burner. They had to deal with something they saw as being far more threatening: a report made by a national committee on civil rights that would have affected the practice of segregation.

Mr. Byrnes was elected as governor just before the pretrial hearing for the aborted Civil Action No. 2505. Although that lawsuit was withdrawn, he was aware of its implications. In his January 1951 inaugural address, the new governor recommended that South Carolina float $75 million in bonds to equalize schools and school facilities. Almost simultaneously Mr. Hollings's committee made its report to the legislature, recommending a 3 percent sales tax be levied to finance a school improvement program that included new buildings, increased teachers' pay, and implementation of a statewide school transportation system.

Urging immediate ratification of the sales-tax plan, the new governor proposed to devote most of the funds to improving black educational facilities. On April 19, 1951, the General Assembly approved the tax levy, and less than two weeks later the governor signed the bill. Almost immediately the State Educational Finance Commission was established to allocate the tax revenue, and E. R. Crow was appointed its director. It was in this capacity that the defense called Mr. Crow to the stand.

On the witness stand, Mr. Crow readily admitted inequality of the state's schools. In fact Mr. Figg had conceded the same thing about facilities in District 22 at the opening of the trial, a complete about-face from the "not guilty" plea originally entered. Although he had begun his preparations for the trial using the information supplied by Mr. Rogers, Mr. Figg was a meticulous lawyer who didn't rely on hearsay. He visited the Summerton schools and was appalled by vast inequities between the student facilities. No self-respecting lawyer would argue they were equal. So he decided it was best to admit the situation up front and to present plans for improvement. My father thought Mr. Figg's acknowledgment of the inequalities was a good lesson for Mr. Rogers "who had misrepresented the truth."

Mr. Crow testified that large sums of money would soon be spent to equalize the schools, with more than four hundred thousand dollars becoming available on July 1. As soon as the money was in hand, the Department of Education would begin building and improving facilities throughout the state. When asked a question about desegregation of students, the Educational Finance Commission's director unequivocally stated that integrated schools would not work in South Carolina and that black people did not want their schools to be desegregated.

Thurgood Marshall and his team were taken aback by the admissions of inequality. Their witnesses had stacks of evidence to disprove any claim of equality, but those carefully constructed presentations were useless with nothing to refute, and there was almost no opportunity to argue whether segregation violated the Fourteenth Amendment. Not that it, or any other evidence presented by the plaintiffs, would have mattered. Both Judge Waring and Judge Timmerman, with their strong and opposing opinions, undoubtedly knew how they were going to vote before the trial began. Most likely, Judge Parker also knew he wasn't going to shake the southern establishment's boat. The trial ended in a mere two days. The Clarendon County people went home, far more quietly than they came, wondering what would happen next.

June 1951

Not knowing when a verdict would be reached but confident that almost any decision would be a great step forward, NAACP members arranged a June 17 testimonial meeting to honor the plaintiffs. Fifteen hundred people came to Liberty Hill Church for the occasion. The speakers included John McCray, editor of the *Lighthouse and Informer,* as well as both the president and the secretary of the South Carolina Conference of NAACP Branches. Standing at the pulpit in a church designed and built fifty years earlier by my great uncle, Rev. De Laine gave an electrifying account of how the groundwork had been laid for the *Briggs* case and of the uphill journey the people of Summerton had endured. As he spoke, the fearlessness and determination that had characterized his leadership spread through the chamber, inspiring all who heard. From the moment he rose to speak until he sat again, rounds of applause reverberated around the auditorium.

Six days after the testimonial meeting—and one month after the Charleston trial—the district court rendered its decision. It was ruled that South Carolina's laws were not in violation of the Fourteenth Amendment, and on that basis the request to order the abolition of segregation was denied. However, the court did

June 17, 1951, testimonial meeting in Liberty Hill AME Church showing key local and state NAACP figures: (from the left) E. E. Richburg (secretary, Clarendon NAACP), Modjeska Simkins (secretary, state NAACP), J. W. Seals (treasurer, Clarendon NAACP), S. J. Montgomery (chair, executive committee of state NAACP), J. A. De Laine, Harry Briggs (plaintiff in Briggs), John McCray (editor, *Lighthouse and Informer*), J. S. Boyd (president, Clarendon NAACP), James N. Hinton (executive director, state NAACP), Eugene A. R. Montgomery (field secretary, state NAACP). Mr. Montgomery is presenting a merit award to Mr. Briggs. Photograph by E. C. Jones. Courtesy of the De Laine Family Collection

find that black students in Clarendon County had not been provided equal facilities and opportunities. To correct that condition, it was decreed that the schools must be equalized immediately and that the school authorities were to make a report concerning the actions taken in response to the directive within six months.

Rev. De Laine, displeased with the decision, said, "To me, granting the county six months to see if they are going to make progress is like granting a maid six months to see if she is going to give a baby the milk she hasn't been giving all along. Is it right for a judge to give a criminal time to continue his crimes?"

He was comforted, however, that the decision was not unanimous. An irate Judge Waring vehemently dissented and wrote a lengthy and scathing dissenting opinion in which he let no point go unchallenged. He summarized the reason for the lawsuit by stating, "This case was brought for the express and declared purpose of determining the right of the State of South Carolina, in its public schools, to practice segregation according to race."

He explained that "the plaintiffs allege they are denied equal educational facilities and opportunities and that this denial is based upon difference in race." Then he stated that, before the case was brought to trial, "The defendants . . . alleged that all facilities are adequate and equal." Judge Waring noted that at the beginning of the trial, the "defendants' counsel announced that they wished to [admit] inequalities in respect to buildings, equipment, facilities, curricula, and other aspects of the schools." This, he declared, was duplicitous.

He was distressed that his peers, two federal court judges charged with the obligation of dispensing justice, had allowed the defendants to file the statement of concession and to consider it as an amended answer to the charge. With their acceptance of the ploy, his colleagues had permitted the defendants to avoid the real issue that brought the case before the court.

By merely considering the case as another separate-but-equal case and failing "to meet the issues raised," he said, "the entire purpose and reason for the institution of the case and the convening of a three-judge court would be voided."

His dissenting opinion was a tour de force. Expounding on the consequences of irresponsible judicial action, he wrote, "If a case of this magnitude can be turned aside and a court refuses to hear these basic issues by the mere device of admission that some buildings, blackboards, lighting fixtures, and toilet facilities are unequal, but that they may be remedied by the spending of a few dollars, then, indeed people in the plight in which these plaintiffs are, have no adequate remedy or forum in which to air their wrongs."

And he foretold what would happen "if this method of judicial evasion be adopted." His words, written in 1951, predicted that, "these very infant plaintiffs now pupils in Clarendon County will probably be bringing suits for their children and grandchildren decades or rather generations hence in an effort to get for their descendants what are today denied to them."

He disagreed with giving the defendants time to address the existing problems for, "if [the plaintiffs] are entitled to any rights as American citizens, they are entitled to have these rights now and not in the future." And the reprimand he gave his colleagues for their disgraceful evasion of justice was blunt and strong. "We should be unwilling to straddle or avoid this issue, and if [this is] the type of justice to be meted out by this Court, then I want no part of it."

Judge Waring's dissenting opinion pointed out that "the United States adopted the 13th, 14th, and 15th Amendments . . . to wipe out completely the institution of slavery and to declare that all citizens in this country should be considered as free, equal, and entitled to all of the provisions of citizenship." With this in mind, he declared there was no need to study the many arguments and opinions concerning the meaning of the Fourteenth Amendment. As he wrote, a person "of ordinary ability and understanding of the English language will have no trouble in knowing that . . . this Amendment . . . was intended to do away with discrimination between our citizens."

He also addressed the concept of race, appropriately raising a series of thought-provoking questions concerning the assignment of individual human beings to specific races.

What possible definition can be found for the so-called white race, Negro race, or other races? Who is to decide and . . . what test are we going to use in opening our school doors and labeling them "white" and "Negro"? The law of South Carolina considers a person of one-eighth African ancestry to be a Negro. Why this proportion? Is it based upon any reason: anthropological, historical, or ethical?

If it is dangerous and evil for a white child to be associated with another child, one of whose great-grandparents was of African descent, is it not equally dangerous for one with a one-sixteenth percentage? And if the State has decided that there is danger in contact between the whites and Negroes, isn't it requisite and proper that the State furnish a series of schools one for each of these percentages? If the idea is perfect racial equality in educational systems, why should children of pure African descent be brought in contact with children of one-half, one-fourth, or one-eighth such ancestry?

He answered his questions very succinctly, writing, "To ask these questions is sufficient answer to them. The whole thing is unreasonable, unscientific, and based upon unadulterated prejudice."

Again and again the institution of racial segregation had been justified by citing the 1896 *Plessy v. Ferguson* decision. However, Judge Waring dismissed any such arguments, saying, "The reasoning . . . in [that case stemmed] almost completely from a decision . . . made many years before the Civil War when the Fourteenth Amendment had not even been dreamed of." Furthermore, he most appropriately pointed out, "we are not called upon to argue or discuss the validity of the *Plessy* case."

In commenting on the sad state of South Carolina's educational facilities, Judge Waring observed that the 1951 State Educational Act had just been adopted and that one of the witnesses for the defense, Mr. Crow, had been employed to "handle monies if and when the same are received sometime in the future." In criticizing the act, the judge noted, "nowhere is it specifically provided that there shall be equality of treatment between whites and Negroes in the school system." Clearly he was skeptical that the funds would be distributed equitably. He also noted that "there is no guarantee or assurance as to when the money will be available. As yet, no bonds have been printed or sold. No money is in the treasury. No allocation has been made [nor] application blanks . . . printed. Can we seriously consider this a bona-fide attempt to provide equal facilities for our school children?"

In summarizing his position, Judge Waring declared, "I am of the opinion that the system of segregation in education adopted and practiced in the State of South Carolina must go and must go now. *Segregation is per se inequality.* . . . If the courts of this land are to render justice under the laws without fear or favor, justice for all men and all kinds of men, the time to do it is now and the place is in the elementary schools where our future citizens learn their first lesson to respect the dignity of the individual in a democracy."

The closing words of the opinion, the last official opinion Judge Waring would write, were, "I had hoped that this Court would . . . make a clear cut declaration that the State of South Carolina should follow the intendment and meaning of the Constitution of the United States [and] not abridge the privileges accorded to or deny equal protection of its laws to any of its citizens. But since the majority of this Court feel otherwise, . . . this opinion is filed as a dissent."

15. *Verdicts*

No question is ever settled until it is settled right.
ELLA WHEELER WILCOX

Determined to prevent the horrifying situation of a six-year-old black boy sitting at a desk next to a six-year-old white girl, South Carolina's lawmakers moved rapidly to equalize school facilities. Proceeds from a newly approved 3 percent sales tax financed a massive school improvement program. Less than six months after Governor Byrnes took office, Mr. Crow and his colleagues on the Educational Finance Commission had laid the groundwork for a remarkable building program—one to which the state would ultimately commit $100 million for constructing and improving schools over the next three years. One of the commission's first successes was the consolidation of more than 1,000 school districts into fewer than 125 and, in the process, dispensing with many small rural schools by building a number of larger, more centrally located ones.

AUGUST–OCTOBER 1951

In an August 1951 speech at the University of South Carolina, Mr. Crow tried to make some white teachers understand the need for a $75 million bond and the new sales tax. The program his commission was overseeing, he said, "constitutes nothing less than an 'Educational Revolution.' It is the kind of revolution we must have because we have had neither the wisdom nor the statesmanship to solve our problem by evolution." He then described another revolution that was occurring simultaneously, "a 'Sociological Revolution' forced upon us by necessity to avoid the effect of possible adverse Federal Court decisions."

The self-acknowledged segregationist revealed himself to also be a realist by saying, "In achieving the objectives of this program, we . . . must pay for stately mansions built by the labor of slaves. We must pay double for our years of neglect. And we must pay, too, for the devastating effect on our state of all the leather-lunged demagogues who have ridden into office by whooping up the race issue. We-shall-have-to-pay-until it hurts."

On a different occasion Mr. Crow said the same thing in another way, but he was more specific about how the money would be used: "We must pay for the

The Lee Elementary School was one of several one-room schools in Clarendon County. Almeta De Laine (the wife of a distant relative of Rev. De Laine) conducted classes in this building for many years until 1951, after which it was abandoned. Courtesy of the De Laine Family Collection

inequalities administered under the pretense of Separate-But-Equal; we must pay for the transportation of Negro school children which formerly have been neglected; we must pay for the replacement of the miserable buildings; and new modern buildings must be built out of this money."

Even though South Carolina's educational revolution proceeded rapidly, the NAACP was not going to settle for a stopgap solution. Its freedom fighters had no intention of abandoning *Briggs* and its challenge to the institution of segregation. In July, one month after the district court delivered its verdict, the NAACP's Legal Defense Fund filed an appeal. As a constitutional challenge, *Briggs*—the case that came out of Clarendon—was able to go directly to the U.S. Supreme Court, bypassing the court of appeals and becoming the first challenge to public school segregation to reach the nation's highest court. Other lawsuits making similar challenges were not far behind.

The Kansas case was already in the pipeline. It involved a group of parents who were unhappy, not because their schools were inferior, but because their children had to walk past white schools to reach their assigned black schools. The secretary of the NAACP's Topeka branch had written to the New York headquarters in August 1950 to say the group was ready to test the segregation law in court. The request had been put aside. Only after Judge Waring dismissed the equalization case from Clarendon County was the request reviewed. Satisfied that the Topeka complaint would make a strong case (and that it would attract donations), the legal team filed *Brown et al. v. Board of Education of Topeka* in the U.S. District Court of Kansas in February, two months after *Briggs* was filed. On August 3, 1951, the three-judge district court in Kansas unanimously denied the *Brown* plaintiffs the relief for which they had prayed.

Meanwhile, in Clarendon the *Benson* slander case still dogged Rev. De Laine. Although his fine was slashed to $2,700 on appeal, it still went unpaid. His adversaries must have been very displeased; they had boasted of how they would break him and make him pay the costs of the parents' petition, yet he had paid nothing and did not seem to be suffering. An effort was made to attach his property, but the Clarendon County sheriff could locate no property in J. A. De Laine's name. The judgment was declared *nulla bono*—a Latin term meaning no property was found that could be seized to satisfy the judgment.

The instigators of the slander lawsuit were not willing to accept that result, so a second court action was initiated to contest the transfers of my father's property. To their consternation, the judge ruled the transfers were legal. When it became clear that the only way of possibly collecting damages was through an involved legal effort, something finally happened that really hurt Daddy financially. Something very suspicious.

Our Summerton house and two outbuildings, structures that were all less than sixty feet outside the town limit, were completely destroyed by fire in the same month that the Kansas segregation case, *Brown,* was appealed to the Supreme Court. With our family living in Lake City and the house no longer being guarded by supporters, a fire roared through the house on the night of October 10. The town's firemen, dressed for firefighting, arrived and parked their fire truck. Refusing to fight the fire because the house was outside the town limits, they watched the flames lick skyward, engulfing and consuming everything inside the house: our stored furniture, my cousin's mortuary materials, and my aunt's household goods. The firemen watched until nothing remained except the masonry of the chimneys and the porch.

The fire was said to be mysterious, and speculation was rife whether the fire had a bearing on my father's role in the desegregation case. An official report later confirmed what we already knew: the fire was caused by arson. Rumors implicated a man whom Rev. De Laine had helped many times, but who always needed money because of an alcohol problem. He is said to have burned his benefactor's home for a small payment of less than the proverbial thirty pieces of silver.

Nearly two years earlier, when the deed for our house was transferred to Dr. Adams's name, my father had also tried to transfer the insurance. However, the insurance broker, a Summerton man, wouldn't make the change. Because the insurance was still in my father's name, the court was able to attach the entire insurance payment for the destroyed property, even though it was several times

Members of the De Laine family standing on remains of the family's Summerton home, October 10, 1951: (from the left) J. A., Mattie, Joseph Jr., Ophelia, and Brumit B. De Laine. At the top of the small hill, approximately at the center of the photograph, was the home of Harry and Eliza Briggs. Scott's Branch School was behind the photographer, on the other side of the road. Photograph by E. C. Jones. Courtesy of the De Laine Family Collection

greater than the fine. Both our home and the payment for its loss were gone. Mr. Benson's backers had finally succeeded in making the preacher pay.

But J. A. De Laine was not ruined. Every square foot of the several hundred acres of land he owned, except the two small parcels that he gave away, was still safely in the names of trusted relatives and friends.

DECEMBER 1951–MARCH 1952

The NAACP lawyers immediately appealed the ruling handed down by the district court for the Kansas lawsuit, *Brown et al. v. Board of Education.* That case arrived at the Supreme Court three months after the case that came out of Clarendon. However, no action had been taken on the *Briggs* appeal. The six months that the defendants had been given to file a progress report was not yet up, so, technically, *Briggs* was still being litigated in the lower court.

On December 20, with three days to spare, their lead attorney, Mr. Figg, submitted the report. Satisfied with claims made by the defendants, Judge Parker wrote an open-ended, inconsequential order instructing the defendants to file additional reports at later dates. Judge Waring obstinately refused to sign the order because it was simply a delaying tactic that could be stretched out indefinitely. So, on January 8, 1952, Judge Parker simply forwarded the report to the Supreme Court, making no final disposition of the case.

Twenty days later the Supreme Court—perhaps reluctant to address the issue of segregation—vacated the district court's prior decisions and sent *Briggs* back to it, asking the lower court to take any action deemed appropriate in light of the report, and to give its views on the case. The case for which Rev. De Laine had worked so unrelentingly was completely removed from the Supreme Court's docket. *Briggs* would have to begin its journey to the highest court of the land all over again.

The case was reheard in district court on March 3, almost three years after the public meeting that advertised the equalization effort. This time, however, there was no voice to speak for common sense and fairness—Judge Waring had resigned his post. Sitting in judgment on the circuit court with Judges Parker and Timmerman was Judge Armistead M. Dobie. Judge Parker again presided as the defendants presented a supplementary report of equalization steps taken since December. Ten days after the hearing, the three judges issued a unanimous verdict stating, "Beyond question . . . [the] defendants have proceeded promptly and in good faith to comply with the court's decree."

The judges were correct, the defendants were complying with the decree. Accomplishments in Clarendon County included the consolidation of District No. 22 with several other districts and the appropriation of money to construct modern school buildings. Plans for two new elementary schools had been approved and contracts let for their rapid completion. Another contract had been let to convert the existing Scott's Branch building into an elementary school. A new district high school for black children, already 40 percent completed, would be ready for occupancy by August. These building projects for the consolidated district would involve the expenditure of $516,960 to "unquestionably make the school facilities afforded Negroes within the district equal to those afforded white persons."

There were other changes. Teachers' salaries in the district had been equalized by local supplement, as should have been done earlier. The curriculum had also been equalized, bus transportation instituted, and $21,522.81 spent for furniture and equipment in the black schools. Students would no longer have to sit on boards suspended between two chairs. The lower court's verdict concluded with the approving statement, "The State of South Carolina is earnestly and in good faith endeavoring to equalize educational opportunities for Negroes."

April–October 1952

Some people blamed the governor for South Carolina's new sales tax, calling it "Jimmy's tax." However, a *Lighthouse and Informer* reporter found that white merchants in Clarendon County called it "De Laine's tax." Schoolchildren at Scott's Branch went even further, calling the school buses "Rev. De Laine's buses" and their new school building the "De Laine Building."

The feverish effort to equalize the schools brought unparalleled and fundamental changes to the schooling of South Carolina's children. A mere two and a half years after S. E. Rogers and the school trustees reported that black schools in District 22 were better than the white ones, all three of those old black school buildings had been abandoned or renovated. By the end of October, every black child in lower Clarendon County would attend school in a modern building, and bus transportation would be provided for those who needed it. District 22, along with Districts 5 and 26—the districts that caused the confusion in the *Pearson* bus case—had ceased to exist.

Five years after Rev. De Laine asked Hammett and Levi Pearson about suing for bus transportation, the youngest Pearson children rode on a public school bus to a consolidated school that was equipped with indoor toilets and water fountains, as well as being maintained by a janitor. They were among the first black students in the state's history that rode to school via publicly funded transportation. And it wasn't just people in Clarendon County who benefited. Throughout the state the construction of new schools was the order of the day, and school buses took children to black schools.

Many black people in the state thought the improvements were due to the generosity of their "good" school officials. In this regard Daddy wrote, "Some who sat on their 'do nothing seat' said, 'It had to come.'" Knowing better, he commented that they were wrong in that "things don't just happen, you've got to make them happen."

As welcome and as long overdue as the changes were, the schools could never be equal as long as segregation existed. The discontent simmering in Summerton had broken free, and from out of Clarendon came a demand from a people ravenous for freedom from repression, single-minded in their determination to break free of the status of second-class citizenship, and implacable in their challenge to enforced school segregation. By the time May came and *Briggs* began its second journey to the Supreme Court, the *Brown* case had already been docketed. On June 9 the Court placed the two cases together, with *Brown* as the lead case, and scheduled oral arguments for the beginning of the Supreme Court's 1952 fall term.

Perhaps in deference to the impending national election, the hearings were postponed. By that time the NAACP's Legal Defense Fund had appealed a third segregation case to the Supreme Court. The district court in Virginia had heard *Davis et al. v. County School Board of Prince Edward County, Virginia, et al.* in February and decided it in March. The decision was appealed in July. The NAACP's team now had three cases, from three different states, that addressed the issue of whether public school segregation infringed on Fourteenth

Amendment rights in the Supreme Court. Thurgood Marshall and his associates made a motion for *Davis* to be argued along with *Briggs* and *Brown*. The motion was granted.

December 1952–December 1953

With arguments for *Briggs, Brown,* and *Davis* scheduled for its first session in December 1952, the Supreme Court took notice of still another segregation case. This one was pending in the District of Columbia's Circuit Court of Appeals. Since the District of Columbia is not in a state, the lawsuit, *Bolling et al. v. Sharpe et al.,* could not claim infringement of Fourteenth Amendment rights. Therefore, unlike in the other three cases, *Bolling's* lawyers were arguing that segregation deprived them of due process of law as guaranteed under the Fifth Amendment. At the request of the high court's justices, *Bolling* was moved to the Supreme Court's docket and scheduled for argument immediately following *Brown, Briggs,* and *Davis.*

Less than a month before the four cases were to be argued, the attorney general of Delaware appealed a pair of segregation cases that he had lost to NAACP lawyers in his state's supreme court. His appeal to the United States Supreme Court was granted. However, to the Delaware lawyer's displeasure, the case—*Gebhart et al. v. Belton et al.*—was scheduled for hearing along with the NAACP's cases. Thus, a total of four Fourteenth Amendment cases were to be heard consecutively. The single Fifth Amendment case would be heard immediately thereafter.

The hearing dates were scheduled for December 9–11, 1952, with *Brown* being first on the docket. Perhaps it was thought that, since Kansas was not in the Deep South, the listing would make the nation understand that segregation was not solely a southern issue. The decision was probably a good public relations move, but it doomed the case that came out of Clarendon to obscurity and ensured that *Briggs* would not be hailed as the case that ended segregation.

The hearing proceeded according to plan and by a stroke of luck, my father—the man responsible for starting it all—got into the courtroom to witness the proceedings of the trial of the century. But like everyone else, he would have a long wait for a verdict. During posthearing deliberations, the justices asked for clarification of certain questions before they would try to come to a decision. They restored all five cases to the Supreme Court's docket, and the lawyers would have to reargue them on December 9, 1953.

Rev. De Laine also had the opportunity to witness the Court's second round of deliberations. He recalled, "When the 'Nine Old Men' filed into the courtroom, there was a new face in the center. This was not the face which looked as solid as a stone, but a smiling face of one who felt his presence would be a blessing in the court. It appeared [that] all the old justices graciously accepted him as chief."

The chief justice who had presided at the first hearings, Fred M. Vinson, was no longer among the living. His replacement, Earl Warren, inherited a deeply

divided Court. My father's observation suggests that the associate justices had readily accepted Chief Justice Warren as a conciliator.

As *Briggs* and the other desegregation cases became national news, people throughout the country became curious about Summerton, the unknown back-woods town whose black citizens dared to challenge the institution of segregation. Carl Rowan, a reporter from the *Minneapolis Morning Tribune,* came to Summerton and interviewed a number of individuals. Rev. Seals's statement to him succinctly explained the motives of the plaintiffs. "We ain't asking for anything that belongs to these white folks. I just mean to get everything for that little boy of mine that any other South Carolina boy gets."

Other investigators reported that some black people were happy with the status quo. However, when Mr. Rowan questioned Gilbert Henry about that, Mr. Henry patiently said, "Listen mister, let me explain. There are Uncle Toms and belly draggers. Nobody fit to bear the name Negro is for segregation. What Negro . . . is satisfied when he is half naked as a jay bird?"

During a speech at St. Mark Church, my father addressed the idea that black people were in favor of segregation. He asked his audience, "Isn't it hypocrisy when a person of the Anglo-Saxon race takes a reporter to a Negro and asks him if he wants his children to mix with the white children? Doesn't any sane person know that if the Negro says yes, reprisals will soon be taken?"

As *Briggs* achieved recognition, outsiders sought to be in the limelight that accompanied the case. They began pushing Rev. De Laine, Rev. Seals, and the Pearsons into the background. As these undeserving people tried to take credit for the genesis of *Briggs,* facts were distorted and conflicting statements made—even in strategic places. Displeased with what was happening, Clarendon's NAACP members decided to emphasize the pivotal and vital role that Rev. De Laine had played in all events leading to the filing of *Briggs.* Key facts about the case were published, along with references to reprisals inflicted on people and to my father's financial losses. A last entry in the list noted that, instead of dampening determination, the reprisals had served "to stir the fighting spirit."

May 17, 1954

More than five months passed following reargument of the desegregation cases with no word from the Supreme Court. Then, around 1:00 P.M. on May 17, 1954, with almost no advance notice, Chief Justice Warren announced that a decision had been reached. My father observed, "The long awaited Supreme Court decision—which had kept us in a [state of] high tension from eagerness for a favorable decision and [which was responsible for] the insults and reprisals we had undergone for at least six years—was handed down." A single verdict was delivered for the four Fourteenth Amendment cases, followed immediately by a verdict for the Fifth Amendment case.

The Court had unanimously decided that "separate educational facilities are inherently unequal," that "segregation is a denial of the equal protection of the laws," and that, "in the field of public education, the doctrine of 'separate but equal' has no place." In other words the "nine old men" had declared that segregation based on race was illegal and had to go.

Immediately all five cases—which would collectively become known as *Brown v. Board*—were restored to the docket. A decision needed to be made about how the defendants should proceed in view of the verdicts before a directive could be issued.

The announcement was big news, and, as Rev. De Laine observed, the decree "was destined to change the educational, political, and social course of the nation." Major coverage was given to the verdict by the national news media. *Newsweek*'s assessment was typical: "The Supreme Court this week smashed the last of the legal barriers that stood for generations between white and Negro Americans. . . . It was the most momentous court decision in the whole history of the Negro's struggle to achieve equal rights in the United States and the result will be nothing short of a social upheaval."

Not everyone voiced approval of the decisions. Unsurprisingly some white people sadly called the day "Black Monday." Others—like E. E. Colvin, pastor of Immanuel Baptist Church in Florence, South Carolina—tried to use their stature as community leaders to maintain the status quo. "If our Negro friends will listen to reason and continue the practice of segregation on a voluntary basis, we can have peace and harmony, but, just as surely as you live, if we permit the spirit of hatred to dominate our thinking and our conduct, we can bring on something that will do as much damage in the long run as the War Between the States did a hundred years ago."

Although both men were Christian ministers, Rev. De Laine and Rev. Colvin had totally different philosophies, having experienced life in totally different ways. Perhaps even the God they worshiped was not quite the same one. That would not have been surprising because the religious practices of many white Christians indicated that black people went to a different heaven after death and that they got there through different pearly gates.

On hearing the Supreme Court's verdict, my father recalled, "I sprang to my feet and went to Green's Funeral Home to see if they had heard the news. On my way, I saw many red-faced people who said there would be another civil war before integration happens."

June 1954–March 1955

South Carolina's educational revolution was almost complete by the time the U.S. Supreme Court made its iconoclastic ruling. Hundreds of schools—such as those at Liberty Hill, Spring Hill, and Silver—that once served South Carolina's black children had been abandoned. The little Bob Johnson School, just beyond the

Pearson place, had closed more than ten years before the South Carolina educational revolution began. But others, equally disgraceful, had continued to operate until South Carolina's attempt to save segregation permanently shuttered their doors. By 1954 the new Scott's Branch High School building had been occupied for a year and a half.

Dotting the state were 2,500 brand new classrooms in 200 hastily constructed, consolidated schools that served mostly—but not exclusively—black children. White schools were also improved. Every county in the state now had a modern school building for black students that cost at least two hundred thousand dollars. The rural students who attended those schools were transported by public school buses. I doubt that any thinking person mourned the loss of the shacks that had served too many of the state's children. Rev. De Laine observed, "Satisfaction had come to those who were the subjects of discrimination, but justice was delayed."

Rev. Richburg became principal of a new high school in Orangeburg County. My mother and the rest of the elementary school teachers at Lake City Colored School moved their classes into the former high school building where they enjoyed more space and better facilities. BB had the privilege of spending his senior year at the brand new Carver High School. In a mere four years, South Carolina's educational revolution—spurred and goaded into being because of Rev. De Laine's efforts—had directly touched the lives of more South Carolinians than had the American Revolution of 1776.

Rev. De Laine had dreamed that someday black children would attend schools with proper heating and enough classroom space, but the new buildings were beyond his wildest dreams. As he watched the blossoming of the new edifices, he had no regrets for his losses. It mattered not one whit that he would never teach in one of them.

With Jay and me already in college, only BB would ever walk the halls of one of those schools as a student. That, too, was all right with my father. It wasn't for us that he had fought so long and hard, that he had put himself in a position where men tried to silence him by any possible means. It was for all children—the ones whose guardians had signed the petition, the ones whose parents could neither read nor write, the ones whose fathers had fought in foreign lands for rights they themselves were denied, the ones whose mothers cooked for people who wouldn't sit next to them, and the ones whose families had never learned to hope. It was for the children of the oppressed—as well as for the children of the oppressors. To him the new school buildings were signs of hope for all generations to come, for the descendants of heroes, scoundrels, leaders, handkerchief heads, belly draggers, educational and political gangsters, and even white supremacists.

Each of the hundreds of new yellow school buses needed a driver. High school boys, black and white—who were at least sixteen years old, 5 feet 2 inches tall, and over 110 pounds—were hired to do the job for their respective segregated schools. Having driven a variety of vehicles along narrow, rutted backcountry roads and over shaky wooden bridges, the teenagers were usually well experienced. After taking and passing a three-day bus driver training course, they each earned a salary of twenty-five dollars a month, regardless of length of the route or number of riders on the bus.

In September 1954, BB (weighing 111 pounds) was certified to have his own bus route—one of thirteen for the Lake City colored schools. His route covered approximately forty-nine miles, and more than one hundred students often packed themselves into his fifty-six-passenger bus. It made Daddy profoundly happy to see his son in the driver's seat of a school bus. For that bus to be filled beyond capacity with black boys and girls suffused him with a sense of fulfillment. The loss of his job, his home, and his money paled in comparison to what he had succeeded in helping to gain for so many.

On March 15, 1955, the state superintendent of education pompously itemized the tremendous educational strides the state had made from 1944 to 1954. The long article in Columbia's *State* newspaper reported that the value of the state's school buildings had almost doubled between 1951 and 1955 and that school enrollments quintupled since 1944. The number of buses and the number of students transported had practically doubled since the state began paying the total cost of transportation in 1951. It is noteworthy that the article failed to make any association between the *Briggs* case that came out of Clarendon and the educational advances, or between improved educational opportunities for black children and increased enrollment.

April–May 1955

Although the Supreme Court had ruled that segregation must go, the task of desegregating the schools of the Deep South was daunting. The problem of how to enforce the Court's ruling created complex problems. Ultimately the Court convened, April 11–14, 1955, to address the various problems. It was then that S. E. Rogers—the school board's lawyer—declared to the venerable justices of the highest court in the United States of America something to the effect that "the white people are not going to have any Negroes going to their school."

Incredulous, Justice Frankfurter asked if he meant to say that the Supreme Court's order would not be obeyed. Mr. Rogers answered that was exactly what he meant.

It was probably in recognition of such belligerence that the Supreme Court equivocated when it issued its final decree on May 31, 1955. In essence the court passed the buck and remanded the task of accomplishing school desegregation to the district courts. The directive given was for the district courts to do whatever was "necessary and proper to admit the parties to these cases to public schools on a racially nondiscriminatory basis *with all deliberate speed.*" That ruling is perhaps the only one in the history of the U.S. Supreme Court that allowed justice to be executed at the convenience of the guilty party.

JULY 1955

The Fourth Circuit Court of Appeals met on July 15 in Columbia to consider the directive. Eager to see what would be done about the Supreme Court's decree, Rev. De Laine went to the hearing over which Judge Parker presided. According to my father, the judge announced, "The Supreme Court has reversed our decision and declared segregation unconstitutional in the public schools. [It has] said you can't segregate the races. But it did not say you have to mix them."

4
After 1955

16. *New Evil*

O God, the heathen have defiled thy holy temple
PSALM 79:1 (VARIATION)

For five years our family enjoyed life in Lake City. The community enveloped us with warm acceptance, and the town truly became our home. Rev. De Laine still journeyed to Summerton occasionally, but other than overseeing the farm, his work in Clarendon was finished. Still a good shepherd to his flock, he frequented the byways of Lake City and surrounding farms—always dressed in suit and tie or clerical collar—spreading good cheer, teaching, and ministering to the lost and the saved, the hopeless and the happy, the illiterate and the educated.

AUGUST–SEPTEMBER 1955

The summer of 1955 moved along pretty much as we expected. My mother enjoyed a well-earned vacation from teaching. My brother Jay, drafted into the U.S. Army immediately after college graduation, was serving our country as a medic in far away Korea. Eighteen-year-old BB had just graduated from high school. He had a summer job driving a charter bus, legal for someone so young because of a technical loophole. He was often away from home. I was nineteen and would return to college for my junior year in mid-September.

My father avidly read the newspapers, listened to the radio, and discussed local, national, and world events with anyone he could. He was aware that diehard segregationists across the South were displeased with the Supreme Court's decisions and that some influential southern men eagerly worked to stir up hatred. Under the guise of patriotism, they denounced the Supreme Court and tried to discredit the NAACP by accusing it of brainwashing African Americans. Daddy was dismayed by Judge Parker's statement during the 1955 district court hearing, which had added fuel to the segregationists' rage and undermined the intentions of people previously willing to accept the decision. The Supreme Court had called for "all deliberate speed," and the segregationists had interpreted that as meaning "never."

Bent on continuing to deny black people their constitutional rights, segregationists organized themselves to resist the court order. The mainstream news media in the South willingly provided excellent avenues for the dissemination of anti-desegregation propaganda. Facts were misrepresented and any point that could be used to discredit black people or liberal white people was magnified. As if the presence of black and white children in the same classroom were undemocratic and could destroy the nation, claims were made that "Communists are trying to make us integrate."

Bitter in his defeat, S. E. Rogers looked for a way to preserve segregation, white supremacy, and the "honored southern way of life." He found his Rosetta stone in Mississippi. During the summer of 1954, rebellion against the *Brown* decision had given birth in that state to an organization whose members were determined to "keep the Negro in his place." Known as the White Citizens Council (WCC), the organization and its members were dedicated to crushing any leadership that advocated integration. Their goal was to apply economic pressure to "troublemakers" who advocated compliance with the *Brown* decision.

Enlightened in WCC techniques of terrorism by economic pressure, Mr. Rogers returned to Summerton fired with missionary zeal. He began to travel extensively around the state, organizing local councils and working to gain the support of South Carolina's leading citizens. Under his guidance, WCC chapters proliferated throughout South Carolina's predominately black areas. Its membership is said to have grown to include almost all leading white men—grocers, farmers, bankers, mayors, doctors, and lawyers. Men who never would have deigned to join the Ku Klux Klan—businessmen, civic figures, and religious leaders—were willingly recruited. Because membership soon included the men who served as policemen, judges, and government servants, the WCC was the law. Anyone who dared defy "the Council" was destined for disaster. And any member of the NAACP was a marked person.

Under Mr. Roger's expert tutelage, WCC members learned how to put the economic squeeze on people. Recalcitrant black tenants were to be evicted from their homes. Teachers who belonged to the NAACP were to be fired. Credit was not to be extended. White shopkeepers were forbidden to serve certain black customers. Goods were not supposed to be delivered to black stores. Only the bravest and most humane white people dared to break the rules lest they, too, suffer. The few white suppliers who helped "troublemaker" shopkeepers had to do so covertly, dropping off supplies in isolated places.

In August 1955, Mr. Rogers succeeded in organizing a White Citizens Council in Clarendon County. One of its founders was the county's superintendent of education, L. B. McCord—the same man who had testified against Rev. De Laine in the *Benson* trial. Then, intent on spreading the venom of hatred and the gospel of economic reprisal, WCC missionary Rogers made his way out of Clarendon to our town in Florence County.

On the night of August 26, Mr. Rogers held an organizational meeting in Lake City that was attended by several hundred white men. Rev. De Laine did not find out exactly who was present or exactly what was said. However, word got back to him that the lawyer had advised the assembly, "The nigger preacher y'all are feeding is the real backbone of the desegregation movement. Y'all got to get rid of him before y'all can stop the others."

That was when life changed for our family. That very night the night riders took to their cars, obeying Mr. Rogers's advice. Three of us—my mother, my father, and I—were in the house when the ketchup bottle hit. Startled, we went to the front porch to see what had happened. Red sauce was splattered on the wall and on a rocking chair. Pieces of glass and orange peels were on the floor. No real harm was done, and none of our property was broken. My mother surveyed the mess and attributed the act to "some crazy person." I naively wondered why anyone would do such a thing. If my father suspected any serious foul play, he didn't show it, but he did report the deed to the police.

Real terror against Rev. De Laine had begun. As he observed, "When Bishop Reid sent me to Lake City using his 'Godly Judgment,' he didn't foresee the low, undermining strategy of the Summerton lawyer who failed a total of six times to stop the Negro's quest for justice in courts of law. He hadn't seen the egotistical racist becoming executive secretary of the White Citizens Council in a desperate attempt to preserve segregation [and keep] the scales of justice unbalanced. Bishop Reid couldn't even see how that smug bigot would influence the minds of some white people to become as bent on destroying Negroes' aspirations for first class citizenship—and with as little remorse—as a wolf that kills a rabbit for a meal."

A careful man who was determined he would never be the rabbit, Rev. De Laine still maintained the habit of keeping his guns greased and his "powder dry," ready for use if needed.

Four nights after Mr. Rogers's visit, the night riders struck again, this time breaking a living-room window. BB was at home that night. He reported the vandalism at the Lake City police station. The supposed enforcers of law and order listened indifferently. Then one of the uniformed men snidely asked, "You sure that wasn't your Daddy's car?"

Some policemen came and thoroughly examined the scene. They carefully picked up every shard of glass from the broken window—"to be taken back to the station for fingerprint examination." When BB pointed to some very clear tire prints beside the road, the lawmen suddenly spotted a "speeder," jumped into their squad car and sped away, destroying the tire prints.

After that we began to be extra careful. We closed our window shades early in the evening and never went near a window at night if the lights were on.

One evening around that time, Rev. De Laine stopped at a filling station. A sharecropper signaled him from the shadows to give a warning, "They say you the backbone of the school segregation suit 'n they gonna git you out of the way. I'm telling you, Rev., you better watch out for yourself and don't stay 'round in no public places 'cause Mr. Floyd say they gonna run you from here. Or else bury you." The man was scared, constantly looking around, alert to notice if anyone was watching. "He said you was on the TV and that you the one suing the state." For a man whose livelihood—such as it was—depended on the whims of an angry segregationist, the sharecropper's action was nothing short of heroic.

The third time the night riders struck was during the day. At noon on Saturday, September 3, several cars passed our Lake Street residence and the adjacent church parking lot. With their occupants making a lot of noise, the cars turned at the corner onto Church Street and headed toward town. One of the cars, a Buick, returned a few minutes later, and its occupants threw a barrage of rocks at our house.

Perhaps my father had foreseen that the harassment was going to continue and was mentally prepared. He and BB immediately jumped into our car and chased the Buick to get the license plate number. The car, carrying five white men, moved slowly, and he had no trouble in overtaking it. Once Daddy had the license number, E 10-472, he drove more than twenty miles to file a report at the sheriff's office in Florence.

The reception he got there was similar to the one BB had gotten in Lake City the first time we complained. A policeman disdainfully recorded the complaint, telling Rev. De Laine, "Preacher, I think you need glasses. You can't see well enough to copy a correct license number."

Meanwhile the Buick returned and stopped near the parsonage. Seeing it, my mother quickly got pencil and paper to record the license plate number, which was E 10-472. She sent me to the Lake City police station to report the matter. I walked the three-quarters of a mile to the station and was back home before my father returned.

Rev. De Laine didn't come straight home. He, too, went to the Lake City police station to make a report. The officer on duty interrupted him, saying, "Why you making such a big thing of it? That's the same thing that gal of yours reported awhile ago. You scared she didn't come down here?"

Nevertheless the county sheriff came to the parsonage along with the Lake City police chief to investigate. Refusing an invitation to enter the house, they asked the three of us to sit in the back seat of the squad car. While we were there, Mother declared, "If they don't let us alone, I'm personally going to shoot 'em."

Rev. De Laine recognized the folly of her words and quickly interjected, "Oh, no. We don't want to do that."

Ignoring him, Police Chief Maxie Hinds turned to Mother, saying, "I don't blame you. I'd shoot 'em myself."

Having a good idea of the law concerning the protection of property, Rev. De Laine calmly told the chief, "If I shoot them, you would be the first to arrest me. Isn't it illegal to shoot anybody on the street or in a public road?"

"Well, now," Chief Hinds drawled, "That's another thing." He paused, and then brightened to say, "But if they come on the property, you can shoot 'em."

At perhaps twenty feet from the house, Lake Street was much closer to my parents' bedroom than most parts of the church's property. Acutely aware of this, my father commented, "They don't need to come on the parking lot to hurt us."

The police chief didn't let that reality stymie him. Instead he helpfully suggested, "You could shoot to mark the car." Giving justification for that course of action, he said, "The number you gave us is a dealer's number. So many people try cars out that the wrong person could be apprehended. Now, if the car was marked when it got back to the dealer's place . . ."

The next few days brought more drive-bys with yelling and gunfire. After each occasion Rev. De Laine reported the incident to the police. Except for the time when one of the officers said, "Ah axed them boys not to do that," the police tried to accuse BB of being the perpetrator. Told that my brother was not in town, the law officers would ask, "How about the church members?" Or they would dismissively say, "Oh well, it's just so many NAACP members doing these things."

In small towns little events usually make big news. Thinking newspaper reporters would investigate and take pictures, my father didn't have the broken window fixed. But, in spite of the familiarity of the local and state press with the name De Laine, not an inkling of the Lake City happenings appeared in any newspapers. Wanting the acts made public, members of St. James Church delegated someone to find out why the *Florence Morning News* had been silent on the subject.

The editor, a man who reported the news without bias, had heard nothing of the incidents. Checking up on the lead, he called the Lake City police. After questioning the police chief, the young editor interviewed Rev. De Laine. Only after he saw the evidence did he realize how incomplete the police chief's report had been.

Moore's Esso station on Church Street was a block from our home. My father thought Leroy Moore, one of the station's owners, "could reasonably be classed as a respectable public servant." But he said, "The other young fellow was nasty with his words and acts. He seemed to think that filthy language and . . . trying to show off made him important." Immediately after Mr. Rogers's visit to Lake City, the young men who hung around Moore's began to harass me whenever I walked by. When I left for college around mid-September, the youths redirected their attention to my mother and began to harass her. A favorite tactic was to suddenly accelerate one of the cars kept parked at Moore's and speed toward her as she passed.

A few minutes after the second time that happened, the humble white woman who lived across the street from us walked out to meet Mother when she turned the corner. Discovering what had occurred, the woman's already pale skin blanched even further. She said, "That's what I come out here for. I wanted to tell you that my boys ain't in this thing. I keep telling them we might be poor, but we ain't no trash. Me 'n my husband know y'all is good people, and it's just wrong how them boys keep bothering y'all."

Confused, Mother asked what she meant. The woman replied, "Even though people call us white trash, you and the preacher has been nice to us. Y'all must pray and be careful. You and the preacher got to be real careful."

The neighbor's words put great fear in my mother. Our house was not well buffered by other homes. Only the church parking lot was between it and Church Street, a major thoroughfare. On the other side of Church Street was a large field and the town's sewage tank. Behind and at the far end of the parking lot, St. James Church was the last building in town. Beyond it was the swamp, a no-man's land. Any person with malice in his heart could easily reach our home unobserved.

By the time my father came home that evening, my mother was near the breaking point. Her report of the day's events visibly annoyed him, but he was a man slow to lose his composure. He reassured her with his usual response. "Pshaw, Mattie, you oughtn't to let little things bother you so much. You could die from just worrying."

In spite of the reassurances he gave, my father lodged a complaint with the Esso Standard Oil Company office in Columbia. His letter stated, "The employees of your service station on the corner of Church Street, in Lake City, South Carolina seem to be using the place as a base for terrorism." After giving details of two incidents, he added, "This is being reported to you because I do not believe the ESSO Standard Oil Company upholds lawlessness. I shall keep my family away from this station and ask that they not interfere with any of us."

Five days later a reply arrived from the manager of personnel and public relations. It expressed regret that Daddy "should be subject to the alleged discourtesies . . . [but] the Esso Standard Oil Company is not responsible for the behavior of its dealers or their employees." Disclaiming any control over the station and indicating that an independent merchant operated the station, further assurance was given that "we do not approve of discrimination or any overt acts by anyone . . . but . . . you can feel assured that your complaint will be passed on to the dealer." Satisfied that his complaint had been noted, Daddy stapled the letters together and filed them away.

Saturday, October 1

On the evening of October 1, a curious thing happened. Perhaps twenty-five white people assembled by the sewage tank on the other side of Church Street. Neither BB nor I was at home, having both left for college, but our parents watched as a hole was dug with a tractor. Two loads of trash were emptied into it, and a huge bonfire was made. The entire crowd left after the hole was covered. My parents didn't know how to interpret the event, but later they heard there was a cross in the fire.

Unlike Summerton, Lake City certainly did have a Ku Klux Klan group—just as the mayor had told my father. When we first moved to the town, there were frequent reports of Klan meetings and cross burnings, and it was not unusual to hear of robed men riding through black neighborhoods. My brother Jay had even witnessed a Klan meeting and cross burning a few miles away. Perhaps the bonfire by the sewage tank was evidence of Ku Klux Klan activity.

Sunday, October 2

The timing of the bonfire was probably coincidental, but it happened the Saturday before Rev. De Laine was to leave for the AME Church's annual Palmetto Conference (of which St. James Church was a part) that would be held in Charleston. The following morning dawned fair and beautiful, and an unusually large crowd came to church. During the previous few weeks, Sunday attendance had consistently been larger than usual, with some people coming out of curiosity, while others were showing their defiance to the WCC. Almost everybody, young and old, knew they were indebted and owed the blessings of school bus transportation and new school buildings to the activities of Rev. De Laine. They also knew of the connections between the Supreme Court's rulings on public school segregation and the rise of the WCC.

In addition they had heard of the previous day's cross burning and were eager to hear what their pastor would say. Lake City's black policeman, Mr. Gray, was there in uniform, although he was not a member of St. James. Always courteous toward Rev. De Laine, he was the same that morning. However, my father suspected the policeman had been sent to the church as part of a war on his nerves.

The curiosity seekers in the congregation must have been disappointed for the pastor spoke not a word about recent events. Nor did he mention leaving. He hadn't thought of the morning as his last Sunday before the annual conference, a time when many AME preachers gave "Farewell" sermons. For him it was simply business as usual.

Later in the day he walked several blocks to visit some shut-in members of the congregation. Coming back, he turned onto Church Street for the last stretch before getting home. As he passed Moore's, he noticed a couple of white youths in a car beside, but not actually on, the property of the Esso station. One of them asked, "You know where the city limits is?"

Obligingly my friendly and helpful father gestured ahead toward the swamp, saying the edge of the town was "from right there, right at that bridge."

The youth Daddy called a "fat-headed young man from High Hill" called out, "Do you know how to get out?"

Recognizing the situation for what it was, Daddy said nothing else and continued homeward.

Monday, October 3

The annual conference would begin on Tuesday and continue until Sunday. Since Rev. De Laine planned to be away during that time, he ran several errands on Monday. Everywhere he went that day, black people cautioned him with same message, even if different words were used each time: "They say they're going to get you."

At one intersection he was forced to stop and wait a few moments because the driver of the car in front seemed undecided and was obstructing the traffic. At the same time a policeman was issuing a traffic ticket to a black motorist on the left of the intersection. The motorist in front finally proceeded out of the intersection, allowing Rev. De Laine to turn. The police officer promptly left the man to whom he was issuing a summons and pulled my father over. Daddy reported, "He told me I didn't stop at the stop sign. I argued with him, indicating I had stopped not only for the traffic sign, but also because of the motorist obstructing the intersection and that I was there long enough to see him issue a ticket to the parked motorist." Recognizing that Rev. De Laine was emphatic and had witnesses, the policeman turned and left.

My father knew some white people had hatred in their hearts and mischief in their minds, but he assumed the things that were happening and the rumors flying were tactics intended to frighten him. He often commented that fear begets more fear. If given the chance, he used to say, fear can turn the fainthearted into out-and-out cowards. Furthermore he had faith in God and often quoted the scripture that read, "Yea, though I walk through the valley of the shadow of death, I will fear no evil: for thou art with me."

Fear is one thing; common sense and precaution are entirely different. That night, as he had done almost every night since the night riders started their reign of terror, Rev. De Laine stayed awake, guarding his wife and his home.

Tuesday, October 4

Annual conferences of the AME Church are pretty much like any other conference. Pastors and delegates exchange views, give reports, and attend workshops. However, on the last day, always a Sunday, the pastors were officially given their pastoral appointments for the next year. Typically the pastor and several members from every church attend their conference. That October in 1955, members attending from St. James would include Webb Eaddy, the first man my father had met when he came to St. James and whose house was less than twenty feet from the parsonage. Early on Tuesday, Mr. Eaddy and Rev. De Laine took the eighty-mile journey together. Mis' Eaddy and my mother stayed in Lake City, and, because so many strange things were happening, Mother would sleep at the Eaddy's place.

In the five years that he pastored in Lake City, Rev. De Laine had steadily increased his presence in the Palmetto Conference. No longer an outsider, he now had positions on many committees. So although he said the nights of staying awake to guard his home had left him feeling "weary and broken," his time at the Charleston meeting was to be filled with various duties. Tuesday seemed to drag on interminably, and my father looked forward to a night of unbroken sleep. When mealtime came, he discovered that the combination of fatigue and unexpressed worry had deprived him of his appetite. Nevertheless he allowed himself to be taken in the evening to a nonchurch meeting where he was introduced to J. Arthur "Joe" Brown, an official of the local NAACP branch.

WEDNESDAY, OCTOBER 5

Mother was sleeping soundly when Mis' Eaddy awakened her. "Mis' De Laine! Mis' De Laine! Wake up. The church on fire."

Flames leapt high from the burning church, lighting the sky with an eerie glow. A temple of God was being consumed. Without delay the town's firemen got the blaze under control before it spread. And they did not leave until every spark had been extinguished. Nevertheless their fast and efficient efforts were no match for the raging fire, and the edifice was reduced almost to rubble.

The next morning the church members examined the devastation. With tears streaming down their faces, the women of the church sobbed, lamenting the loss of their new furniture and songbooks. "We worked so hard to buy them. Now they're gone and there is not even a place for us to attend services."

THURSDAY, OCTOBER 6

St. James's pastor got the awful message on Thursday. Jolted by the news, he was genuinely distressed for the first time in eight years of fighting, harassment, and persecution. He was worried about my mother, his helpmate of twenty-four years. The message that he received had said nothing about her. After talking with Mother by telephone, he learned she and Mis' Eaddy were all right, only frightened. He couldn't leave immediately because he was highly involved in the program that day. So he remained in Charleston, "in person but not in mind. As soon as I could reasonably get away from conference obligations, Brother Eaddy and I went to Lake City." There was nothing the two men could do except console their wives.

The church was badly damaged, practically burned to the ground. Only the frame remained. Rev. De Laine noted, "When I went into the hull of the church, I discovered either gasoline or kerosene powder all over the floor—from the communion room, over the pulpit furniture and choir loft, and down the aisles. Even the benches revealed that criminal setting of fire had to be the case."

Walking through the ruins, sadness engulfed my father's heart. Almost five thousand dollars' worth of new pulpit furniture and pews had been destroyed.

The losses also included a Hammond organ and the building itself. Lacking fore-sight—or perhaps simply trying to save money—the members had not bought adequate insurance. The church and its contents were insured for less than the cost of just the new furniture. Staring at the ruins, he remembered the claim that his father, as presiding elder, had built the church in the early part of the century. He also recalled that the church was said to be built on the site where the black postmaster was burned to death in 1898.

Shaking his head in disbelief, my father walked to the pulpit one last time. There he saw the charred Bible from which he had read scripture so many times. Although burned on every side, the compact paper prevented it from being com-pletely consumed. It was open, either fortuitously or deliberately, to an interest-ing page. At its lower corner was the last verse in the fifth chapter of the book of Judges. Daddy read, "So let all thine enemies perish, O Lord: but let them that love him be as the sun when he goes forth in his might."

He left the church and went to the Eaddy house. Shortly afterward the fire inspectors and sheriff called him outside and asked an idiotic question, "How did it happen?"

My father was incredulous. "I had been eighty miles away and they asked *me* how it happened," he said.

Although he reminded the officials of previous incidents, the sheriff tried to blame black people. Rev. De Laine said, "I really felt outdone when the sheriff advanced the theory that my son and some other boys probably did it for some spite. He knew the treachery that had been going on and yet he tried to accuse my son."

Not knowing my brother's whereabouts, the sheriff had shown his prejudice and callousness by trying to blame arson on him. Fortunately BB had not been in Lake City since entering college as a freshman six weeks earlier. Later my dad rightfully observed, "This kind of accusation has ruined many innocent people of color." He also recalled the words of a familiar hymn, "God moves in mysterious ways." If BB had come home to Lake City that weekend, his reputation and life could have been destroyed.

Late in the afternoon my father returned to Charleston where he found that the bishop had arranged to transfer him to a church in Bermuda. The head of the church had furthermore announced—to the entire annual conference—that Rev. De Laine would be leaving the country immediately. My father flatly and unam-biguously told the bishop he was not going to leave.

Friday, October 8

On Friday, when Mother got home from school, she found an unusual looking letter. It bore an 11:00 A.M., October 7, postmark and was addressed to "Rev. J. A. Delane. Collard. City." Contrary to her practice, she opened the letter and, with alarm, read the almost illiterate message.

J. A. Delane

We have been notified by the best of authority that you are the one that started school segregation mess at Manning, S.C. and that you was run out of manning four dirty work there. so you come to Lake City to continue your filthy work. Maby you dont know Lake City but you are going to find out real soon. Several hundred of us have had a meeting and pleged our selves to put you where you belong, if there is such a place. I wonder if ever heard about the Negro Postmaster that was send to Lake City and was notified to leve. He refused. However he left, but in a coffin. So we have decided to give you 10 days to leave lake City and if you are not away by then rather than let you spread your dirty filthy poison here any longer. We have made plans to move you if it takes dynimite to do so. This is final.

The letter exhibited a degree of hatred that was far beyond my gentle mother's understanding. She instantaneously decided she was not going to face such evil alone and got a friend to drive her to Charleston.

My father was glad to see her, but he exasperated her by acknowledging as a compliment the implication that several hundred people recognized the power of his teaching. He remained a model of equanimity, a bulwark in a time of storm. If the letter caused him any perturbation, it was well hidden. Comforting my distraught mother, he told her, "Don't worry. Nothing's going to happen to us. God is on our side."

Wisely he immediately sought out the NAACP leader he had met on Tuesday evening. Seeing the letter, Mr. Brown straightaway took my father to Charleston's police headquarters where he was escorted to the office of the chief detective. The chief recognized him the moment he entered the room. With a superb recall of faces, a well-honed memory for fact, and an eye for detail, the officer probably deserved his position. He was the kind of man who would do a job thoroughly yet admit the limits of his abilities.

Reading the missive of hate, hearing the tale of harassment, and knowing Rev. De Laine's background, the detective did what was required. He made copies of the letter for the Federal and State Bureaus of Investigation, as well as one for my father's records. Then he assigned a man to protect my father as long as he remained in Charleston.

The story was immediately picked up by the news media, and reporters were eager to question Rev. De Laine. One man gave the impression of being fair, sincere, and determined to tell the story objectively, but most seemed intent on collecting evidence to condemn the NAACP. No matter what the twist, Rev. J. A. De Laine was front-page news.

The annual conference continued, and my father performed his duties as required, with the Charleston detective always just a few feet away. Unable to forget that someone had it in for him, my father's stomach roiled and it was difficult for him to force food down. Yet, even to my mother who knew him so well, he seemed a man of steel, fortified by an inner strength that gave him the resources to face all outer threats completely unafraid.

Still trying to get the stubborn man to consent to leave Lake City, Bishop Reid summoned my father. In the Episcopal Room, a place that served as the leader's office, the bishop reported on his latest effort. "I just talked with Bishop Nichols who told me to send you to him. He is offering you a church in Newark, New Jersey, or one in Washington, D.C. The choice is yours."

Responding, Daddy drew his breath and declared, "No, Bishop. I don't want to go."

Stunned by this reply from a man whose church had just been burned and who carried a threat to his life in his pocket, the bishop exclaimed, "No!? My God, De Laine, why not?"

Three months earlier my parents had visited New York. Finding the hustle and bustle of city life not to their liking, they wanted no part of it. Searching for an answer that would neither offend the bishop nor belittle his efforts, Daddy slowly tried to explain: "We don't like the city." "We're southerners and country people." "I'm too old to make such a change." "I fear my ability to survive in those sophisticated circles." "Our families are here." "Too much politics."

Bishop Reid couldn't believe what he was hearing. He tried hard to persuade my father, relating how interested Bishop Nichols was. He enumerated the advantages of the move and emphasized the dangers of remaining—all to no avail. My father was unmoved, and his decision remained unchanged. His heart would never leave Clarendon County.

Rev. De Laine left the Episcopal Room. The issue still weighed uneasily on the bishop's mind.

SUNDAY, OCTOBER 9

Sunday came, the final day of the annual conference and time for the ensuing year's pastoral appointments to be announced formally. Every pew in the large church was occupied, and standees filled the side aisles. People waited for official announcements of what most already knew. The hubbub of last minute arrangements was interrupted by the blare of the loudspeaker. "Rev. De Laine. Rev. De Laine, please come to the Episcopal Room."

The bishop spoke only after they were alone. "I'm bothered, De Laine. I don't want to send you back to Lake City. For the third time I'm asking you to change your mind. What do you say now about going to Bishop Nichols? Both of the two places are still available. How about it?"

My father looked at the balding, round-faced man. "Bishop," his answer came, "five years ago you said God had directed you to send me to Lake City and

I didn't want any part of the place. Now, since God directed you to send me there, I am determined to stay until God tells me to leave. Or tells you to move me."

Ignoring the introduction of God's directions into the conversation, the shorter man spoke again, "I've looked and looked for a suitable place to send you in South Carolina. Only three places are open that are commensurate for a man of your standing." The bishop named the places.

Rev. De Laine's retort came fast and positive, "Every one of those places is a Ku Klux Klan– or White Citizens Council—hole. I'd be jumping out of torment into hell." He drew his breath and continued, "I'd rather stay where I am and fight it out."

"Then you're determined to go back?"

"If you send me."

A few minutes later Rev. De Laine's name was the first to be called when Bishop Reid began to read the appointments. The church leader prefaced the appointment by saying, "I don't believe Lake City is Mississippi." He must have tried to close his ears and mind to the congregation's audible gasp that came after he read, "Rev. J. A. De Laine, St. James Circuit, Lake City."

The Charleston detective and Mr. Brown, the NAACP leader, remained with Rev. De Laine until he left for Lake City. Before leaving, Daddy felt obliged to do one more thing. "I wrote a letter [of thanks to the chief detective] for the protection offered to me and mailed it to Harry Jenrette, the TV broadcaster. I told him that when I left Charleston's city limits, I would be in the hands of South Carolina and Lake City."

Riding home with Mr. Eaddy, my parents were more relaxed than either had been for days. My father's presence and his constant reassurance that "nothing's going to happen, don't worry" stilled my mother's fear. He bolstered his own confidence with the comforting words of the forty-first Psalm, "The Lord will deliver him in time of trouble. The Lord will preserve him, and keep him alive; and he shall be blessed upon the earth; and thou wilt not deliver him unto the will of his enemies."

For the journey back to Lake City, the St. James delegation formed a motorcade to keep their pastor's car from being alone on the homeward journey. Perhaps it was a good thing they did for, at one point, several carloads of white men were parked along the highway. At that particular place, a uniformed state trooper stopped their lead car and signaled the others, including Daddy's, to keep moving. They obeyed, then stopped and parked a bit farther on. Some of the men walked back to see why the lead car was stopped. After a bit of tongue lashing and harassment by the officer, all were allowed to drive away.

In Lake City the "homeless" members of St. James Church had held afternoon services at the black high school. Ever the caring shepherd, Rev. De Laine wanted to go by to reassure his flock. Near the school, on a dirt road usually avoided by white policemen, they met several members. Wanting to greet his returning pastor, one member pulled his car parallel to my father's and stopped. Immediately a white police officer arrived, arrested the man, and took him to the police station, accusing the driver of blocking traffic. In the excitement no one thought to accompany the arrested man. But on his way home, my father remembered and announced he would go to the station.

The church members had already let him know about their fears: "It ain't safe for you 'round here. We heard the police got guns stacked a foot high 'round that police station." Mother echoed their concern and objected strenuously to his plan. But iron-willed and concerned, my father drove to the station anyway. Upon arriving, he found the man from his church had already been released and was walking toward his car. A white man at the station had recognized him and advanced the money for his fine.

My parents headed for home. Daddy would spend another night watching and guarding.

17. *Armageddon*

I consider my life worth nothing to me, if only I
may finish the race and complete the task. . . .

ACTS 20:24

The next morning, Monday, October 10, Daddy chauffeured Mother to school and then, as was his habit, went to the high school's little library to read for a while. Before long one of the teachers drew a chair close and began to admonish him for accepting reappointment to Lake City. She said, "Rev. De Laine, if I were you, I would leave this place."

"Why?" he queried. "I haven't done anything that I need to run from."

She talked at him, trying to find a vulnerable spot in his seemingly impenetrable armor. "You have a good wife and three fine children to live for. You ought to think about them. They need you too much for you to think about staying here. Your life is too valuable to be thrown away by some worthless person."

Unabashed and looking squarely at her, he replied, "I'm here because I realize that if some cowardly skunk wishes to steal up on me in the dark, that will be my fate. As for my family, thank God I have lived to see my children large enough to run for themselves, if necessary. And I trust that my wife will be able to take care of herself. They are far more prepared to take care of themselves than most people."

He was immovable. Giving up, the woman dropped her head and cried until my father felt sorry for her. But he did nothing to ease her distress.

Leaving the library, he visited the site where one of his church members was building a house. There another person began to tell of something he had just heard. Apparently the Ku Klux Klan had held a rally to organize a parade, the sole intent of which was to get my father. Flippantly Rev. De Laine advised the men, "Tell them to come on, I'll be there."

His body was weary and his mind needed respite from the rumors and threats, from the begging and pleas. Nights of guarding and days of guardedness had exacted their toll. He went home, his eyes closing before his head touched the pillow. Hypnos, the Greek personification of sleep, would wait no longer to collect his due.

Daddy snored lightly. The clock ticked on. The doorbell rang. And rang. Then the knocking started, loud and commanding. No one answered. The car was at the house, so the puzzled visitor peeked in the windows. Seeing a figure on a bed, the man became alarmed and walked two miles across town to find Mis' De Laine at the school.

A string of horrified "what ifs?" stampeded through Mother's mind. Hurriedly arranging for someone to watch her class, she asked another person to drive her home. As she fumbled to open the kitchen door, it yielded, helped from the other side. His eyes wide, my astonished father asked why she was home so early.

When she explained, he gave his familiar little snort of a laugh and said she worried too much. "I was just sleeping."

While his first visitor was going to find my mother, another had been successful in awakening the clergyman. They all wanted to make him aware of a bombing that had taken place not too far away. The terrorists were busy dispensing their wares of terror and destruction. The levelheaded pastor listened, then opined, "If our people would just mind their own business, the hatemongers would give up and settle down. All they want is attention."

He drove Mother back to school to complete the day. A few hours later he picked her up. Although their agenda for the late afternoon was to travel to Florence to see a doctor, they gave some other teachers a lift to their boarding place and were invited to eat an early dinner there. While they tarried, a messenger brought a telegram from Bishop Reid. It contained yet another attempt to persuade Rev. De Laine to leave the state.

Dumbfounded both by the messenger being able to locate him and by the content of the telegram, all conversation left my father. Simultaneously my mother's fears began to rise again. Before they left Lake City for Florence, she insisted on going by the house of her school principal. She wanted to give him her class register because, if she got her way, she wouldn't be in school the next day. However, no one was at his home, and they went on to Florence.

The doctor let my father use his telephone to call the bishop. Once more Rev. De Laine told his superior, "I went to Lake City because God directed you to send me there. At that time I felt like I was being sent to torment. Now that I am in torment, I don't intend to run to another state unless God tells me to go."

Listening to Mother's concerns, the doctor told her, "I don't see why Reverend should jeopardize himself and you. I wouldn't go back to Lake City tonight if I were you. It's too risky." When she replied that Daddy was determined to return, the doctor suggested having him talk to the president of the Florence chapter of the NAACP before they left the town. Mother tried to get my father to do so, but he countered with his stock response, "You worry too much."

She pleaded to go to Columbia, saying her mother would be worried. He retorted that her mother also worried too much. She tried arguing that Lake City wasn't safe. He claimed that he was too tired and didn't want to go somewhere else. Mother was persistent, begging him to at least go to Sumter where they could stay with a friend.

His final word on the matter was to the effect, "Mattie, I'm tired. I just want to go to sleep. In my own bed. Now, will you please shut up?"

In twenty-four years of marriage, he had never before spoken to her in that way or asked her to shut up. The issue was closed. They got home around seven that evening.

Before he could get in bed, a member of the church board came to apprise him of arrangements for the evening's meeting. Rev. De Laine told the man to proceed as best they could; he was too exhausted to attend. A few minutes later Officer Gray came, saying, "They sent for you to come to the police department. Two reporters are there who want to talk with you. And Mr. Ballard from the *Florence Morning News* said he will be back to see you about ten o'clock."

My father trusted neither the request nor the man. It was nearing nine P.M., and an eight o'clock curfew was in effect in certain black sections of town. The request could have been a ruse to get him into the wrong part of town, where a white policeman could justifiably arrest him. Or perhaps after Mr. Gray delivered him to the station, the black policeman would be sent somewhere else, leaving the white men to do whatever they wanted. Either way he would be framed, and the public would never learn the truth. His fate would be publicized as a case of justice having been done to a rebellious black person. If he lived to appear in court, his testimony, the words of a black man, would have no standing against the testimony of a white man, especially if the white man were a policeman.

Taking no chances, he emphatically told Mr. Gray, "The church furnishes a living room for me to entertain my guests. Anybody who wants to talk with me will have to come here. That goes for white or black. I'm not going to the police headquarters to see anybody. Goodnight, Mr. Gray."

The policeman softly responded, "I don't blame you, Reverend."

Again Daddy went to bed, only to be disturbed around ten o'clock by the arrival of the reporter from the *Florence Morning News*. The man was amazed that anyone would stay in a Ku Klux Klan–infested area after receiving threats such as Daddy had. My exhausted father was not moved. "When the reporter left, I went back to sleep."

Soon afterward Rev. Seals arrived from Summerton. He brought two members of his church with him, and they all wanted to offer words of encouragement. My father awoke long enough to greet them, but asked permission to remain in bed. Leaving the entertainment of the goodwill ambassadors to my mother, he was soon asleep again.

Opening the back door to see the visitors off, my mother was surprised that the light between the house and the church was no longer burning. One of the visitors commented that the light must have just blown out because it was on when they arrived. As the visitors said their goodbyes, Rev. Seals advised Mother to go inside and close the door before they left. She replied, using the same words my father often said to her, "Don't worry 'bout us, Rev. Seals, we'll be all right."

From inside the house, she watched the car leave the parking lot. Appreciative of the visit and hoping their friends would get home safely, she went back to grading student papers. Then the quiet of the night was broken by loud talk and laughter. Surprised that someone would be passing at that time of night, she lifted the window shade a fraction of an inch and peeked out. A group of white men—who had come from the far end of Lake Street where no white families lived—stopped briefly under the street lamp, then turned onto Church Street, and disappeared from view.

A few minutes later a car slowed in front of the house. Sounds like gunfire ripped through the night. Or was it just the sound of firecrackers? Again Mother went to the window. At least four cars were moving slowly down Church Street. Glinting in the light from the street lamp, she saw gun barrels projected from the windows of the two front cars. Then flashes of light accompanied more sounds. My mother rushed to my sleeping father, urging him to wake up.

Daddy had already started his repetitive message of "Don't worry" when another shot was fired. Instantly alert, he was up and, in quick reflexive actions, turned out the lights and grabbed a gun. Eight more shots rang out. By the time he got to the window, the last car was pulling out of sight. Creeping to his side, my mother had already begun to plead, "Let's leave. We can't stay here."

The hand holding the sixteen-shot 0.38-gauge Winchester rifle dropped to his side, and my father's free hand drew his wife close. "Don't you see, Mattie, I can't leave. It's no use trying to run from my shadow. They'd find me. Or some other hatemongers would find me. They'd catch me running, and they'd lynch me. I wouldn't stand a chance. Running is more dangerous and less honorable than staying to know what I'm running from."

Looking down at my trembling mother, the tenderness and love he felt for her caused him to pause. But his resolve was firm, "I'm not leaving, but you'd better get out."

Taking her by the hand, he led her into the kitchen where he stopped. "Stand right here 'til I can see what's outside." He opened the door, then stood, tense, listening. There was no sound. Cautiously he peered around the doorframe into the darkness of the back yard. The faint outline of a man was barely discernible beside the garage. Jerking his gun to a horizontal position, he demanded, "Who is that? Speak!"

A black man's voice, carrying only as far as its owner intended, came out of the shadows, "Me, Rev. Jes' me."

The shepherd held his fire, knowing his sheep's voice. Mr. Eaddy, our neighbor, emerged from his squatting position, the sawed-off shotgun dropped, but clearly visible. Coming to the back porch, he explained, "They burned the church but I don't mean for them to do anything to you or the parsonage. I'm gonna stick with you."

Touched, but knowing the man was wholly dependent on white people for his livelihood, Rev. De Laine said something like, "Thank you, sir. All I want you to do is to go back in your house and take care of my wife. I'll be here unless God tells me to leave." Then, briefly looking at the house, he commented, "I think I'll stay out here where I can see better."

Bidding him to be careful, Mr. Eaddy and Mother went next door, leaving my father alone in the cool night with the church's burned hull standing like a grim warning. The two men would never see each other again.

Taking a seat beside his car, and almost invisible in the dark, my father prepared to wait out the night—which was just approaching midnight. It wasn't long before the whine of a motor announced the approach of a car. Daddy tensed, his hand gripping the gun. The terrorist's car pulled to the side of the road and stopped. My dad aimed, ready—if necessary—to "mark the car," just as the police chief had told him to do.

Two shots came from the car.

Rev. De Laine was calm. He had never mistreated any of them. He didn't even know who the thugs were that terrorized him in the night. But he was determined he wouldn't run away, not knowing why he was running or from whom he was running. There were at least four occupants in the car. But my father didn't know that. Neither did he know that one of the occupants was Leroy Moore, the "respectable public servant" and co-owner of Moore's Esso Station.

He only knew that someone had shot at his home and that he was going to mark the source of the gunfire. His answering shot, fired almost without aiming, must have both surprised and terrified the snipers. Not knowing how true his aim had been, the excellent marksman—who never shot at living creatures, but who made sure each of his children could handle a gun—pulled the Winchester's lever to throw out the empty shell and reload at the same time. He thought he was moving slowly, fumbling. The car took off, turning onto Church Street toward the swamp. It sped off into the darkness so fast that Daddy was amazed. "If that car didn't have atomic energy, it had some mighty good fuel in the tank. It seemed impossible for a car to get away so quickly."

The night riders were running scared, and my father was running to fire one more shot before the damaged frame of the church blocked his view. "If I missed the car, I regret it. If I hit its occupants, I was shooting at the car. The marking of the culprits was worth my life." He didn't know it then, but the car had been marked. Both bullets had hit the car. Two of the occupants were also hit, probably by shattered metal from the top of the car. There was no further shooting.

Here is Daddy's explanation of what he did and why he did it: "Even a minister of the Gospel can reach a point when patience ceases to be a virtue. The chief of police had said, 'Shoot and mark the car.' He didn't mention that in marking the car, the occupants might also be marked. If the occupants got in the way of the bullet, I was aiming to identify the car. The officers said I might have been mistaken about the license plate number I had previously reported, but that car had an identification mark which no man has ever disputed. I do not believe God would have approved if I had run and hid from the threats of the terrorists. My conscience is void of offense toward both man and God."

To make sure other terrorists were not lurking around, Daddy searched for telltale shadows by the hedge and the low stone wall. Finally, satisfied he was alone, he let his arms drop, lowering the gun. The tension was gone. It felt as though a great burden had been lifted. The car had been marked. The anonymous riders in the night would no longer remain anonymous. Assured that he had done the right thing, my father returned to his lonely observation post and waited. The chief of police had promised to have one of his men pass the parsonage every fifteen minutes. One should come soon.

Seconds stretched into minutes. The bent stop sign at the corner gave silent testimony of a careless driver long since gone. The shell of the burned out sanctuary bore ghostly witness to the reign of hate. No one walked on Lake Street, and no one drove on Church Street. My father was alone in the dark.

The stink from the swamp's stagnant water blended with the stench from the sewage tank. In the night's silence, Daddy had time to think, time to imagine the most preposterous things and to review various recent happenings. Was it possible that the police chief wouldn't keep his promise? Or that the officers of the law were cooperating with the night riders? The thoughts were far fetched, but what other explanation was there for the recent events? That white policeman trying to give him a ticket? The black policeman coming to church in uniform? The failure of the police to tell reporters what was happening? The ready accusations against his son?

Struggling for answers, he kept asking himself questions. Were the Lake City police protectors of the citizens? Or were they perpetrators of lawlessness and injustice, threat, and terror? He said he waited for the police, but nobody came.

My father had told his bishop that God would tell him when it was time to leave. The miracle came as Daddy sat on the wooden back steps of St. James parsonage: "About 45 minutes after the shooting, God whispered in my ears. In my quiet reflection, the Lord said unto me, 'It's time for you to leave here.'"

Ordinarily my father—a most honorable man—told the truth, plain and unembellished (except for the descriptive words he used for irresponsible people). Everyone could trust Daddy's word. But in this case, believing a white lie to be more favorable in God's sight than jeopardizing the life of his emissary, he told one untruth and failed to elaborate on one fact. The truth was that a policeman did come. The fact was that, when God at last whispered his holy advice, he had used the mouth of a human being with a conscience. Mr. Gray, the black policeman, was the emissary that made my father understand he had to leave if he wanted to live. Daddy readily obeyed the "heavenly" message.

"I immediately went into the parsonage and got my handbag, my overcoat, and a few [more] pieces. I put the needed money in my pocket and went out for the last time," he said. Outside the back door, key in hand, his mind raced. Although he had forgotten his earlier need for sleep, he remembered his firearm. Was there anything else that ought to be done? He was locking the door when he remembered Mother hadn't taken a key. Leaving the key in the door, he got in the car and drove out of the churchyard into the empty streets.

He thought no one knew when he left, no one except the person peering from the white family's window directly across the street. He wondered if Mother and the Eaddys heard when the car started. But he wasted no time and took off in the same direction the night riders had taken.

He had no choice. Crossing the swamp minimized the likelihood of being seen and would take him quickly to U.S. Route 52, the Florence road. He said, "I sensed the Night Riders had taken the High Hill Road and I was going the other direction. When I was about to enter Highway No. 52—about one mile from the parsonage—I had to slow down for a yield sign. There was a filling station in the fork of the road. It must have been an all night station. Or the proprietor might have been one of the terrorists."

In any case, when my father slowed down, three men sprinted to a car and started out behind him. Oh, God! The night riders! Throwing caution to the winds, Rev. De Laine floored the accelerator, and his Mercury shot off into the night. The other car followed suit, the night riders having spotted their prey. Whizzing past darkened farmhouses and deserted fields, Daddy drove like a madman, more frightened than he had ever been. The pursuers had the advantage. There were three of them. He was armed but alone—and he had to drive. A well-placed shot from behind could have been fatal.

Approaching the little town of Scranton, he took his foot from the accelerator. The speedometer registered eighty in the thirty-five-mile zone. He didn't want to get caught for speeding but, even more so, he didn't want to be caught by his pursuers. No one was in sight, not even a drunk. He stepped on the accelerator again, pressing it to the floor, going as fast as the 1953 Mercury would take him.

His car zoomed on into the night. Trees blurred into streaky, dark blobs that blended with, and hid, an occasional lighter blob. The car behind seemed to be keeping the same speed. Daddy passed a car, his attention glued to the white stripe that stretched ahead. He passed another car. And another. Then the pursuers' car was no longer in the rearview mirror. Whether they had become confused or had run out of gas, he neither knew nor cared. His accelerator wasn't released until he reached the Florence city limits. There he intended to ask the sheriff for asylum. He should have known the sheriff was not on his side.

Back in Lake City the last barrage of shots resounded through the still of the night. They echoed from the grotesque shell of the burned-out church. They reverberated up and down the quiet streets, shaking the souls of those who were awake to hear them.

The people in the house next to the parsonage huddled together, two of them trying to comfort the third. My mother wanted to go to my father, but Mr. and Mis' Eaddy restrained her: "You can't do anything. He said you must stay here."

The sounds died down. Minutes ticked by. Forever, it seemed. A car motor started and moved away. Then once again there was the silence of the October night. The night wore on.

"I believe that was Rev's car leaving. I'm gonna take a look."

Gun in hand, Mr. Eaddy crept through his back door, just far enough to see that the Mercury was no longer there. He faded back into his house.

Hearing the words "Rev's car's gone," Mother's sadness swelled beyond measure. That night of October 10, 1955, brought the darkest, the iciest, the windiest, and the rainiest hours she ever experienced. For her the darkness plunged deeper than pitch-blackness. In her brain a tempest raged. Torrential rains, whipped by gale force winds, beat at her sanity. Fear engulfed her with a bitter cold. There seemed to be no refuge. The man who had firmly refused to be intimidated by threats and who would not let his determination be weakened by pleas from the fainthearted was not there to comfort her. Her husband, a pillar of steadfastness, a Rock of Gibraltar—a man she had never known to commit a selfish act, either with his family, his students, or his parishioners—was gone. Where? She didn't know. What fate would befall him? She dared not imagine. That altruistic gentleman who sacrificed and went out of his way to help others was now himself in need of help.

Her hands wrung, tears streamed down her face. Several times she drifted off into a fitful sleep; awakened each time by horrifying dreams. She dreamt of burning houses, burning crosses, burning churches; ghostly visions of men in sheets, men in cars, men with guns; fearsome, unreal sounds of stones striking board, of shattering glass, of shots piercing the darkness. Nightmares of cars driving in the night. Terrible visions of half running, half falling through lonely corridors fraught with danger, always calling, "JA! JA! Where are you? JA, please answer me." And after each episode, she awoke, bathed in a cold sweat, reaching for her absent husband, shivering with fear in that lonesome October night.

Awake, she prayed unceasingly, her never-ending prayer repeated over and over, "Oh, God, our help in ages past, our hope for years to come, our shelter from the stormy blast, and our eternal home. Take care of him. Please, God, take care of him."

Mis' Eaddy didn't sleep peacefully either. Her concern for the clergyman was less intense, less personal. Haunting her was the fear of her family's own future. She and her husband had jeopardized themselves by being Good Samaritans and taking in their neighbor. "Suppose the night riders come for us? Oh Lord, what will we do? When 'they' find out, will they get us too?"

She, too, fell to praying. "Oh, God, our help in ages past, our hope for years to come, be thou our guard while troubles last, and our eternal home."

Mr. Eaddy didn't try to sleep. He stood vigil with his shotgun, peering out through the windows whenever he dared. But he also kept the faith. Occasionally he adjusted and caressed the shotgun that rested on his knees, acknowledging— more than praying—to God, "Under the shadow of thy throne, thy saints have dwelt secure; sufficient is thine arm alone and our defense is sure."

My father went to a friend's house in Florence. There local NAACP leaders and church colleagues prevented him from contacting the sheriff and helped him escape from South Carolina.

On October 11, 1955, a warrant was sworn for his arrest.

Rev. J. A. De Laine's concluding words about that night were, "I will leave the way I went and my destination for future posterity to find out."

And now . . . I go . . . not knowing the things that shall befall me—Acts 20:22

Epilogue

'Tis the set of the soul
that determines its goal,
and not the calm or the strife.
ELLA WHEELER WILCOX

R ev. De Laine found sanctuary in New York State, where the governor
refused to grant extradition. However, the AME Church never gave him
any official recognition for his role in the struggle for racial equality. Furthermore
it gave him only token support as a minister, despite promises made before he left
South Carolina. His first assignment was to start a new congregation in the western part of New York State, but no financial assistance was forthcoming to achieve
the goal. Two years later he was transferred against his wishes to the New York
City area and given a pastorate with less than thirty members. In 1958 he was
assigned to a small church in Brooklyn whose members had requested him ever
since he fled South Carolina. As he had done in Buffalo, my father built up the
congregation by attracting new members who hailed from South Carolina. He
and my mother bought a house in Queens, New York, where they lived until 1971
when Daddy retired and moved to Charlotte, North Carolina.

My father died on August 3, 1974, twenty years after the Supreme Court's historic decision, never having returned to his beloved Clarendon County and with
a warrant still out for his arrest. Even with his death, the AME Church, to which
he had steadfastly retained his allegiance, failed to acknowledge officially his gift
to America.

In 1994 a well-wisher requested that the warrant for his arrest be removed.
The request was denied with the explanation that, if Rev. De Laine looked for a
job, the prospective employer had a right to know his history. At the time my
father had been dead twenty years. If he had still been alive, he would have been
ninety-six years old. The arrest warrant was finally removed on October 10, 2000,
forty-five years after it was issued.

My mother taught in the public schools of New York State for seventeen
years, her income giving my parents financial security. After her retirement in
1973, she joined Daddy in Charlotte. My father's treasure, support, helpmate, and
best friend for forty-three years died in 1999, twenty-five years after his demise.

Their children—my brothers and I—achieved professional successes that would have been impossible had we remained in South Carolina. In a remarkable bit of irony, BB became the director of safety and driver education for North Carolina's largest school district during the first year of court-ordered busing that was intended to desegregate its schools.

The Lake City home where my parents had lived, St. James parsonage, was searched the day after the shooting. There police found a microscope bearing the name of a doctor from New York State. Contacted at the address on the case, the doctor's parents were told by South Carolina authorities they had recovered the stolen microscope. The couple informed the officials that the instrument was the lawful possession of a young South Carolina man named J. A. De Laine, Jr., who was serving his country as an army medic in Korea, along with their son.

Unlike South Carolina's educational revolution of school equalization, the national revolution of public school desegregation did not occur quickly. It has been more like the Hundred Years' War. In 1965, ten years after the Supreme Court called for desegregation to proceed "with all deliberate speed," the courts had to issue a desegregation order that forced Summerton to stop "deliberating" and to integrate its schools immediately. In spite of the townspeople's intense resistance, five black students attended the previously all white Summerton High School that year. Perhaps to prevent further desecration of its sacrosanct halls, the school was permanently closed the following year, and the formerly all black Scott's Branch High School was kept open. Every white student was taken out of the district's schools—either to be sent to an integrated public school in nearby Manning or to be placed in a local, newly established private school—and Scott's Branch remained all black. Fifty years after the *Brown* decision, in the year 2004, white parents in Summerton were still managing to keep the town's public schools segregated.

In Clarendon County, particularly in the Summerton area, the reign of hate and retaliation continued for more than fifteen years. It is almost impossible to describe, and equally impossible to imagine, the extent to which the black people of Clarendon County were made to suffer because of their quest for equality. The retaliation that began in 1948 with Levi Pearson being denied credit continued and intensified over the course of the following years.

Threats and derision became commonplace. The plaintiffs suffered loss of jobs, homes, and opportunities for their children to pursue higher education. More tenant farmers and sharecroppers were evicted. Annie Gibson and her family were actually dispossessed from their home on Christmas Eve. For a while, before finally moving to Gipp Street, they had to live with relatives. Mis' Annie's daughter was deprived of a college education because of the family's sudden destitution.

Lucrisher Richardson and her family were also evicted, as was her brother-in-law Lee Richardson and his family, from the land they had rented and farmed.

Mis' Lucrisher's family was able to find accommodations in town, but Mr. Lee was not so fortunate. He had to move several times. With no job, no credit, and no home, many days he had no idea of how he would provide food or shelter for his wife and children. A man of the soil, he refused to leave the area in which he had lived all of his life. Because of the kindnesses of relatives and lifelong friends, he and his family managed to survive. Ultimately one of the *Briggs* supporters made it possible for him to get a small homestead.

Susan Lawson, a single mother and sharecropper, was able to get through what would have been her leanest of times because a supporter rented her an acre of his land. He apologized that he was unable to offer more. Nevertheless, during the three years that she lived and farmed that one acre, she netted more money and lived better than she had in her previous years of sharecropping. Life improved even more for Mrs. Lawson when she remarried in the mid-1950s and moved to her husband's place.

Henry Scott was evicted at harvest time. For most of that year, he had toiled in all kinds of weather so that he could bring in a good harvest. However, he was denied the opportunity of reaping the ripened crops. Survival was a challenge. Nevertheless Mr. Scott stayed in the Summerton area. For the rest of his life, the man who, on June 8, 1949, had roused the parents with his emphasis on the need to get organized, supported himself and his family with what he could grow on two acres of land.

None of the farmers could buy seed for crops, get cotton ginned, or use credit at the stores they formerly frequented. Landowner plaintiffs James Bennett, Gilbert Henry, Robert Georgia, Frederick Oliver, Edward "Bubba" Ragin, "Big" William Ragin, and Gabriel Tindal could no longer rent land to increase the acreage that they farmed. To buy supplies and sell crops, they had to go outside of Clarendon County and rely on the help of relatives who lived elsewhere. Bennie Parson put up with such indignities until 1959, when, disgusted with the difficulties of obtaining supplies and selling produce, he moved his family to New York, where he became a welder. He never looked back and never regretted his role in helping to bring the dawn of desegregation.

Harry Briggs had to leave the state to find work to support his family, which remained in Summerton. Hazel Ragin got no further work as a housepainter. Until his death, he earned his living as a hunting and fishing guide for tourists. Although Rebecca Richburg's husband was not fired and they could not be evicted from their home, they too suffered. They were not given credit, and they supported their fellow petitioners by going to other counties to shop.

Wholesalers refused to sell to plaintiff Mary Oliver (as well as to other small business people like "Monkey" Smith), and delivery men refused to deliver goods. If supplies needed to be replenished for Oliver's café, someone with a large vehicle had to travel to Columbia, or even farther away, to find vendors. The only local middlemen who dared sell them provisions did so covertly, exchanging goods in out-of-the-way, wooded areas. Mis' Mary's regular patrons were also feeling the economic pinch and had even less discretionary money than usual for her fish sandwiches and jukeboxes. Somehow the family and the café made it through those awful years of threats and retaliation. In 2004, more than fifty-four years after Mis' Mary signed the first petition, the café was still in operation.

Onetha Bennett died not long after the Supreme Court's verdict. I was told that Mose Oliver, the handyman to whom my father gave a piece of property, left town, but I don't really know what happened to him.

The black petitioners and supporters in Clarendon County remained undaunted in spite of their sufferings. The outspoken Gilbert Henry, who had questioned the removal of a picture in the school, continued showing significant leadership, strength, and courage. In spite of reprisals, and because he still had dependents in school after the 1954 Supreme Court decision, he signed the updated petition in 1955 where *Briggs* plaintiffs whose children were no longer in the school were replaced by parents of current students. At the time of his death, he was still actively involved in civil rights efforts, serving as secretary of the Clarendon County branch of the NAACP.

The unremitting perseverance of unassuming people like Lee Richardson commands admiration and respect. Economic pressure did not make him recant. Forcing him to move his home more than once could not make him bow his head. Even when his white neighbor blocked access to the road leading to his house, he continued to stand firm. The act only showed the stupidity of the perpetrator. Mr. Lee—and the other heroes of Clarendon County—was like the apostle Paul, who said, "None of these things move me."

Although Rev. Seals and his wife lost their teaching jobs, he refused to the leave the area. Like many of the women, his wife went to New York for protection and to find work, sending money back to support those left behind. Their thirteen-year-old grandson, whom they were rearing, was sent to live with relatives. In 1956 the Seals's home was mysteriously destroyed by fire. Rev. Seals died in 1973 at the age of eighty.

I don't know how long Rev. Richburg continued as principal of the high school in Orangeburg County. However, until he passed away in 1960, members of his family—like all suspected supporters of the case—were victims of retaliation. They were refused service in stores, credit for farm essentials, loans from banks, and rental of farm equipment. Relatives in the North, my father, the NAACP, and others publicized the plight of the Clarendon County people for a while. In response people such as Walter Reuther of the AFL-CIO and A. Philip Randolph of the Pullman Car Porters, a couple of New York–area Jewish groups, and other northeast organizations provided food and financial assistance to some of the affected farmers. The AFL-CIO advanced more than forty thousand dollars to a Manning cooperative for the purchase of a combine. However, no merchant in South Carolina would sell the piece of equipment to the cooperative without proof that the purchaser was not from Clarendon County. Ultimately arrangements were made to procure the equipment in another state.

If it hadn't been for Judge Waring's strong convictions and his action at the pretrial hearing for the equalization lawsuit in November 1950, *Briggs, Brown,* and *Davis* would not, could not, have been brought to the Supreme Court at the same time. Like the people from Clarendon County, Judge Waring also paid a heavy price for taking a stand against the ruthlessly unfair system. After the *Briggs* trial, the ostracized judge resigned his post and left South Carolina to live in exile in New York City. He died in early 1968 at the age of almost eighty-eight, and his body was returned to Charleston for burial. Fewer than a dozen white persons and more than two hundred black people attended the funeral in his hometown.

Reverdy Wells never got a college scholarship. He was conditionally enrolled in a South Carolina college before being drafted into the armed forces. Upon completion of his military duty, the high school valedictorian was denied admission to another college. He made the agonizing discovery that his high school transcript had been altered so that it consisted of all failing grades. His corrected transcript was delivered to him in 1991. Reverdy, who never earned a college degree, died around 2007.

With the help of Harold Boulware and South Carolina's NAACP branches, Clarendon parents continued to pursue their children's rights. In April 1960 some of the *Briggs* plaintiffs went to court again, asking that segregation be ended in their school district. Their lawsuit was aborted, but parents in other parts of the state later filed similar suits and won. Mr. Boulware's vital role in bringing *Briggs* to trial was virtually ignored by the NAACP, and he never received adequate acknowledgment for his careful groundwork. Later in his career, he became the first black person to be appointed as an associate judge for the municipal court in Columbia, South Carolina. Subsequently he went on to serve as a judge in the Richland County judicial system and in the family court of the state's Fifth Judicial Circuit. He passed away in early 1982 at the age of sixty-eight.

The names of many foot soldiers in the Clarendon County struggle for equality have been lost. The acid of neglect and erosiveness of time have reduced their individual bitter tribulations to not even a brief footnote in history. Those history-making heroes are now all gone. After the tragic death of Willie "Bo" Stukes, Onetha Bennett was perhaps the next *Briggs* plaintiff to die. Harry Briggs, the lead plaintiff, breathed his last in 1986. When Annie Gibson made her final transition in 2001, the *Briggs* plaintiffs were no more. And with the passing in 2007 of James Brown, the Esso truck driver who was one of the first petitioners to lose his job in the quest for equality, the last of the bravest heroes that ever lived in Clarendon was gone.

The deeds of those brave women and men of *Briggs* were great gifts to our nation that we must treasure. *Dawn of Desegregation* is their saga, and it illustrates how a few courageous people with strong convictions can triumph and actually change the course of history. The ripple effect from *Briggs* and the other *Brown* cases resulted in major changes in all sectors of American society, leading to many things—handicapped ramps, maternity leaves, and job protection for older people—now taken for granted as rights guaranteed under the Fourteenth Amendment.

On September 9, 2004, in the year of the fiftieth anniversary of the 1954 *Brown* decision, Rev. J. A. De Laine, along with three other Clarendon people whom he inspired to action, was posthumously awarded a Congressional Gold Medal, the most distinguished award that can be bestowed by the United States Congress. It was given in recognition of his contribution to the nation as a pioneer in the effort to desegregate public schools. The award was finally approved because of the persistence of South Carolina's first black congressman in more than one hundred years, Representative James E. Clyburn. However, it is fitting to acknowledge that the effort was initiated by U.S. Senator Ernest F. Hollings, the white man who, in 1951, was the head of the committee that recommended the sales tax that funded South Carolina's educational revolution.

Once every five years the University of South Carolina's Museum of Education posthumously honors individuals who have furthered the practice of education in South Carolina and the nation. In 2006 the Reverend Joseph Armstrong De Laine—a man fired from his job as a Clarendon County educator—was inducted into the Museum of Education's Hall of Honor and became a member of this exclusive group.

I fought the good fight, I have finished the race, I have kept the faith.—2 Timothy 4:7

Notes and Sources

General Sources

For additional information on J. A. De Laine, the reader is referred to the following sources:

Joseph A. De Laine Papers, University Libraries Digital Collection, University of South Carolina, Columbia. Available online at http://www.sc.edu/library/digital/collections/delaine.html (accessed September 3, 2010).

J. A. De Laine, "Our Part in a Revolution," *AME Christian Recorder* (Nashville), 1966–70 (ca. 150 installments).

For general information about the *Brown* lawsuits, education in South Carolina, and NAACP efforts in the state during the 1940s, the reader is referred to the following works:

W. Lewis Burke and Belinda F. Gergel, eds., *Matthew J. Perry: The Man, His Times, and His Legacy* (Columbia: University of South Carolina Press, 2004).

Richard Kluger, *Simple Justice: The History of "Brown v. Board of Education" and Black America's Struggle for Equality* (New York: Vintage Books, Random House, 2004).

Peter F. Lau, *Democracy Rising: South Carolina and the Fight for Black Equality since 1865* (Lexington: University Press of Kentucky, 2006), esp. chap. 4.

Julie Magruder Lochbaum, *The Word Made Flesh: The Desegregation Leadership of the Rev. J. A. De Laine* (Ph. D. diss., University of South Carolina, 1993).

Juan Williams, *Thurgood Marshall: American Revolutionary* (New York: Three Rivers Press, 1998).

Tinsley E. Yarbrough, *A Passion for Justice: J. Waties Waring and Civil Rights* (New York: Oxford University Press, 1987), esp. chap. 7.

1. Briars of Discrimination

The source of much of the data about schools was Julie Magruder Lochbaum, *The Word Made Flesh: The Desegregation Leadership of the Rev. J. A. De Laine* (Ph. D. diss., University of South Carolina, 1993).

For a brief discussion of education funding in South Carolina, see Ada Louise Steirer and James C. Hite, *Historical Development of South Carolina's State and Local Revenue System.* Strom Thurman Institute Working Paper Series (Clemson, S.C.: Strom Thurmond Institute of Government and Public Affairs, Clemson University, 2005).

The NAACP Legal Defense and Educational Fund Inc. (LDF) worked in the courts to secure equal justice. At the time of the events being discussed, it was popularly referred to as the NAACP.

Senator W. B. Harvey's remarks regarding busing appeared in the March 13, 1943, edition of the *Sumter Daily Item,* reprinted from the *Charleston News and Courier.*

In a 2005 telephone interview with the author, Willard Strong provided information
about the history of the Santee Cooper Hydroelectric Project and Lake Marion.

Daisy De Laine Block was a major source of De Laine family information.

Information about the 6-0-1 law was found in W. W. Carpenter and L. E. Flowers,
"Evaluation of Certain Plans of Financing Education in South Carolina," *Peabody
Journal of Education* 7, no. 1 (1929): 37–41.

Roberta Mack Prince provided much of the information used in this and other chapters
related to Society Hill Church.

2. Spokesman for the Disenfranchised

Although the reservoirs of the new Lake Marion were full enough to begin generating
electric power within two months after closure of the gates in 1941, it took several
years for the lake to reach its final size. The digging of the beds for the two reservoirs
was the largest land-clearing project ever undertaken in United States.

The Pearson cousins, Jessie and Ferdinand Pearson, provided most of the information
used in the account of the classes for veterans.

In addition to the Pearson cousins, the men who signed the letter of July 6, 1946, requesting classes for veterans were George Harvin, Jessie Ranton, Bertice Lemmon, Elven
Walker, Fladger Harvin, and Samuel Nelson.

Information concerning the parents' bus came from Jessie Pearson, Ferdinand Pearson,
J. A. De Laine, Jr., B. B. De Laine, and Clara Gipson McKnight.

4. Ups and Downs

An article in the March 15, 1955, issue of Columbia's *State* newspaper discussed both the
reintroduction of twelfth grade and teachers' salaries.

See Tinsley A. Yarbrough's *A Passion for Justice: J. Waties Waring and Civil Rights* (New
York: Oxford University Press, 1987) for information on Judge Waring's rulings.

5. Transition

Several documents erroneously refer to S. Isaiah Benson as I. S. Benson.

Reverdy Wells was the source of the information about Mr. Benson's relationship with the
senior class.

The six others who attended the meeting with Thurgood Marshall were Hammett
Pearson, his wife Charlotte, and son Jessie; Levi Pearson and his son Willie (not
Ferdinand); and Ravenel Felder, a Davis Station World War II veteran and local
teacher.

Information about Mr. Benson's teaching activities is in the record "Hearing before
County Board of Education." Held on October 1, 1949, a copy of the report appears as
appendix B in Julie Magruder Lochbaum's *The Word Made Flesh*.

Among the eighteen senior class students who composed the letter to the authorities
were Reverdy Ragin, Gussie Ragin, Eva Brown, Robert "Buster" Georgia, Jr., Israel
Bowman, Phynise Pearson, Edna Watson, and Paralee Mitchell.

"Handkerchief head" is a term that Rev. De Laine often used to describe sycophants or
lackeys.

The J. L. Miller quotation was made in the presence of J. A. De Laine, Jr., in Manning,
South Carolina, in 1991.

The quotation from Thelmar Bethune is from *Transcript of Proceedings: Commission on Civil Rights in the Matter of South Carolina.* Advisory Committee. May 22, 1964, Manning S.C. Hart & Harkins. Shorthand and Stenotype Reporting, 930 F Street NW, Washington 4, DC.

6. June 8

The pamphlet mentioned is by J. A. De Laine and others, "The Clarendon County School Segregation Case," undated pamphlet, De Laine Family Collection.

J. A. De Laine, "Speech," undated, De Laine Family Collection.

J. A. De Laine, E. Richburg, E. Ragin, and R. Georgia, "The Clarendon County School Segregation Case (Revised)," undated pamphlet, De Laine Family Collection.

"Crawfish" is a colloquialism that means to retreat or go back on one's promise.

7. Across The Rubicon

"Big" William Ragin was one of several Summerton men with the same given name.

J. A. De Laine and others, "The Clarendon County School Segregation Case," undated pamphlet, De Laine Family Collection.

The petition to reinstate teachers was sent as a letter from Josie G. Ragin and forty-three others to the superintendent and trustees of School District Number 22, Clarendon County, July 25, 1949.

Documents taken to the state superintendent's office included sworn statements from Rosa S. Montgomery and Maggie D. Stokes, dated June 20, 1949.

The decision from the trustees was in an untitled, undated document from Chariman R. M. Elliott, G. S. Kennedy, and J. D. Carson (clerk), trustees of School District No. 22, Clarendon County.

Confirmation of the date of the students' hearing was a notice, "Notice to Committee on Action," from L. B. McCord to the Committee on Action, September 23, 1949.

The board's decision in regard to the students' petition was given in a document from L. B. McCord, A. J. Plowden, and W. E. Baker entitled "Decision of the County Board of Education on Case of S. I. Benson and Summerton Board of Trustees," October 1, 1949.

A reiteration of the parents' request that no teachers be discharged was in a letter from R. G. Oliver, Gabriel Tindal, William L. Ragin, Robert Georgia, Edward Ragin, and J. A. De Laine addressed to "Honorable School Officials," dated October 4, 1949.

8. An Offer That Was Refused

The fourteen-year-old boy, George Stinney, lived in Alcolu, South Carolina.

9. Warnings

Those who signed the equalization petition to the Board of Trustees for School District Number 22, Clarendon County, South Carolina were from the families of Onetha Bennett, Harry Briggs, Henry Brown, James Brown, Robert Georgia, William Gibson, Gladys E. Hilton, Gussie Hilton, Lila Mae Huggins, Blanche Johnson, Lee Johnson, Mary O. Lawson, Susan Lawson, Frederick Oliver, Mary Oliver, Mose Oliver, Bennie Parson, Jr., Edward Ragin, Hazel Ragin, Rebecca Ragin, William Ragin, Lee Richardson, Lucrisher Richardson, E. E. Richburg, Rebecca Richburg,

Henry Scott, Esther Singleton, Willie M. Stukes, and Gabriel Tindal. The petition was signed on November 11, 1949.

The word "paps" refers to teats or whatever babies might suckle for nourishment.

The date given for the McKnight murder was based on the recollection of B. B. De Laine.

The pseudonym, Mr. Crawler, was used because the man has not been identified in print previously.

10. SHOWDOWN ON MAIN

The Esso brand of fuel oil ceased to exist in the United States on January 1, 1973, when it was formally replaced by Exxon.

The information in this and the following chapter about James Brown was compiled from a 1994 conversation with James Brown and a 2004 letter from his daughter, Euralia Brown Craig.

11. A NOT-SO-MERRY CHRISTMAS

The history of Gipp Street and information about Hazel Ragin was provided by Sarah Ellen Ragin Williams, his daughter.

Denia Stukes Hightower provided a written account of her father, Willie "Bo" Stukes.

Devout Christians Harry and Eliza Briggs were members of St. Mark AME Church, where he was sexton and she sang on the choir. Some of the information about the couple came from Nathaniel Briggs, the youngest of their five children.

The source of information about Mazie Solomon was a tape-recorded interview conducted by Joseph A. De Laine, Jr., and B. B. De Laine in July 1991.

The incident concerning Robert Georgia's mules and wagon was recounted in the *Transcript of Proceedings. Commission on Civil Rights in the Matter of South Carolina.* Advisory Committee. May 22, 1964, Manning, S.C. Hart & Harkins. Shorthand and Stenotype Reporting, 930 F Street NW, Washington 4, D.C.

John Wesley Richburg supplied information about his parents (Rebecca and John Hazel) and Senn's Mill. Additional information about Frank W. Josey and Walter B. Senn, Jr., came from the Senn's Mill Marker at 3 Cantey Street, Summerton, South Carolina.

Celestine Parson Lloyd supplied information about her parents, Bennie and Plummie Parson.

12. LIAR, LIAR

For a description of S. E. Rogers, see J. B. Martin, "The Deep South Says 'Never!'" (Part 2) *Saturday Evening Post,* June 22, 1957.

J. A. De Laine, "An Open Letter. A Summary of Incidents in the Summerton School Affair," letter postmarked January 1950. De Laine Family Collection.

Document. "Before the Board of Trustees of School District No. 22, State of South Carolina, County of Clarendon: In Re: Harry Briggs, et al., Petitioners, Decision of the Board. R. M. Elliott, Chairman; C. D. Kennedy, J. B. Carson, Clerk, Trustees of School District No. 22, of Clarendon County, South Carolina. Summerton, S.C. February 20, 1950." De Laine Family Collection.

Decision of the Board. Before the Board of Trustees of School District No. 22, County of Clarendon. February 20, 1950. De Laine Family Collection.

The events of the night the papers were scattered around town was recounted to Joseph A. De Laine, Jr., by Robert Georgia, Jr.

Beatrice Brown Rivers provided some of the information about the role her father, Henry Brown, played in finding the duplicating machine.

Benson v. De Laine was heard in the Court of Common Pleas, State of South Carolina, County of Clarendon, on August 21, 1951.

13. Moving On

Summerton is a small town, and many of the petitioners were related, as noted in the text. Additionally Annie Gibson's parents reared their niece Gardenia Martin Stukes— wife of Willie "Bo" Stukes—and the two women grew up as sisters. At least two petitioners were related to Rev. De Laine by marriage. One of Lucrisher Oliver's uncles had been Rev. De Laine's brother-in-law, and a brother-in-law of Annie Gibson had been married to Rev. De Laine's niece. Both of these men were deceased by 1949.

Names of the men listed as members of the board in District 22 are Chairman R. W. Elliott, J. D. Carson, and George Kennedy. Other men listed by name were L. B. McCord, chairman of the county board of education and county superintendent of education, and the two other county board members, A. J. Plowden and W. E. Baker. The last named defendant was School District 22 superintendent H. B. Betchman.

November 17 may not have been the actual date of the pretrial hearing for the equalization case because, in one place, Rev. De Laine gave the pretrial date as October 17.

The hunting group included Edward Ragin, Robert Georgia, William Ragin, Hazel Ragin, Frederick Oliver, and Gilbert Henry.

Civil Action No. 2657, *Briggs et al. v. Elliott et al.*, was filed at the U.S. District Court, Eastern District of South Carolina, Charleston Division.

Request for Dismissal, Civil Action No. 2505, *Briggs et al. v. Board et al.* was filed at the U.S. District Court, Eastern District of South Carolina, Charleston Division on December 26, 1950. Stipulation of Dismissal, Civil Action No. 2505, *Briggs et al. v. Board et al.* was filed at the U.S. District Court, Eastern District of South Carolina, Charleston Division on January 5, 1951.

14. Federal District Court

Civil Action No. 2657, *Briggs et al. v. Elliott et al.*, U.S. District Court, Eastern District of South Carolina, Charleston Division, was heard on May 28, 1951, and decided on June 23, 1951.

In the description of the testimonial meeting given in an installment of "Our Part in a Revolution," Rev. De Laine was citing a *Lighthouse and Informer* report made by John McCray.

In the excerpts from Judge Waring's dissenting opinion, the paragraph format has been altered to facilitate reading.

15. Verdicts

Information about Mr. Crow's speeches came from Rev. De Laine's summaries, which were probably based on articles in the *State* newspaper.

C. T. Rowan, "Jim Crow's Last Stand (Part 3)," *Minneapolis Morning Tribune,* December 1, 1953.

Rev. De Laine gave a speech as an invited guest at St. Mark AME Church. The first page of his undated notes was misplaced; page 2 begins "in the school. Thus there . . ." A reference made to *Briggs* awaiting a Supreme Court decision places the speech prior to May 1954.

The *Newsweek* article appeared on May 24, 1954.

E. E. Colvin, "Segregation in Light of Word of God," *Florence Morning News,* September 2, 1954.

B. B. De Laine supplied information about school bus drivers. In 1954 the salary of newly hired bus drivers was twenty-five dollars.

The judgments in the desegregation lawsuits were given in the following cases:

Brown v. Board of Education, 347 U.S. 483 (1954) decision, (U.S. Supreme Court reargument). U.S. Supreme Court.

Bolling v. Sharpe, 347 U.S. 497 (1954) Argued December 10–11, 1952. Reargued December 8–9, 1953. Decided May 17, 1954. U.S. Supreme Court.

Brown v. Board of Topeka, 347 U.S. 483 (1954). Reargument. Decision rendered May 17, 1954. U.S. Supreme Court.

Brown v. Board of Education, 349 U.S. 294 (1955). Opinion and judgments. May 31, 1955.

16. New Evil

For information about the origin of the White Citizens Councils, see "New Anti-Negro Groups Spring Up in South; Economic Pressure Is Weapon," *State,* November 21, 1954; Julian Scheer, "The White Folks Fight Back," *New Republic,* October 31, 1955, 9–12; John Bartlow Martin, "The Deep South Says 'Never!'" (part 2), *Saturday Evening Post,* June 22, 1957.

Details of what happened during August and September 1955 are based in part on the following sources: J. A. De Laine, "My Last Sunday in Lake City," undated document; J. A. De Laine, "The first part of this is lost" (notes); J. A. De Laine, "An Open Letter. A Summary of Incidents in the Summerton School Affair," January 1950; "Lake City Pastor's Home Is Bombarded," news clipping [*Florence News,* 1955?]. All in the De Laine papers.

The letter from J. A. De Laine to the ESSO Standard Oil Company was dated September 19, 1955.

The letter from H. M. Dreyer, manager of personnel and public relations with ESSO Standard Oil Company, to J. A. De Laine was dated September 22, 1955.

The De Laines did not have a telephone, and messages were sent through a member of the church.

Descriptions about Mrs. De Laine's reactions came from a news clipping with the text of a speech that she gave at a Baltimore NAACP rally at Sharp Street United Methodist Church, Baltimore, on January 22, 1955. The newspaper was probably the *Afro-American.* Additional information came from an untitled page of her notes.

17. Armageddon

Leroy Moore was identified as an occupant in the car hit by bullets from Rev. De Laine's gun in an article in the *State,* October 21, 1955.

Rev. De Laine sent a letter to a news reporter, Harry Gianaris, on October 13, 1955, explaining why he shot at the passing car.

An article in the *Charlotte (N.C.) News*, Friday, October 21, 1955, titled "S.C. Faces Battle to Regain Minister," said the bullets that shattered metal of the car probably hurt the occupants.

The account of what happened in Lake City after Rev. De Laine fled is based on a page from Mattie De Laine's notes.

EPILOGUE

In a *New York Post* article dated December 4, 1955, Ted Poston reported the attempt to accuse Rev. De Laine of the theft of the microscope.

Ruby Gater, who worked for Robert "Monkey" Smith when she was a teenager, described how she would go to secluded areas to pick up supplies for her employer.

Index

Note: JAD refers to J. A. De Laine

Adams, E. A., 14, 18, 26; friendship with JAD, 117, 126–28, 154
African Methodist Episcopal Church (AME Church), 13, 14, 17, 41, 92, 190; conferences, 41, 58, 173–79; motto, 14; organization and policy, 15, 41, 92, 126, 174, 190; pastors, 18, 111, 137. *See also* De Laine, J. A., and AME Church; *and individual churches*
agriculture classes, 21, 24, 115
Allen, Richard, 92
Allen University, 14, 15, 66, 126; Board of Control, 35, 126, 128; summer school, 24–25, 61, 66
AME Church. *See* African Methodist Episcopal Church
Anderson, Maceo, 40, 42–43
Antioch / Zion Hill circuit, 127
Armistice Day, 82–84, 138
arson: of the De Laines' Summerton home, 154; of the Lake City church, 175–76
attendance (school), 7, 8, 121

Baker, Frazier (Lake City postmaster), 127
Baker, W. E. (Clarendon school board member), 142
Banks, Lester, 47
Belton, Mattie. *See* De Laine, Mattie
Benedict College / Allen University Summer School, 24
Bennett, James. See under *Briggs* plaintiffs
Bennett, Onetha. See under *Briggs* plaintiffs
Benson (lawsuit). See *Benson v. De Laine*
Benson, S. Isaiah, 41; financial accounting, 49–51, 67, 73; grievance rehearing,

72–73, 74; neglected duties, 42–43, 78; resignation, 75–76, 81, 100; Scott's Branch principal, 42, 57, 68; slander lawsuit, 116, 133, 154; student grievances, 48–54, 57, 64–65, 69
Benson v. De Laine, 111, 116–17, 124, 168; verdict, 133–34, 154–55
Betchman, H. B., 64, 137, 141–42; conference with JAD, 74–78; De Laine house, 79, 81; lawsuit defendant, 133, 141; school positions, 40, 51, 119; student grievances, 40, 51, 60, 65, 73–74; teachers rehired, 81; Seals, 92–93, 104, 112; "Warning Benson" papers, 125
Bethune, Thelmar, 48
Bible passages: Hosea 10:12, 100; Judges 5:31, 176; Luke 8:5–15, 100; Luke 16:23, 97; Luke 8:8, 102; Psalm 41, 179
black high schools (in Clarendon County), 10, 12, 23, 27, 35, 46
black people, 3, 70–71, 79; economic status of, 4; educational status of, 5, 7, 13, 89; response to equalization effort, 76, 131, 138; told to resign from NAACP, 112
boats. *See* drowning
Bob Johnson Elementary School, 15, 27, 160
Bolling et al. v. Sharpe et al. (District of Columbia), 158, 159
Boulware, Harold: desegregation, 145, 194; equalization effort, 41, 46, 87, 117, 132; grievance rehearing, 71–73; *Pearson* lawsuit, 27–28, 33, 35–37, 44; voter registration, 34, 36
Boyd, J. S., 34, 36, 48, 148
Briggs. See *Briggs et al. v. Board et al.; Briggs et al. v. Elliott et al.*

About the Author

OPHELIA DE LAINE GONA, formerly a medical school professor, is retired from the University of Medicine and Dentistry of New Jersey. In addition to scientific publications, Gona's previous writings include articles about her father and the *Briggs* lawsuit.